Stories *from*
the
Sagebrush
**CELEBRATING
NORTHERN NEVADA
AT THE MILLENNIUM**

Dusty Darbin, eleven, learns horsemanship during his summers staying with his grandmother, Deanna Adler, in Paradise Valley, Nevada.

...I find myself reflecting whimsically on how very much like the sagebrush the people are, at least in the hinterland that makes up most of Nevada, setting down roots and thriving in unlikely places, hardy and resilient, stubborn and independent, restrained by environment and yet able to grow free.
  Robert Laxalt, Nevada: A Bicentennial History

Stories *from* *the* Sagebrush

CELEBRATING NORTHERN NEVADA AT THE MILLENNIUM

WRITTEN BY DON COX

PHOTOGRAPHS BY JEAN DIXON

PAINTINGS BY RON ODEN

**From the *Reno Gazette-Journal* series
MILLENNIUM 1999-2000
Northern Nevada at the Turn of the Century**

PUBLISHED BY THE
NEVADA HUMANITIES COMMITTEE

Publication of this book was made possible through the generous support of the following foundations and corporations:

E. L. Wiegand Foundation
John Ben Snow Memorial Trust
International Game Technology
The E. L. Cord Foundation
The Bretzlaff Foundation
Wells Fargo

The quotations on the section divider pages are from the following sources:

Crum, Steven J. *The Road on Which We Came: A History of the Western Shoshone*. Salt Lake City: University of Utah Press, 1994.

Wright, William [Dan De Quille, pseud.]. *The Big Bonanza. 1876.* Reprint, New York: Alfred A. Knopf, 1953.

East of Eden, West of Zion: Essays on Nevada. Edited and with an introduction by Wilbur S. Shepperson. Reno: University of Nevada Press, 1989.

Beebe, Lucius. *The Central Pacific & the Southern Pacific Railroads*. Berkeley: Howell-North, 1963.

Starrs, Paul F. *Let the Cowboy Ride: Cattle Ranching in the American West*. Baltimore: The Johns Hopkins University Press, 1998.

Laxalt, Robert. *Nevada: A Bicentennial History*. New York: W.W.Norton, 1977.

Book design: Nancy Peppin
Text editor: Barbara Land
Index: Jean Stoess
Prepress services: Reno Typographers
Printing: DynaGraphic Printing

© Copyright 1999
Nevada Humanities Committee

ISBN 1-890591-05-X

First Printing October 1999

A Halcyon Imprint of the
Nevada Humanities Committee

Contents

A thousand thanks...

The making of a book like this involves imagination, knowlege, skill and a lot of teamwork. From the first glimmer of an idea to the finished volume, the Reno Gazette-Journal *and the Nevada Humanities Committee have had the help of talented people.*

Both organizations are eager to thank the many northern Nevadans who shared their stories and the team of specialists who conducted town meetings in their communities. On the next few pages, newpaper publisher Sue Clark-Johnson and Humanities executive director Judith Winzeler mention some specific names. Author Don Cox, in his own distinctive voice, here adds a few more:

The best cookies were served in Austin, the healthiest food at Pyramid Lake. There was a complete meal in Genoa and a great restaurant in Eureka.

We did a lot of eating on the tour of towns and cities in northern Nevada that resulted in a *Reno Gazette-Journal* series, *Northern Nevada at the Turn of the Century,* and this book, *Stories from the Sagebrush.* At every stop, volunteers baked cookies. In Genoa, which claims to be the state's oldest white settlement, they fixed dinner. On the Pyramid Lake Paiute Reservation they made sure we got plenty of fruit.

During the weeks when we stayed home there were were regular meetings of the advisory committee that guided the project from start to finish. The group ate a lot of submarine sandwiches and potato chips. Too bad they didn't go with us to Eureka, a well-preserved Nevada mining town where Nancy Brewer, a graduate of the French Culinary Institute in New York, kept her Jackson House Restaurant open late, just for us.

That certainly made Jim McCormick happy. He was hungry after moderating a discussion among at least thirty Eureka citizens who talked about the past, present and future of their historic town. We had a gathering like that at each stop. McCormick, emeritus professor of art at the University of Nevada, Reno, was one of four volunteer moderators on our millennium tour. He took turns with the others: Reno artist Mary Lee Fulkerson, UNR emeritus professor of history Jim Hulse and *Gazette-Journal* columnist Rollan Melton.

At each of his appearances, Hulse reminded the audience that the *Gazette-Journal* had come to town simply to look at the life of the place and its people — without needing a fire or other headline-grabbing event to get us there.

Melton, a career northern Nevada journalist, delighted us all by bringing along his wife, Marilyn, a funny and outspoken lady. Both Meltons had a lot to do with transforming the project from a newspaper series into a book.

In every town we needed a good guide, somebody who really knew the place and loved talking about it. Wally Cuchine was our man in Eureka. Cuchine, director of the Eureka Opera House, knows where the bodies are buried in his town's seven cemeteries. Laura Tennant was the woman in Dayton. Tennant, a longtime resident and local newspaper reporter, knows where the gold is buried in the backyards of her town.

In Carson City there's a guy named Guy — Guy Louis Rocha. Officially, he's the state's assistant administrator for archives and records. For us, he was a tour guide to all of northern Nevada, the historian who separated fact from fiction, always just a telephone call away.

Out on the road, when you're hauling a sound system from town to town, you need somebody who knows how it works. Our expert was Sequoia Fowler, who also helped with the heavy lifting.

Ed Shur, an eastern kid who'd never seen sagebrush before he came to Nevada, was the newspaper editor in charge of the series and the boss who did every job that wasn't assigned to somebody else — which was a lot. In the office, Donna Warren and Janis Laycox made sure the whole operation didn't fall apart.

Even when you think you have everything covered, there's always the unexpected. That's why the unnamed guy in Virginia City was important. He held the light so we could see where to plug our equipment into an electrical socket in the Storey County Courthouse. Without him, the show couldn't go on.

Hope he got a cookie.

Don Cox

A newspaper records more than history

Of all the institutions it takes to make a town go, we believe a newspaper — the medium of record — must take a lead in requoting history. That's what we do, year round, but to chronicle the end of one millennium and the coming of another the *Reno Gazette-Journal* wanted to do more.

To provide a richly textured tapestry, we needed to look at northern Nevada through the eyes of the people who live here and to visit the places they call home. We realized the importance of talking to the people who keep those communities alive — of digging into their past, present and future.

And so we did. Tonia Cunning, our executive editor, started well ahead of time in 1998, assembling an advisory board of Nevada arts and humanities leaders to help with the project. Led by Kathie Bartlett, chairman of the Nevada Arts Council, these advisors exchanged ideas and came up with a plan for a series of town meetings in selected northern Nevada communities. The *Reno Gazette-Journal* invited everyone concerned about each town to come and talk and listen.

At each meeting we heard from mayors and PTA presidents, parents and students, waiters and farmers and retired workers. Moderators for these gatherings included *Gazette-Journal* columnist Rollan Melton, Nevada artist Mary Lee Fulkerson, University of Nevada, Reno emeritus professor of history James Hulse and UNR emeritus professor of art Jim McCormick.

Meanwhile, a team of *Gazette-Journal* staffers had been selected to attend the meetings, explore on their own, and bring a year-long newspaper series to life. The planned features would run approximately three Sundays per month, beginning in January 1999 and ending by Nevada Day 1999.

Senior reporter Don Cox was assigned to write the stories and assistant photo editor Jean Dixon was named project photographer. Graphics director Ron Oden, while supervising page design for the series, later created a hundred and twenty oil-on-linen paintings to illustrate the weekly features. Don, Jean and Ron have described their experiences in separate notes that appear with their photographs in this front section of the book.

The Gazette-Journal's senior projects editor, Edward H. Shur, was editor and supervisor for the newspaper's millennium series. Two years earlier, he had edited another year-long series that became reporter Frank Mullen's successful book, *The Donner Party Chronicles*, with photographs by Marilyn Newton. Copy editor Glen Feighery, also a key player in the Donner Party series and book, now worked with Jean and Ron on the presentation of the millennium series.

On the road, from town to town, our team found a treasury of individual stories that could fill a library. As their collection of notes and images grew, the team recognized a common concern in most of the small communities. Residents want to preserve what they have without interference from the outside world. They want to keep their communities the way they are, free from the ills of some big cities. At the same time, they wonder how their communities will survive. If economic improvement means growth, will it also mean the loss of small town comfort?

The biggest surprise for our team was the attitude of many small town high school students and recent graduates. Most of them say they like small town life and are not eager to go anywhere else. The few who would leave home say they fear the town is getting too big.

Back in our office, as the weekly features progressed, *Gazette-Journal* editors started looking beyond the newspaper series. From their earliest meetings, advisory board members had talked about preserving the millennium series as a future book. Recalling the success of the Donner book, published by the Nevada Humanities Committee, the board turned to one of its members.

As executive director of the Humanities Committee, Judith Winzeler had been involved in every step of the process to transform Mullen's newpaper columns about the Donner party into a hefty volume on bookshelves. Now she offered to approach her committee with the millennium idea. Once again, the *Reno Gazette-Journal* undertook a partnership with the Nevada Humanities Committee.

Winzeler describes her committee's approach to the book in her remarks following this page. Humanities members supported the idea, raised the funds for publishing a book, and *Stories from the Sagebrush* emerged. We believe Don, Jean and Ron have captured people's hopes, dreams, desires and optimism in these pages. As you read, we hope you'll visit northern Nevada along with them.

Sue Clark-Johnson, publisher
Reno Gazette-Journal

Great horned owls perch in a tree in Winnemucca.

From all of us, special thanks to these community organizations: Fleet Reserve Association Ladies Auxiliary of Carson City, Bristlecone Convention Center, White Pine Chamber of Commerce, Eureka Opera House, Dayton Valley Community Center, Genoa Town Board, Nevada State Library and Archives, Carson Valley Improvement Club, Lyon County Courthouse, El Capitan, Duckwater Shoshone Tribe, Austin Courthouse, Austin Chamber of Commerce, Stockmen's Hotel & Casino, Fernley Town Complex, Storey County Courthouse, Hillside Elementary School, Dresslerville Community Council, Mason Valley Chamber of Commerce, Fallon Convention Center, Sparks High School, Gerlach General Improvement District, Pershing County Community Center, Paradise Valley Community Hall, Walker River Paiute Tribe, Tahoe Douglas Senior Center, Incline High School, Carson Valley Middle School, VFW Ladies Auxiliary, Reno, Pyramid Lake Paiute Tribe

Small town Nevada is alive and well

Stories from the Sagebrush reveals the richness of our Nevada heritage. The people portrayed in these pages connect with the places where they live, creating a sense of community. At a time when so many critics seem concerned about the absence of civic virtue, here are hundreds of stories of people living in community. Civic pride is alive and well in small town Nevada.

In a state that is growing rapidly, these stories can provide newcomers and longtime residents with a shared understanding of the state's history and current condition, bridging the gap between city dwellers and rural citizens.

At the same time, the book can open a window through which others may observe Nevada's cultural heritage and people. In a more practical sense, the book can contribute to the vitality of northern Nevada by advancing cultural tourism, economic development and historic preservation.

A project of this magnitude is possible only with widespread community support. We found that support in every town where local people hosted the newspaper's millennium team. At the *Reno Gazette-Journal*, the project became a labor of love for Don Cox, Jean Dixon and Ron Oden.

Executive Editor Tonia Cunning worked with the citizen advisory committee and never wavered from her belief that this was an exceptional project. The newspaper team was spirited, tenacious and able to produce an amazing series on deadline while assigned to other tasks as well.

Books, of course, are produced with a different set of design and editing rules. The production team that worked with Don, Jean and Ron in redesigning the newspaper series for book publication was equally dedicated. We are grateful to graphic artist Nancy Peppin whose design for this book reflects the intense sunlight and sharp shadows of the Great Basin landscape. Patty Melton, design consultant, contributed to the artistic quality. Text editor Barbara Land provided a liaison between journalism and scholarship.

Invaluable partners in transferring graphics from newspaper files to the pages of this book were Tim Kist and Rob Nemeth at Reno Typographers and Marjie Swiatek and Bill Price at DynaGraphic Printing. In the Humanities office, staff member Mary Toleno and student intern David Parsons were meticulously conscientious manuscript readers. Stephen Davis's carefully crafted prose helped us secure the grant funds that made this book possible.

Those who believed in the project enough to offer financial support include Kristen Avansino, president of the E.L. Wiegand Foundation; Rollan Melton, trustee of the John Ben Snow Memorial Trust; Brian McKay of International Game Technology; William O. Bradley of the E.L. Cord Foundation; and Michael Melarkey, representing the Bretzlaff Foundation. Special thanks go to Mendy Elliott who arranged for Wells Fargo to purchase copies of the book to be distributed to schools and libraries.

Judith Winzeler, executive director
Nevada Humanities Committee

Clues to the future in Nevada's past

As it awaits the end of the twentieth century and anticipates the second millennium, the northern portion of the thirty-sixth state looks back on a history of profound change. *Nevada*, the Spanish name meaning snow-covered, was first applied to this land more than one hundred and forty years ago. Even earlier, explorer John C. Frémont called this arid, mountainous region *the Great Basin*.

In the 1840s, when Mexico claimed most of the Great Basin, its western reaches were inhabited only by the Washoe, Northern Paiute and Western Shoshone tribes. Now some five hundred thousand Nevadans call it home. The landscape has been transformed by mining, railroads, highways, and agriculture. Legislated industries such as casino gambling, easy divorce, and quick marriage have shaped the cities. Tourism and light industry have left their marks. Most of the state is federally managed by the Bureau of Land Management, the Forest Service, and the Departments of Defense and Energy.

Yet, despite the impact of 150 years of change, rural Nevada sustains an allure that captures the imagination. Basque-American writer Robert Laxalt calls it "the other Nevada." East of metropolitan Reno, one still finds a remote corner of the nation rich in culture, history and folklore. It is so sparsely populated that it would have — if it were a separate state — the smallest population in the nation, with less than one-half a person per square mile. Minus the cities, this rural state would still cover more than 100,000 square miles and would rank as the eighth largest state in the union.

What does the future hold for northern Nevada? A century ago, when the area's mining industry was depressed, thousands of people abandoned the Silver State. Then, beginning in 1900, new mineral discoveries reinvigorated the dying economy. Today, while conditions are not as gloomy as they were at the last turn of the century, the mining industry is depressed once again and Nevada's monopoly on legal casino gambling has been gone for almost twenty-five years.

Reno/Sparks, northern Nevada's flagship metropolis, appears to be at a crossroads. Sprawling on the fringe of the "other Nevada," the twin cities are still growing in every direction engulfing neighboring communities such as Lockwood. Gaming-driven tourism is still their life's blood, even though warehousing and light industry have brought significant economic diversification in the latter half of the twentieth century.

In recent years, cities and towns like Elko, Ely, McGill, Eureka, Winnemucca and Austin have seen mining companies close or cut back operations, laying off thousands of workers and curtailing their exploration. Mining will come back — it always has — but what will the impacted communities do in the meantime to bolster their sagging economies?

Other communities are prospering despite the cloudy future of mining and casino gambling in northern Nevada. The changes are dramatic. Fernley, a sleepy farming community for most of its twentieth-century existence, is now a booming industrial center in northern Lyon County. New businesses are attracted by Fernley's abundance of undeveloped land, lower taxes than neighboring counties and the state's freeport tax exemption. If Fernley town leaders cultivate the nearby Pyramid Lake Paiute Tribe in adjoining Wadsworth, the town can benefit from the Truckee River water settlement and share in future development.

Fallon, the Churchill County seat of government, also has changed dramatically during its one hundred-year existence. Once an agricultural oasis in the desolate Lahontan Valley, Fallon has become a military town, home of TOPGUN, the prestigious flight training unit at the ever-growing U.S. Naval Air Station. Residential subdivisions are springing up where alfalfa fields once spread to the horizon. New residents include a growing senior population.

Gardnerville, Minden, Dresslerville and Genoa also find their bucolic way of life at risk. Twenty-five years ago, these Carson Valley communities were surrounded by dairy farms, fields and ranches. Today the battle is over open space and greenbelts amid rapidly proliferating housing tracts and custom homes. The Carson Valley has become a bedroom community for Carson City, Reno and Lake Tahoe Stateline casinos.

Dayton, another growing bedroom community, was a prosperous milling town during Virginia City's nineteenth-century mining boom. Then the town settled down to become a quiet agricultural enclave on the Carson River through most of the twentieth century. Today Dayton is growing bigger every year. Light industry has found its way to the area and a four-lane U.S. highway runs through town. Moderately priced houses have sprung up south and east of the river and many homeowners commute to work in Carson City or Reno/Sparks. New schools, a library, super-market, senior center and golf course are all products of the last twenty years.

Carson City, once the nation's smallest state capital, now has more than fifty thousand residents. After the 2000 U.S. census, Nevada's capital city will be designated an urban area, one more link in the growing Sierra Megalopolis, a population corridor stretching some eighty miles from Cold Springs north of Reno to Topaz Lake south of Gardnerville. There are very few farms and ranches left in the valley, and the city's population density is among the highest in the state. The east side of the city is dotted now with new industry, but open space has been set aside for parks, trails, and wildlife habitat along the Carson River and on the Carson Range. Heritage and cultural tourism are recognized as mainstays of the local economy.

Yerington, Hawthorne and Schurz on the Walker River Paiute Reservation are all linked to the fortunes of the Walker River and the dying Walker Lake near Hawthorne. In their efforts to save the lake, Hawthorne leaders and U.S. Senator Harry Reid have focused on Weber Dam, currently scheduled to be reconstructed on the Paiute reservation. The dam and reservoir will affect all upstream users of water from the Walker River, including Yerington. That city has experienced modest growth in the twentieth century. Downtown looks like Mayberry, USA, with a few casinos sprinkled in. Yerington's agricultural character still prevails, nourished by relatively abundant water in the Mason Valley.

Hawthorne, like Walker Lake, has been dying a slow death in recent years. The Mineral County seat of government, which relies heavily on the Army Munitions Depot for its economic livelihood, wants to enhance the recreational offerings of Walker Lake to attract tourists. The need is for more water from the Walker River to find its way to Walker Lake.

Some places in the "other Nevada" seem almost frozen in time and probably don't want to change much. Gerlach in Washoe County, Paradise Valley in Humboldt County, Tuscarora in Elko County, and the Duckwater Shoshone Reservation in Nye County fall in this category. These are out-of-the-way places that have not been impacted by the spillover of urban Nevada.

Gerlach is a remote railroad outpost, gateway to the Black Rock Desert. Paradise Valley looks like a scene out of the 1950s "Lassie" television series. Tuscarora, a shadow of its mining glory days, is quiet and quaint, uncompromised by the commercialism found in some revitalized frontier towns. Duckwater is

Guy Rocha in his Carson City office

a preserver of traditional Shoshone folkways. Serene in its isolation, and faced with the issues of sustaining the tribe in a remote location, Duckwater escapes the myriad problems of other tribal communities adjacent to urban expansion.

Northern Nevada clearly has an uncertain future. Natural resources such as minerals and water are finite and need to be managed wisely. Agriculture will play a diminishing role in the state's future economy, but expanded promotion of existing special events, and the creation of new ones, will help to fill voids in state and local coffers. Legislated industries, like casino gambling, may go the way of easy divorce.

But northern Nevada has one resource that is only beginning to be developed systematically and marketed to the world. Cultural tourism can play a major role in our future. Nevada — particularly northern Nevada — has always been a polyglot society composed of people from virtually every ethnic, racial, and religious background. These immigrant Nevadans and their offspring have left their mark on the state. Much of that heritage is found in the "other Nevada." With its mixture of Native Americans, western frontier tradition and varied immigrant experience, northern Nevada could attract tourists from around the world.

This book, with its vivid snapshots of northern Nevada at the turn of the millennium, captures a moment in time. It also has the potential to advance cultural tourism by engaging northern Nevadans to think creatively about shaping a prosperous future by investing in an adventurous past.

Guy Louis Rocha, assistant administrator for archives and records

Don Cox

Don Cox, in Genoa, on the second day of the tour.

T he text of this book is a conversation, actually a series of conversations, that started in October 1998 with Bob Cox (no relation) and ended in June 1999 with Betty Keife.

Cox and Keife aren't famous. They're not celebrities. They're not public officials. They're people from northern Nevada telling their stories. That's what's in this book: individual stories. A lot of them. It's Cox, Keife and others like them talking about their past, present and future.

In two cardboard boxes under my desk, there are 149 cassette tapes and 35 notebooks filled with those conversations. It's amazing what people will tell you when they're just talking. A lot of it's in the book. Some of it's not. There isn't enough room.

Edna MacDiarmid, a woman in her 90s and a neighbor of Cox in Dayton, remembered eating tacos with Marilyn Monroe when the actress was in town in 1960 for the filming of *The Misfits*. Monroe died two years later.

"Marilyn used to come over with her tacos," MacDiarmid said. "She was very gracious and very nice."

In Hawthorne, residents struggled to explain the economic problems their town faced with cutbacks and layoffs at the Hawthorne Army Ammunition Depot, a huge ordnance storage facility opened in 1930. Jerry Bryant, a high school student, said it best:

"Technology has advanced. We're stuck with leftover technology nobody wants."

In Reno, Don Carano is relatively famous. He owns one of the big casinos, the Eldorado, and part of another, the Silver Legacy. But Carano, a Reno kid, likes talking about childhood incidents.

"I lasted in Catholic school two days," Carano said of his education experience as a ten-year-old. "I got kicked out. Somewhere along the line, the family decided I should go to Catholic school. I didn't last a week. I didn't get along with (the nuns). For some reason, we didn't see eye to eye."

In the first conversation, Cox gave directions to the site of Nevada's first gold discovery — in Dayton — as if he were telling you how to get to the corner market.

"When you go into Dayton, if you turn right at the light and stay on Main Street, the next place is Steve Saylor's house, the artist. He's pretty famous. Gold was discovered right where he lives."

In the last conversation, Keife described the lifelong process of filling the barn next to her Wadsworth home with pieces, big and small, of Nevada history:

"You just start collecting. You just bring something in and add it. Pretty soon you can't get the car in."

That's like the two cardboard boxes. You just keep adding to them. Pretty soon they're filled with history.

Jean Dixon

Jean Dixon and Uncle Herman in Dresslerville

While growing up, I spent many hours waiting for my mother as she took pictures, mostly of nature. Ruth enjoyed the whole process of slowing down and noticing the beauty surrounding her. I would wait with her while she maneuvered her tripod into the perfect position to capture an uncurling fern. And wait while she waited for a shorebird to stand still at the ocean's edge. I was often restless and bored during these outings. I was more interested in taking pictures of people in motion. That's why I became a photojournalist.

Ruth died nearly five years ago, but her passion for life and photography has stayed with me and blessed me throughout this project. She was there when I pulled over to photograph a hillside of wild irises on Austin Summit. And again, as I waited for an enormous thundercloud to turn the deepest shade of pink in the sky above Schurz. The images in this book would have made her smile. I hope that they will make the readers smile too as they turn these pages and meet the many characters and places along our northern Nevada travels.

My thanks to my partners in the project, Don Cox and Ron Oden. I thank them for their patience as they waited (and waited) for me to take pictures, sometimes stopping the Jeep without warning to photograph a scene while the light was just perfect. And a special thanks to Glen Feighery, our copy editor who in each Sunday's newspaper made our Millennium package sing.

My thanks also to my husband, Joe Gosen, whose support and loving encour-agement helped keep me focused through-out the project. And hugs to my daughter, Jessie Aikin, who finally accompanied me on a road trip after wondering when I would ever be done traveling to all those "foreign lands."

Jessie is a thirteen-year-old city kid who couldn't imagine the charm of anyplace rural — that is until we spent the weekend in Eureka. She spent a Sunday afternoon riding a huge gray horse named Steel with the Etchegaray kids and that's all it took. She was smitten with rural life and ready to relocate, leaving the mall and fast food behind. She even suggested we move our family to Eureka, a town of 900 people. Of course, she would need a horse of her own.

Over ten months, I shot over 300 rolls of film for this project. I edited about 11,000 images down to 328 photographs for final consideration in the book, which came together only because a wonderful collec-tion of northern Nevadans graciously agreed to let me photograph them, often without notice. It was a privilege.

This project allowed me to slow down and, like Ruth, to notice the beauty sur-rounding me. I am forever grateful.

Ron Oden

Ron Oden finishes a sketch while waiting for Jean and Don in Yerington.

No matter how brilliant or common the remnants of human effort, absorbing and collecting them is a rich experience. This tour was important to me, not just for the selfishly satisfying act of placing a bookmark in time, but for the fulfillment of visiting, seeing and recording the braided truth and lore of northern Nevada.

The simple act of painting a subject dignifies it, which commands the viewer's attention. For any particular reason an artist might wish to manipulate the image to suit his purpose. In this book, my paintings were intended to be truthful and relatively accurate. Occasionally, I chose to heighten the emotional value of a work, such as the road to Duckwater, or Ely's Ghost Train, but for the most part, I painted real people, places, and things, resisting beauty for honesty. I think of these works as "painted book notes" that I hope will provide a clear, honest, and informational picture of my experiences in a creative context.

Art is to be seen, and the greatest compliment an artist can be given is for someone to spend time viewing his or her works. It was a privilege to work on this wonderful and meaningful project. Let me express my many thanks to my gifted colleagues Don Cox and Jean Dixon, and to all who made this book possible. Most importantly, let me express my appreciation to those who will spend the time to turn these pages and follow our trail through a millennium tour of northern Nevada.

According to their oral tradition, the Newe were placed in their homeland by the Creator, whose complexion was the same color as that of the natives. Once placed on the land, two native women instructed the coyote to carry a large, pitched water-basket with him on his journey into the Basin area. Coyote was specifically told not to open the lid. Moved by irrepressible curiosity, he periodically opened the basket during his trip. The beings concealed inside jumped out here and there. The Newe believe this explains why they live over a large area.
  Steven J. Crum, The Road on Which We Came

Native People

A small willow basket woven by Dresslerville resident Shirley Frank

Dresslerville

Washoe children learn to respect all of nature, including water, on their tribal lands.

The whistle blows on a divided past

Backdrop for Dresslerville: the majestic Sierra Nevada.

A s a girl, Betty Flint couldn't wait to leave home. "We were always looked down upon, being Indians," Flint said of growing up in Carson Valley as a member of the Washoe tribe. "We had to live with (whites), work with them and, you know, get along. I was glad to get married and get out of here."

Flint was gone for forty years. She and husband John lived in the San Francisco Bay area. They raised a family. Now that their kids are grown, Betty and John have returned. They live in Topaz on the Nevada-California border, outside the tribe's Dresslerville community, but she spends much of her time in Dresslerville re-learning what she'd forgotten. History. Traditions. A way of life.

"The language, I spoke the language before I moved to the city," Betty said of her native Washoe tongue, "but I got away from it. I couldn't teach it to my kids, but it's coming back to me now."

So are many other things, such as the painstaking preparations for the annual cultural dinner, a meal of traditional Washoe foods such as pine-nut soup, acorn biscuits and rabbit served to hundreds of Indian and non-Indian guests during the Christmas season. Flint and other tribal elders spend weeks picking, peeling, cooking and grinding pine nuts as their ancestors did it for hundreds of years.

"It's hideous work," Flint said with a slight smile. Much of it is done in the back yard of Dresslerville's senior center. In winter the weather is cold as Washoe women sit on the ground, cooking pine nuts with hot coals in willow baskets.

"The coals flavor the pine-nut soup," explained Theresa Jackson, Betty Flint's aunt. "The pine nuts have their own flavor, but the coals help. It's the only way you can do it, the traditional way, step by step."

The inside of the senior center is warm, but most of the women keep working outside because that's what their ancestors did. "It's our culture," Jackson said when she came inside. The eighty-two-year-old is a keeper of traditions. She knows how to weave baskets, grind the pine nuts and to remove the bitterness from acorns by leaching them with water.

"The acorn is so bitter, you can't put it in your mouth," she said.

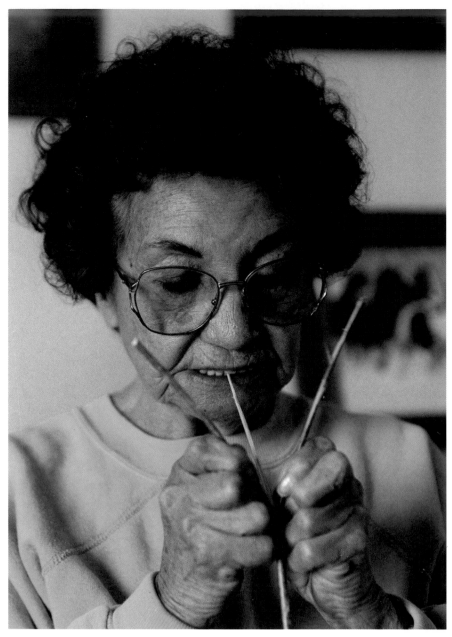

The first step in basket weaving: Dresslerville resident Theresa Jackson, 82, splits a willow branch into three sections to prepare willow thread. She has taught the art to her daughters and granddaughters.

Today it's not easy to find acorns and pine nuts for the dinner or willows for weaving baskets. Development in Carson Valley has turned much of the land into subdivisions.

"There are very few places where you can find willows in the valley," said Jackson, who must be careful not to pick willows that have been sprayed with pesticides. "You really have to check the willows out. You can tell the ones that have been sprayed. You can smell the stuff on them. We used to have lots of good strong willows. That's why we had beautiful baskets. They were strong and

healthy. Today, they're not."

Jackson also knows the stories of her tribe. She recalled her father making blankets of rabbit skins. "When you're skinning the rabbit, there was a certain way the whole skin was in one piece, no breaks in it," she said. "He had a small knife. He'd put the handle in his mouth. He'd let the knife part stick out. He'd have this rabbit skin. He'd pull it apart. He'd cut it and cut it."

The tribe has many other old stories, such as the whistle that blew in the nearby Minden-Gardnerville area at 6:00 p.m. daily. "I used to wonder how my grandma moved so fast to get out of town when the six o'clock whistle blew," said JoAnn Martinez, a long-time Dresslerville resident. "We had to rush to get out of town. We used to run down the street to get out of town."

After 6:00 p.m., Indians weren't allowed in town. "I remember that whistle," Jackson said.

When they were in town, Indians didn't mix with white people. "If you went to the movie theater, you sat upstairs," Martinez said. "You couldn't sit downstairs."

Restaurants also were divided between Indians and whites. "There was a nice Chinese family," Flint said. "He had places for the Indians in the back of his restaurant."

The town had another place the Indians liked. "I remember this woman," Jackson said. "She had an ice cream parlor. She would let us come in for ice cream. You could buy it, but you couldn't sit in there and eat it. You had to go out and eat it." That was the situation for Indians in Carson Valley for the first half of the 20th century.

"At certain times, they had to get out of town," said historian Guy Rocha, a state archivist who studies and maintains records of Nevada's past. "There was plenty of discrimination when it came to Washoe Indians. There were Indians and non-Indians and the Indians had to know the rules."

Today's Dresslerville kids go where they want to go, eat where they want to eat and do what they want to do. "We don't have to be home at six o'clock," said Liza Murphy, sixteen, a Washoe tribal member and junior at Douglas High School. Still, prejudice remains. "Sometimes they call us 'wagon burners' — just to mess around," Murphy said of her white classmates. "Sometimes they keep saying it and it makes me mad. Sometimes it gets old."

The kids plan to leave Dresslerville. They also plan to return. "Once you stay here all your life, it gets boring," said Toni Arcos, fifteen, who wants to study astronomy. "Once you live here all your life, there is hardly anything else to do. You know who everybody is. You know what's going on this weekend."

But the Dresslerville kids are tied to their community in ways hard to break. "When you're little, everybody hangs around with you," Arcos said. "When you get older, it gets better. With the people you know, the friendships get stronger." That's why they return.

"I just don't want to go and never come back," said Jessie Wright, sixteen.

Before 1917, Dresslerville didn't exist.

Indians lived near their work places, mostly on the ranches of Carson Valley. "Here are the native people just trying to survive," Rocha said. "They were totally dispossessed."

Dresslerville was created outside Gardnerville in 1917 when valley rancher William F. Dressler gave 40 acres to the federal government for a Washoe tribal town. It is now one of five Indian communities where Washoe tribe members live in northern Nevada and California.

"At first we didn't have running water in our houses when Dresslerville first started," Jackson said. "We had these houses made of gray stone. We had wood stoves. I used to call them 'mud houses.' Then we got frame houses."

Today, Jackson tries to keep traditions alive by teaching Flint and others the arts of weaving willow baskets and preparing pine nuts. It's difficult, she said, because fewer people are interested. "We don't have many weavers. It's just the same as learning to do this cultural dinner. It's too time consuming. They don't have time to sit by the hour. You have to pick your willow out. How far are you going to go to find a willow?"

- 1964: Washoe businessman Richard Barrington, owner and operator of Plumas Lumber Co., chosen Distinguished Nevadan by University of Nevada, Reno.
- 1966: Tribal Council organized.
- 1970: Land claims settled for about $5 million.
- 1975: Tribal offices built.
- 1990: Stewart Indian community established.
- 1995: Program started to teach Washoe language to tribe.
- 1998: Government returns 400 acres of Washoe land near Meeks Bay at Lake Tahoe on a lease with tribe.

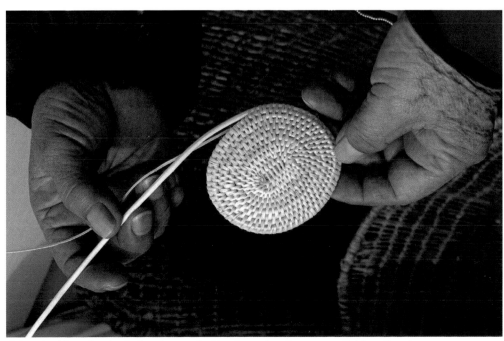

A basket begins to take shape in the hands of weaver Shirley Frank.

Eleanore Smokey, an elder speaker teacher at Washiw Wagayay Mangal school in Dresslerville, helps students learn the language of their Washoe ancestors.

Immersion in language and culture

The Washoe Indians are in danger of losing their language and possibly a lot more. "If you don't have a language, you lose your culture," said Wes Barber, who is learning and teaching his tribe's native tongue at the same time. "When you lose your heritage, dreams die."

The fifty-eight-year-old is trying to keep that from happening. He's part of an effort at the tribe's Dresslerville community to teach children their own language and, with it, their culture and heritage.

"I don't want them to lose it," said Harvey Jim, another leader of the language instruction program. "If you lose your language, you're not considered an Indian anymore."

Every school day in Dresslerville, twenty-three boys and girls between three

Sounding the words: twelve-year-old T'a:ba' (Erik Enos) helps eight-year-old Ma'wi' (Aaron Wallace) with a Washoe language assignment.

Washoe Indian encampment of 1520

This short story about a Washoe Indian encampment in 1520, long before white men arrived in Nevada, was written by twelve-year-old Kyle Little Arrow Bryan, a student in the Dresslerville language school. His story was translated into the Washiw language by tribal elders Amy and Wes Barber, Herman Holbrook, Bernadine James, Dinah Pete and Eleanore Smokey.

Kyle Little Arrow Bryan

Early one morning the men had already gone hunting and the women are trying to get the morning breakfast done. I can already hear the birds singing their morning song and I can feel the morning wind blow across my face. The sun is already high in the sky. The animals are scurrying around trying to find some food. The other Indian children are going into the woods to find something to do.

I like going into the woods to smell the fresh smell of sap and the way the flowers look running across the meadow. My favorite place is where the river runs past the meadow. The day is half gone and the men and women are going to get some pine nuts. The men are knocking down the cones and the women are picking up the pine nuts. The Indian children are climbing up the trees to get the pine nuts and to have fun.

After we picked a lot of pine nuts we started to cook them. At night we sang and we danced and we had a good time. The next day we went to go dig up the pine nuts. After the pine nuts were dug up we started to knock them out of their cones. Everybody was working on the pine nuts. After all the pine nuts were knocked out of their cones, the women started grinding some of the pine nuts up. The men went hunting for deer and *pélew* (jackrabbit).

At the end of the day we all gathered around the fire and started to sing and dance. We sang and we danced all night long. And when the early sun rose we started to pray to the creators for their fine food that they had given us and for the things the creators supplied for us. After the prayer we all started to eat.

Watli?iŋ lew lemċi?a? damo?mo?mo? demlu dơda gaŋa?a?, ċli·lihu ?umtaYaŋa gišuwe?i. Si·su šišimaš weski?im hululugiša. Wadibiluš?aš?eti?a. ?Uċili, ?ida basat, ?ida ċali? hute ḱi?iw lewe? wi·ḱila gisa? bišapu ?igi?. Naŋawŋaŋ gi·sa? dewNeti ?e?gaṗila hute wi·ḱil ɡaṗila ?ida ṗuyli?a?. Lesa? dala?aga le? gaṗila ?rgi šawa? ?ida semiši, sim ta·gim dawyu?uš ?aŋaw gelu diga?la·m dipalal šala? dawyu?uš ?aŋaw ḱe?t?. Dawṗaṗil dakMi·ki latu moċem de Muwe? yegi·ḱula. Waṫa bayu?uš ?išda dime? yakta·dabu. Wu·diŋ wedibaluš ?aš da?mo?mo?mo ?ida ṫelilihu ṫa·gim ?ugilbeti?a ?ida da?mo?mo?mo? ṫa·gim ya·guwa. Naŋawŋaŋ ṗileliwa? ṫa·gim ya·guwa ?ida ṗuyli?a.

Ṫa·gim ya·gu mama? ?udi gese?cga gaya·w?eti?a. Lelum ?išim ?ida šešiši ?ida ɡegum hi·ki ?aŋaw wa·šiw wagayaya?. Dibe? weṗimi?išda ṫa·gim bugayaya ?udi gehumi?a?. Gehumi mama? ?udi de?eglu dik ma·da?a gatḱašilhaya. Milewlew?a? ṫa·gim yatḱašilmama? ?udi ṫa·gim wayu?uš ?aŋaw ?iške le?ew hulew. Da?mo?mo?mo? ṫa·gim dašuwa. Ṫclilihu pelew ?ida memde·wi ṫuYaŋ gišuwe?i. Wapawdaš diyu lelew ?ahuya ?ida ṫanu bo·ṗı lakalelbi? ?aš "diwagayaya? ?ida lo?oš hulew". Dila? diṗal dipek gaša? ?ida tešušluti ?ida galo?oš. Weṗimi?aš ṫa·gim bugayaya? mama? ?udi gawalašu?a? dayu·gili ?ida memde·wi ?adaš, pelew ?adaš, ?ida ?atabi?, dilek ?aš ?um selem mama?udi gehubimi ?udi lemlu hulew.

Above is the short story translated into the Washiw language.

DRESSLERVILLE

- Population: 500.

- Claim to fame: Oldest and largest of Washoe Indian tribe's communities in northern Nevada and California.

- How it got its name: W.F. Dressler, a Carson Valley rancher, donated a 40-acre site near Gardnerville in 1917 for the tribal community.

- Local legend: Dat-So-La-Lee. Born about 1835, she became tribe's most famous basket weaver. One of her ceremonial baskets, which took two years to complete, contains 84,500 stitches. Her works are displayed at Nevada State Museum in Carson City. She died in 1925.

and twelve years old come to classes at 8:00 a.m. in the Youth Center. For five hours, they're taught reading, writing and other basics, all in the Washoe language called Washiw. This is an immersion program, with kids and teachers speaking nothing but the native language. After that, they disperse into different mathematics, computer and tutoring sessions.

"Our language is on the edge of extinction," said School Board Trustee Carla James. "This school is a good avenue." The program, independent of the Douglas County school system which serves Dresslerville, is private and nonprofit, funded with grants and donations. The full-time kids don't attend county schools.

"The kids weren't doing well in the surrounding schools," said Benny Fillmore, one of the program's founders. "There was a lack of pride. We're losing touch with who we are. It came down to our language not being passed on."

Six part-time students attend regular classes in Douglas County schools and come to Dresslerville for language instruction. When the program started in 1997-98, it had ten full-time and six part-time students. Class size is expected to reach fifty by 2000.

"When the elders are gone, we can speak it," said thirteen-year-old part-time student, Yancy Burtt, explaining his reason for attending language classes.

The language is ancient, but only a handful of tribal members speak it. "You could probably count the number of speakers on your hands and toes and my hands and toes," said James, a geologist with the U.S. Bureau of Land Management in Carson City who grew up in Dresslerville and knows only a few words. "I'm not fluent."

The language is dying, school board members believe, because it's not used regularly in Washoe homes. "It doesn't remain with them," Barber said of the tribe's language and children. When he was young, Barber knew the language. Then his grandmother died. "That's all she spoke and that's all I heard," he said. "Then I didn't hear it that much anymore. My grandfather, he spoke mostly English."

Other members of the tribe tell similar stories. They spoke the language as children because their grandparents did. But as the older family members died, so did the language. Along with lack of use at home, Barber said the language was stamped out in the federal Indian schools his relatives attended as children.

"We started losing it as youngsters fifty or sixty years ago," Barber said. "We were taken into these schools and were punished for speaking the language. You'd be severely beaten for it."

Vanessa Bryan, who lives in the tribe's Stewart community in Carson City, doesn't know the language. "When I try to sit with the elders," she said, "I don't know what they're saying. I don't know things about what Washoes do." But she's learning from other family members and her son, twelve-year-old Kyle, who attends the Dresslerville program.

"They're teaching me the traditions that I, as a parent, should have been teaching them," Bryan said. "I don't know my ancestors."

Elder Herman Holbrook helps teach children the native language

Dr. Sharon Malotte, left, finishing her day shift, greets Dr. Loren Simpson as he arrives for night duty at South Lyon Medical Center.

Serving tribal clinics and ER patients

D r. Loren Simpson's foot is heavy on the gas pedal every Thursday when he drives from the clinic in Coleville, California, to the hospital in Yerington.

"At 65 miles per hour, you can make it in fifty minutes," said Simpson, one of the few American Indian doctors practicing in Nevada. A member of the Washoe tribe, Simpson lives in Dresslerville and spends most of his work week in Coleville at one of three clinics in the eastern Sierra operated by the Toiyabe Indian Health Project. That's his regular job from 8:00 a.m. to 5:00 p.m.

On Thursdays, he rushes to the South Lyon County Medical Center in Yerington to start his all-night emergency room shift at 6:00 p.m. When the sun comes up on Friday, Simpson drives back to Coleville to work at the clinic from 8:00 a.m. until noon. The reason for this weekly Coleville-Yerington commute is simple. He needs the money.

"It's to help pay off some bills," said Simpson, a thirty-four-year-old Dresslerville native who returned to the Washoe community near Gardnerville when he finished medical training at the University of North Dakota in 1997.

Simpson didn't set out to be a doctor. As a senior at Douglas High School, he had planned a career in one of two things — construction work or the U.S. Army. But then Simpson changed his mind, went to the University of Nevada, Reno, got a degree in science and went on to medical school. As a student at UNR, he had done volunteer work at Saint Mary's Regional Medical Center and Washoe Medical Center. After college, he went to work as an orderly at Washoe Med.

That's where he met Dr. Sharon Malotte, an American Indian physician. "She asked me if I had applied to medical school," said Simpson, who credits Malotte with pointing him first toward North Dakota and then to the Toiyabe project. Now he specializes in family medicine, along with other Toiyabe doctors who cover an area that stretches from Bishop, California, in the south up to Coleville.

"I do know a lot of the patients and

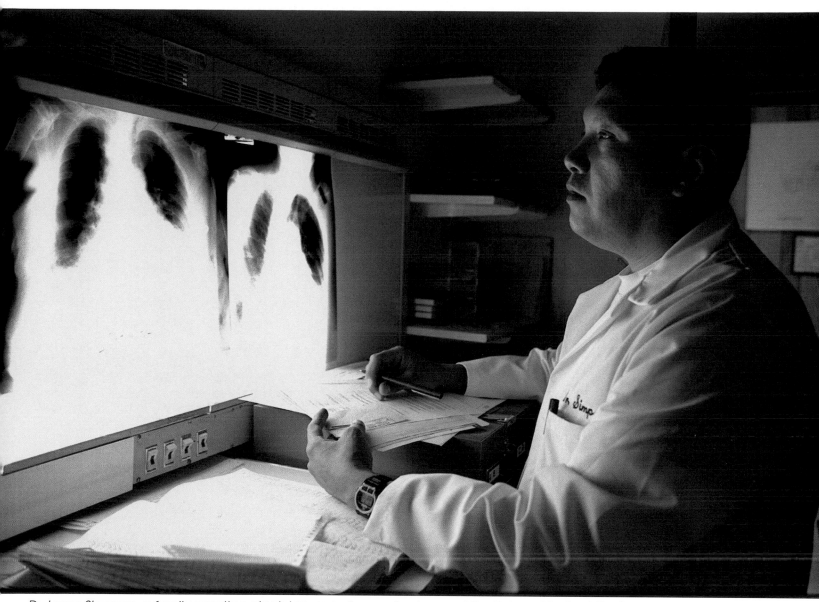

Dr. Loren Simpson, a family practice physician, examines a chest x-ray at South Lyon Medical Center.

their families," Simpson said. "It's the same in Yerington; I see a lot of the people I knew when I was growing up." He said he returned to Dresslerville so he could be with family and friends.

"I do see my family members — my grandmother, my uncles, my brothers," he said. "It's the same at other reservations across the United States as well. That's one of the main reasons I moved home."

Duckwater

For some, the road to Duckwater leads to freedom.

From a rough past, a road runs into the future

On the road to Duckwater, a woman and her dog take an evening walk.

IMPORTANT DATES

- 1863: U.S. signs Treaty of Ruby Valley with Western Shoshone Nation.
- Oct. 10, 1932: Chiefs of Western Shoshone Nation meet in Elko to discuss enforcement of treaty rights.
- 1934: Indian Reorganization Act allows Indians without land to acquire property.
- 1937: Angelo Florio tells two Shoshone men working for him, Wagon Johnnie and Brownie Sam, that he is willing to sell his ranch to the federal government for an Indian reservation.
- 1940: Florio sells ranch to government; it becomes Duckwater Shoshone Reservation.
- 1941: School is opened in old Florio bunkhouse. Stockmen's Association formed to manage livestock on reservation.
- 1942: Government builds first brick houses.
- 1946: Indian Claims Commission authorized by Congress.
- 1949: Public and government schools combined.
- 1955: New school built south of reservation.
- 1971: Reservation gets electricity.
- 1973: Parents withdraw their children from public school and form Duckwater Shoshone School Board.
- Nov. 26, 1973: Duckwater Shoshone Elementary School opens on reservation.
- 1981: Tribe refuses to pay fees to Bureau of Land Management for grazing cattle on 350,000 acres.
- 1984: Tribe contracts for its own law enforcement.
- 1986: First low-rent houses built.
- 1991: Tribe becomes self-governing, receiving funds from federal government, but controls own operations and programs.

D riving down State Route 379, figuring out when you've finally reached the Duckwater Shoshone Reservation is easy: it's where the pavement ends.

Tribal Chairman Tim Thompson knows he lives in one of the state's most remote locations. Drive one hour from Ely on U.S. 6, cross from White Pine County into Nye County, take a right at Currant onto Route 379, go another thirty minutes – and when the road turns from asphalt to gravel, you've arrived.

"I don't even think about it," Thompson said of his out-of-the-way home, "but you can't go to McDonald's." Duckwater has no such thing as fast food. Weekly shopping trips to Ely are made with care. Turning around and going back is difficult if you forget something.

"You make a list," said Thompson, who grew up in a house without running water or electricity. Today, the reservation has no gas stations or supermarkets; no barbershop, video store or restaurant; not even a 7-Eleven.

But despite some of the difficulties, Thompson and the rest of the Duckwater Shoshone seem to enjoy their location beyond the reach of many modern conveniences.

"We're about isolation," said tribal member Doris Allison. "We would rather be out here."

Virginia Sanchez, a descendent of one of the original Duckwater families, grew up in Carson City and then returned to her roots in 1982. "My family is buried out here," said Sanchez, who works in tribal administration. "It's where my blood is. It's got to be that connection, where your people have lived so long. It's where I belong."

Certainly, that's true of Thompson, who returned after living much of his adult life in Reno and Carson City. Thompson retired from Nevada Bell in 1990 and came back to a different Duckwater, a place he hadn't seen much of since graduating from high school in 1961.

"There was no electricity, no water, no telephone," Thompson said of the reservation he knew as a child. "That was living for us. We hauled wood and we hauled water for Mom. Sometimes we'd get a little lazy. We didn't think about Mom washing clothes all day."

Now the tribe operates its own construction company. "We're doing contract work right now," Thompson said. "We're going out for these jobs surrounding the reservation. The two things we're trying to do are roads and reclaiming work on the mines." Thompson and other tribal leaders hope Duckwater Shoshone Construction will give reservation residents a choice.

"Our fun was with riding horses," a resident says of the old days.

They still can leave Duckwater if they want to, or they can stay — and jobs will be available if they do.

Thompson didn't have that choice. He had to leave because the reservation offered him nothing. His brothers, William and Rodney, had to leave for construction jobs in Elko County mines. William Thompson, a single father, now leaves three children — two girls and a boy — behind in Duckwater. Sometimes he works seven days and comes home for four. Other times he works fourteen days and comes home for seven. The kids stay with relatives when their father is gone.

"He hates it," Tim Thompson said of William's long-distance routine. "He's got a home out here. He's got kids going to school." If the construction business booms, William and Rodney will be able to live and work in Duckwater. "We'll solve the problem," Tim Thompson said, "but we're so isolated and remote, there's no way now to work and stay on the reservation."

Along with the construction company, Tim Thompson has his own catfish farm, where he raises and ships fish. He's also waiting for a government environmental

ruling that could allow him to expand the operation.

"I'm brand-new in this business," Thompson said, standing near his feeding ponds crowded with catfish. "I was told it takes three years to raise a nice fat catfish. But we have catfish that were fingerlings a year ago. They're ready for market right now."

In Duckwater, the people are used to fighting for what they want — starting in the late 1930s with two Shoshone men, Wagon Johnnie and Brownie Sam. They worked to get the federal government to purchase a 3,272-acre ranch for sale in the Railroad Valley and turn it into a reservation. They succeeded.

In 1973, parents were unhappy with their children's education at the nearby public school. They wanted to take their kids out of that school and start one of their own on the reservation. They succeeded.

In the 1980s, residents decided they wanted more control over their own affairs and less direction from the U.S. government. They succeeded.

"Yes, they gave us money," Tribal

An artist who preserves traditions and keeps some secrets

Duckwater artist Steven Mike paints scenes and designs on the buckskin surfaces of the drums he constructs at home.

DUCKWATER

- Population in 1998: 298 (age 0-17, 30 percent; 18-44, 32 percent; 45-64, 26 percent; 64-plus, 12 percent; male, 50.3 percent; female, 49.7 percent)
- Median household income in 1998: $19,688.
- Claim to fame: One of three self-governing reservations in the state, which gives reservation direct control of its budget and programs.
- How it got its name: Duckwater Creek flows through the reservation in Railroad Valley in Nye County.
- Local legend: Wii'iddi — known as Chief Blackeye or Willie Blackeye to whites because of the birthmark on his left eye — was Shoshone leader in area before reservation was founded. His descendants live on the reservation.

Steven Mike will show you his paintings and he'll talk about them — up to a point. He won't go into a lot of details about how he creates the artwork on traditional Indian drums made of elk skin, deerskin and rawhide.

"That's my secret," said Mike, who works at his home on the Duckwater Shoshone Reservation. "I don't tell anybody. I learned this by myself. Why should I teach somebody? I'll teach it to my grandchildren, maybe — if I'm still alive."

You've got to have the right wood for the drum frame. Mike doesn't use wood from the reservation because it breaks easily, so he comes to Reno for his wood. The skin has to be prepared for stretching over the frame. And, of course, you have to paint it.

"What you see, you draw," said Mike, who spends eight to ten hours on a single painting. "You see a mountain, you draw it in your mind. Then, you come home and draw it." When Mike paints, he's careful.

"You can't make a mistake on them," he said. "You can't erase it off."

Buckskin drum-tops show the work of artist Steven Mike.

Manager Jerry Millett said of the old system. "They determined how much. They determined what it was you could and couldn't do. They got to decide if you wanted to move some of your law-enforcement money into social services."

Now Congress has changed the government's relationship with reservations, giving Indians a chance for more control. The Bureau of Indian Affairs and the Indian Health Service play a role, but the tribe — which negotiates with the federal government for its budget — spends its own money. Duckwater grabbed the self-governing opportunity.

"We have a tribal government; we have the right to make decisions," Millett said. "We have a school. We have a law-enforcement program. We provide all kinds of health services. We pay the bills." But they still have a fight to finish — the tribe's ongoing dispute with the government about land.

The battle has its roots in the 1863 Treaty of Ruby Valley that the Western Shoshone Nation signed with the federal government. Duckwater's leaders claim the treaty entitles them to a lot more land than the 3,800 acres they have.

"It goes clear back to when the treaty was settled," Thompson said. "Our issues are all based on that. We're still in the process of trying to claim our land rights." A decision must be made: either the tribe accepts a cash settlement or keeps fighting for ground. "I would say the majority wants to settle this thing," said Thompson. "The younger generation wants money. My generation probably wants to hang on."

Duckwater's present boundaries were established pretty much in 1940 when the federal government bought the local ranch. "The government came along and made land assignments out of it," Thompson said. "It ended up with twenty-one land assign-

Young basketball players enjoy a pickup game just before sunset.

An albino catfish is among the hundreds raised by Duckwater Tribal Chairman Thompson.

Thompson and his partner, Deloros Steward, hope to make their catfish farm a successful business on the remote reservation.

ments. We have fifty families now. We need land expansion for farms and other purposes. This is an agricultural reservation. We want to farm and raise cattle."

Duckwater is a pretty spot, with the valley, the creek and surrounding mountains, but some tribal members would rather be somewhere else. "When the reservation was established for homeless Indians, that's how we all came to be here," said Doris Allison, whose family came to the reservation from Smoky Valley south of Austin. "By leaving our own homeland, we lost a lot of our legends and a lot of what we should have been."

Another tribal elder, Douglas George, remembers the early days at Duckwater. "First, there was just a dirt road," he said. "There was no power, no running water. You had to carry water from the springs."

Later, Thompson recalls going off the reservation to a friend's home that had electricity, a telephone and indoor plumbing. "There was a guy south of the reservation, he was my good buddy," Thompson said. "They had utilities. I wondered why we didn't have them." But Thompson never asked his parents. Instead, he accepted life in Duckwater.

"When we were kids, we almost never did go to town," Thompson said of rare trips to Ely. "We never missed it. Our fun was with riding horses. Every once in a while, we went to town in the back of a pickup. We'd get all cleaned up. When we got there, we'd be all dusty."

Millett had a similar childhood. "Nobody had any money to buy toys," he said. "We made our own toys. The one I remember is syrup — Log Cabin Syrup. It used to come in that metal log cabin. It was like a little house."

Thompson remembers one afternoon when he and some other kids were looking around an old log house where his mother had lived before the reservation existed.

"The rancher that lived on that property saw us looking around there one time," he said. "We were looking for relics, horseshoes and stuff. It wasn't long after that he came out with a bulldozer and just knocked it down. There's nothing there now. He was afraid we might claim the land."

School gives a focal point to the community

Keeping the classroom doors open for eighteen students is a struggle, but the Duckwater Shoshone Elementary School is the heart of the Indian community surrounding it. That's why tribal leaders wage an ongoing battle for the school's survival.

"We argue our case," said Jerry Millett, manager of the Duckwater Shoshone Reservation. "It's almost a yearly thing."

The school, sustained by a variety of federal and nonprofit funding sources, was established in 1973 after a revolt by reservation parents. Unhappy with their children's progress, they pulled their kids out of the Nye County School District and brought them home.

"They wanted more involvement in the school," Millett said. "Our kids weren't doing as well as the parents thought they should be doing. There were threats about them having to go to jail if they pulled their kids out." But the parents pushed ahead.

On July 26, 1973, they formed the Duckwater Shoshone School Board. Next they got a $35,000 grant from the U.S. Office of Education. The tribe bought a church building on the reservation and turned it

into a schoolhouse. One teacher was hired. On Nov. 26, 1973, the elementary school opened.

Most Duckwater children from kindergarten through eighth grade attend the school. A few go to a public school near the reservation. Once they're in high school, all the kids ride a bus off the reservation to Eureka and back.

"The community has hung tough over the years to support the school," Millett said. "It's one of the highest priorities here." The school's ultimate governing authority is the U.S. Bureau of Indian Affairs. Every year, reservation leaders must justify the school's existence to the

Duckwater Shoshone Elementary School has its own zoo, complete with goats and ostriches.

BIA.

"We get money from the BIA," Millett said. "There was a time when the BIA sent a representative here and met with the education committee and the Tribal Council and said, 'this is the last year of the school' because there weren't enough kids." But somehow the school, remodeled in 1982, survives. Teachers have been added. The school is an interesting place. It even has a zoo.

"Sometimes the goats will chase the llamas and the llamas will chase the ostriches," said Robert Coggan, one of the school's three teachers. "Everybody chases everybody."

The children are studying the animals. Inside one classroom, four large ostrich eggs sit in an incubator made by students. The kids are waiting for the eggs to hatch. Outside, the students observe ostrich behavior.

"Doesn't he get tired?" asked thirteen-year-old Sheena Thompson, watching Brutus, one of the ostriches, prancing rapidly around the animal enclosure.

Joshua Baca, eleven, has learned something about ostriches. "It doesn't hurt when they peck you," he said. Farmers in Utah gave the ostriches and llamas to the school.

"It was quite a shock for the cattle and horses to see ostriches," Coggan said. "I wanted to get some more animals, but they told me to stop for a while."

The students do more than watch Brutus. "We worked out thirty experiments based on voice recognition and color recognition," said Coggan, who taught in Arizona public schools before coming to Duckwater. "We test the animals' eyes, their hearing. We have recorded some of their vocalizations and mapped out some of their voice variations. We couldn't have done that in a public school setting."

The teachers use what they call an

Joshua Baca, 11, a student at Duckwater Shoshone Elementary School, stays after school to play computer games.

"integrated format" with the sudents, taking one theme — such as ostriches — and building an entire curriculum around it. Along with science, Coggan employs the bizarre bird to teach reading, writing, arithmetic and a variety of other subjects.

"We can put in seventeen subjects a day instead of six. We're teaching skills," said Coggan, who served thirteen years in the Army before coming to Duckwater. Now he says he enjoys the teaching freedom he has on the reservation. He lives in Duckwater because he has to. The largest nearby town, Ely, is a ninety-minute drive. That's a long commute.

Coggan says he doesn't mind the isolation. "I was in the Army so long. In the military, you're in the field nine or ten months a year." Still, Duckwater took some getting used to:

"I just got television, after a year of living here," he said, "and I read a lot."

At Duckwater Shoshone Elementary School, students are incubating four ostrich eggs like this one held by teacher Robert Coggan.

Duckwater Shoshone try to save their past

Reno basketmaker Mary Lee Fulkerson, left, admires a willow cone basket woven by Duckwater resident Evelyn Pete, right.

For Jerry Millett, moving quickly and forcefully appears easy. That's how you succeed: make your point, win the argument, then move on to the next objective. After all, Millett is a leader of the Duckwater Shoshone Indians and he's got to be aggressive. He grew up on the Duckwater Shoshone Reservation, a remote valley in eastern Nevada. Now, he's the tribal manager — the man who's supposed to get things done.

"You make your presentation, I make mine," Millett said. "Whoever talks longer and harder wins." Simple. Direct. But that's not the tribe's way. Although he's a Shoshone, it took Millett some time to understand that.

"I learned from watching the elders," he said. "When we'd have a meeting, they taught me the Indian way. You want to deal with today and the future. The way our people do business is they have to talk about the past and bring that to the present before they can talk about the future." Traditions and customs competing with the ways of the modern world are not just Millett's struggles but Duckwater's.

"We have to live in a culture that's very alien to us because we choose to remain who we are," said resident Doris Allison. "I think of being Indian as a family – not only your immediate family, but the one that surrounds

Father and son bring their memories to the Duckwater town gathering.

Duckwater Shoshone Reservation nestles in a remote valley, seventy-four miles southwest of Ely.

you. That's what helps us survive."

The Duckwater Shoshone are trying to save their past — their culture, their language, their crafts and, most of all, their way of living.

"We should spend time with our young people, telling them what it was like before," Arvilla Mascarenas said. "My son lost the language, but if I talk to him in Shoshone, I'm sure the language will come back to him." Language is the key, and a concern.

"I doubt that we will ever be able to record the language or preserve it because so much of it has been lost," Allison said. "I think it started way back when we were punished for speaking the language."

Many of Duckwater's elders tell stories of their youth at government boarding schools, of being beaten for speaking Shoshone instead of English. Now they talk about trying to recover their history.

"What's important to preserve are the teachings and the way of life of our people.

We have a tendency to forget that," Millett said. "There was a lot of talk about the past and I'm sitting there thinking that we have to decide what we're going to say to Senator Harry Reid."

Millett says he has changed the way he does business. "What I found out is if we do business the Indian way, there is a lot better chance of love, caring and togetherness. Why don't we work out a solution? It makes you feel so much better about yourself when the day is over."

His view of achievement has changed. "In the white man's world, success is measured in dollars and cents. With Indians, success is not measured in dollars and cents. Success is measured in how you get along with your neighbors, how you have family closeness. It doesn't sound like a lot of requirements, but the end result of that kind of success is being happy."

Pyramid Lake

When vandals sprayed graffiti on these tufa rock formations at Pyramid Lake, the rocks had to be closed to the public.

Optimism rises with the water level at Pyramid Lake

Pyramid Lake fishing guide George Molina sets one of his down-riggers.

fter a long summer selling potato chips, soda pop and paper plates to throngs of visitors who stop at his store on their way to Pyramid Lake, George Molina is glad to be back on the water. Molina is starting his fifteenth year as a fishing guide at the lake, where the nine-month cutthroat trout season is open from October until the end of June.

During the season, Molina leaves his wife, Carla, in charge of their Pyramid Lake Store. He searches for trout with clients who come from around the world, all looking for the kind of day Molina remembers from October 1998.

First came the morning: "I had three guys; they landed seventy-nine fish in four hours," said Molina. "I normally take a Thermos of coffee. I never even touched it." They had no time for coffee, or much of anything else, except catching fish. Then, in the afternoon, Molina took a husband and wife fishing.

"I had a retired couple; they caught thirty-five," Molina said. "That was the best fishing they ever had."

In each case, all but two fish had to be thrown back. That's the daily limit at Pyramid Lake. Molina, who quit his job in Reno as a structural-steel detailer to fish, has experienced good and bad days in his years on Pyramid. Lately, fishing has been good.

The lake is the heart of the Pyramid Lake Paiute Reservation. When it's rising, when more Truckee River water is flowing in, the reservation seems to look better. The tribe, in general, appears to feel better.

"It's been a long time since we've seen this much water in our lake and it feels good," said Jeanette Allen, who is trying to revive Paiute traditions as the tribe's language-program coordinator.

Tribal elder Lorraine Wadsworth agrees. "The water has really gone up and our native fish have really come back" she said.

So have other things on the reservation. A new high school is planned, with the opening scheduled for 2001. In the present high school, a collection of portable buildings, students are studying Paiute traditions that many tribal elders fear will die if they're not passed down to the reservation's young people.

"I've always wanted to learn my language," said Kellie Harry, a senior who has attended high school on and off the reserva-

Pyramid Lake Paiute Cultural Center

tion. "I love it. I'm picking it up pretty fast."

Language study is only part of the revival of Paiute culture. The kids are learning the old songs and dances. They're learning the legends. They're also learning the proper way to prepare the Cui-ui fish, the tribe's traditional food from the lake. The Cui-ui is an endangered species, and even though its number is increasing, the tribe consumes only a limited number per year.

"Back in the old days, they used to eat everything," Harry said. "At first, we were just cutting the filets. But Wilson showed us how."

Wilson Wewa, director of the Pyramid Lake Paiute Cultural Center, is a leader of the revival of tradition. At forty-three he isn't an elder, but he spent a lot of time with his grandparents and their friends while he was growing up in Oregon. He learned the traditional ways. Now, he's passing them on.

"My grandparents took me on some of their trips," said Wewa, who oversees the reservation's museum. "I met a lot of old people. I sat at the dinner table and listened to them talk about places and people. I asked a lot of questions. As I got older, the elders knew I was interested in that stuff, so they

started teaching me."

Today, Wewa is teaching and he might be just in time. At Pyramid Lake, the Paiute language is vanishing. If it is going to survive, children must be the ones who carry it on.

"That's who we are, that's what we are about," Allen said. "You need somebody to talk to you every day, or a lot gets lost."

High school principal Randy Melendez, a tribal member, has made the traditions part of his program to attract students to a campus that was dying a short time ago. The teacher, coach and sometime principal from 1980 to 1988, is taking a leave of absence from his administrative post at the Washoe County School District to revive his old high school. When Melendez showed up at Pyramid near the end of the 1997-98 school year, only seventeen students were enrolled at the tribal high school.

"It was seventeen on a good day," said the former Wooster High School star athlete who graduated from the University of Nevada, Reno.

At Pyramid Lake, teenagers have choices: they can attend Reed or Sparks high schools in the Washoe County School District, or Fernley High in nearby Lyon County. That's

Malotte focuses on the big picture

Jack Malotte was asked to paint a large mural on one wall in the Pyramid Lake High School gym. After that, Malotte stuck around to teach art.

"I know a lot of people in this area, so it was easy to fit in with everybody," said Malotte, a member of the Shoshone and Washoe tribes. He grew up in Reno and graduated from the California College of Arts and Crafts in the San Francisco Bay area. At Pyramid Lake High, he painted a mural –– seventy-seven feet long and thirty-eight feet high — of Paiute leaders and Pyramid Lake, the center of the Pyramid Lake Paiute Reservation. He also has painted murals at Lake Tahoe and in Susanville, California.

"Painting on the wall has its advantages," said Malotte, who graduated from Reno's Wooster High in 1971. "You can use a big fat paint brush or rollers. You can get real physical." Here's the disadvantage: "Murals aren't sacred. They usually only last ten years." Or sometimes less.

His art students at Pyramid Lake High paint the walls of their classroom. They paint the walls once, twice, three times or more. Projects are started. More students join in; they add things. The project changes. Once something is started, nobody is sure how it's going to turn out.

"It's had about ten paintings on there," he said of one section of wall. "Everybody adds to it. Some guys get little projects going and they get interested."

But murals aren't Malotte's favorite form of art. He likes something called "mono-printing." Here's how it works:

"You take a piece of Plexiglas, you take oil-based inks. You roll it on there." That's your design. "You run it through a press and you get one print. Then you clean off your glass and start over.

"Each print is different. You get one print. It's more enjoyable than painting on walls."

Jack Malotte, art teacher at Pyramid Lake High School, stands in the doorway of his classroom where the doors, walls and ceiling are an open canvas for student paintings. Large murals are Malotte's own specialty.

PYRAMID LAKE
- Population in 1990: 1,388 (34 percent under 18, 36 percent 18-44, 17 percent 45-64, 13 percent 65 and older; 50.22 percent female, 49.78 percent male).
- Median household income in 1990: $15,660.
- Claim to fame: Home of Pyramid Lake, northern Nevada landmark and one of world's most famous desert lakes.
- How it got its name: Explorer John C. Frémont was said to have named the lake after Pyramid-shaped island. Indian legend says lake was made from tears shed by an Indian woman whose two sons constantly were quarreling. Nixon, community on Pyramid Lake Paiute Reservation that serves as tribal headquarters, was named for U.S. Sen. George Nixon of Nevada. He first was elected to Senate in 1905 and died in 1912.
- Local legend: Sarah Winnemucca, a Paiute in Nevada who lived from 1844 to 1891, is recognized as crusader for Indian rights and education. She presented petitions to Congress and wrote book, *Life Among the Paiutes: Their Wrongs and Claims*. An elementary school in Reno is named for her. But Winnemucca is a controversial figure among Paiutes. Some tribal members, even today, claim she was a traitor, saying she led soldiers to Indian camps. In Pyramid Lake Paiute Cultural Center, display on her includes this: "Sarah Winnemucca. Credited with starting schools in Lovelock and at Pyramid Lake, went on lecture tours across U.S. after Pyramid Lake War of 1860. Sarah has been notoriously known to the Neh-Muh (Indian people) as a traitor and is blamed for many lives lost on a forced march to (an) Indian Reservation in Oregon."

where the Pyramid students were going — to schools off the reservation. Some still do. To revive interest in Pyramid Lake High, the first move Melendez made was to convince reservation kids to attend summer school.

"We said, 'Let's open it up to everyone on the reservation, whether they go to Reed or Sparks,'" he said. "I knew Pyramid Lake kids weren't participating in summer school because they live way out here."

Along with classes, Melendez added something else — a basketball camp. Basketball had been important on the reservation. The high school girls won a state championship in 1981. The boys won in 1987 and 1988. Perhaps Melendez could make basketball important again, and use it to make the school important. Thirty kids showed up for the summer session.

"We tied the basketball into it: morning school and an afternoon basketball camp," Melendez said. "The word got around that we had kind of revived the program."

For the 1998-99 academic year, enrollment reached an all-time high of seventy students. The boys' basketball team, coached by Melendez, finished with a winning record. So did the girls.

"Look at our team, man!" Melendez said, pointing to pictures in his office of the basketball teams. "Look at that up there, all of our junior varsity players, our girls' team and our varsity boys. Half the school is involved. I've always believed these kids wanted to be here and wanted to participate." But first he had to sell the idea.

"I've always believed if you go to a kid and say, 'We're going to have this team. We need you. I'll see you out there tomorrow. I need you out there.' It works extremely well."

Along with basketball, Melendez sold Paiute culture. "We have the language and all that stuff," he said. "Tie it all together, get a good staff, we're off and running." The kids bought it.

"I'd heard what Randy had done livening things up," said Kellie Harry, a basketball player and rodeo performer who switched from Reed to Pyramid Lake High for her junior year. "He's just gotten everything going. I don't regret coming back here. Everyone was looking at high school as a negative thing. He turned it into a positive thing." She says she liked the Pyramid Lake program, but decided to return to Reed so she could graduate with her long time classmates.

Nathan George, heavyweight boxer on the Pyramid Lake High School team, practices in the school's old gymnasium.

Peppy Sampson, a retired Reno construction worker, is coaching boxing. His team has four boys and four girls.

"Randy wanted to try it and see how everything turned out," said Sampson, a long-time boxing coach who runs the team with George New Moon of Wadsworth. "We've got good kids. They train pretty hard and they learn everything." One of them is heavyweight Nathan George, who gives a simple reason for boxing: "It's fun."

So is fishing, which is also a business. The folks who visit the lake contribute an estimated $500,000 annually to the tribe's economy in licenses and other fees. That's why the lake level is important to the tribe. Legislation to settle water disputes among Truckee River users in northern Nevada has helped Pyramid.

"It's still a world-class lake," said Molina, whose wife, Carla, is a tribal member. "Overall, the more water you get, it helps the big cycle of life."

The level is high enough to impress Dave Monda, a biologist with Pyramid Lake Fisheries in Sutcliffe, where the trout-spawning facilities are located and where the fishing boats are put in the water.

"There is a lot more water and the lake level is coming up," Monda said. "The cement blocks in the water used to be on shore." Rising water also threatens the fisheries building. "It's probably going to flood our building," he said. "We built the rock wall to protect it. If it comes up the way it has the last couple of years, we're going to have to get a new building."

Monda is optimistic about the future of the lake and the fish. "This is one of the few places left where it can really be a success story, where you can have trout running back up the Truckee River the way they used to," he said. "A lot of places you can't do that anymore. It's not possible. Here, it is."

Melendez knows about school and difficult times. Once *he* was a student far from home. "That was culture shock; I didn't have a clue," he said of his freshman year at Utah State University.

Melendez could have gone to the University of Nevada, Reno, on an athletic scholarship from high school, but he wanted to get out of town. On the advice of a high-school counselor, he tried Utah State.

"Luckily, there were some other Indian kids at the university," he said. "I had this windbreaker. It was the coldest winter there." He needed a coat. "They had a little Indian center, there were probably thirty Indian kids on campus. We went down to the Indian center where they had these old Army jackets with hoods."

Melendez took one. "I headed across campus," he said. "I saw these two Indian guys. They had their jackets with hoods, too." Melendez ended up leaving Utah State for UNR.

"The Indian kids at Utah were very ill prepared," he said. "At the high school, we want to get them better prepared."

Next door to the high school, in an old wooden building, something else is going on.

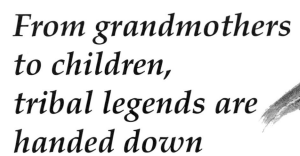
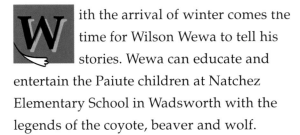

Wilson Wewa

From grandmothers to children, tribal legends are handed down

With the arrival of winter comes the time for Wilson Wewa to tell his stories. Wewa can educate and entertain the Paiute children at Natchez Elementary School in Wadsworth with the legends of the coyote, beaver and wolf.

"These stories are for wintertime," said Wewa, director of the Pyramid Lake Paiute Cultural Center. "During the springtime and summertime, we're not supposed to tell them. It's for fall and winter."

Why? Wewa is surprised to be asked.

"That's what my grandma told me," said the forty-three-year-old Paiute who grew up in central Oregon. "That's what her grandma told her and that's what her grandma told her."

Wewa, who has spent his life learning Paiute tradition and culture, will tell anyone who wants to listen: "The knowledge doesn't belong to me, it belongs to our people." Before being hired in 1998 to operate the tribal museum in Nixon, Wewa was brought to Natchez.

"In Wadsworth, they contracted with me to come down and tell legends to the kids and sing songs," said Wewa, who did the same thing at Pyramid Lake High School in Nixon.

Paiute tribal elders and officials are trying to teach the language and customs to the reservation's youth. The Paiute language is being taught at the high school.

"They hear it every single day," Jeanette Allen, language-program coordinator, said of the high-school students. "You don't hear it once you leave class. They pick up meaningful sentences, things they can use at home."

Charlotte Harry didn't need to learn the language and the legends in school. "I grew up with it," the Pyramid Lake resident said. "People my age just grew up with it." So did Wewa, who wanted to learn and sought out people old enough to teach him.

"It was when I got into my teenage years that I met elders who taught me about basket-making and buckskin," he said. "Some of these elder men taught me how to make drums and sing songs."

But that wasn't enough. Wewa wanted more. "Once you light that fuse of learning, it continues to burn," he said. "It lights other fuses. Pretty soon, you're asking this and asking that. You have to travel to find the people who can fill that hunger for you." Wewa spent hours just listening.

"I found those people, and because I was

White pelicans stand on old pier pilings near the Sutcliffe Marina.

interested in the old spiritual ways, they handed me everything they knew," he said. "I've spent a day sitting under trees outside of somebody's house and listening to stories, listening carefully to what they were saying because I wanted to know."

The Paiute tradition is oral. The stories are told, not written down. People don't always listen; the stories take a long time to tell.

"I have found that a lot of people know fragments of legends," Wewa said. "Somebody will say, 'This is what the coyote did in this story.' But that's all they know. If it's a mixed group, one will say, 'This is how it started.' Somebody will say, 'I fell asleep. I never heard the end.' Somebody else will say, 'Well, this is how it ends.' "

The Paiute creation legend, Wewa said, takes two hours to tell. If parents are trying to tell children in the evening, sometimes the kids can't stay awake that long. "The reason it's fragmented is because of how long it takes to tell," he said. "Probably the reason it's fragmented is because they fell asleep during parts of it as kids."

Wewa has the same problem when he tries to tell the stories to his nephews and nieces: "They want to hear a story. When I'm done telling it, I end up carrying everyone back to their own beds because they fell asleep during the story."

Along with telling stories and explaining legends, Wewa prepares and eats traditional foods — roots, choke cherries, fish and deer. He even convinced some high-schoolers to try the roots.

"The roots I keep at home; they have been elevated to a more sacred food," he said. "I only eat it on Sundays. It's almost like a reward, a birthday cake. It means more to you."

Jamie Stump, a Paiute teenager, heard Wewa's cultural message. He learned native dances and songs. "We go all over to pow-wows," Stump said. That's important to Wewa.

"If our people start to forget those ways, it's going to herald the coming of the end of the world," he said. "All Paiutes talk with no sense of time. It's a general statement. That's why I am a teacher of these ways. I grew up with spiritual teaching. That makes it important for me to pass these things on."

A Lahontan cutthroat trout jumps a fish ladder at Sutcliffe.

Paiutes work to save their language before it dies with the elders

Jeanette Allen counts more than 1,000 words for her dictionary — so far: "One leads to another," said Allen, who heads the effort to turn a spoken language into a written one at the Pyramid Lake Paiute Reservation. Allen and other tribal leaders decided the only way to save their language was to write it down. The ongoing effort started in 1996. Time is running out.

"We're losing it," said Allen, the reservation's language-program coordinator. "We can't teach it fast enough. Learning takes a long time." A recent survey showed that only sixty-one residents spoke the Paiute language fluently.

"The people that know the language are the elders," Tribal Chairman Norman Harry said. "There is a realization that they aren't going to be with us much longer."

The tribe must write its language, Allen said. A dictionary and other books are needed so younger generations can learn the language before it dies out. Only a few attempts have been made to write the Paiute language. Through most of the tribe's history, the language was spoken, not written.

The tribe is basing its dictionary on work church missionaries did in the 1800s when they translated the Bible into Paiute by assigning letters in the English alphabet to sounds in the tribal language.

"The overall goal with the written form is to teach it in school," Harry said. "It may not be exact, but it will be close enough to teach." Recordings are being made of tribal elders speaking the language. "They have developed all of the vowels," he said. "You use the English alphabet and try to convert it into Paiute sounds. It comes close. The letters don't always match."

Until the effort began to print a dictionary, the language was passed from parents to children with the spoken word. But tribal members, in large part, stopped speaking the language.

Often parents of tribal adults such as Harry attended government boarding schools, including the old Stewart Indian School in Carson City, where they were punished for speaking their language. The language started to die because it wasn't spoken enough to be passed on to Harry and others like him.

"I know a little bit," Harry said. "At

The Pyramid

home, it was never spoken. My parents knew it very well, but we all spoke English. We went to public schools." The Paiute language is complex, with different dialects, depending on where you are. "It's very difficult, even with tribes as close as Walker River and Fallon," he said. "The words almost sound the same, but the dialect is a little bit different

"My dad was from Walker River. My mom was from Pyramid Lake. They were constantly giving each other a bad time about the dialects."

The Paiute language has many words. "Some of our words are singular, dual and plural," Allen said. "You use different words for one person standing, two people standing or three. We have a lot of those."

The dictionary, when finally finished, will be a thick one.

A member of the Pyramid Lake Paiute tribe herds cattle north for the summer.

Walker River

A thundercloud turns pink after sunset along Highway 95 near Schurz.

Jobs are scarce in Schurz but customers crowd Big Daddy's

Ex-Marine John Lockwood, an inspector with the Walker River Housing Authority, grew up in Schurz, where he still likes to run near Weber Reservoir.

ohn Lockwood still runs — just not as far or as fast. No longer does Lockwood dash to the top of Black Mountain overlooking the Walker River Paiute Reservation. He isn't a teenage star on the Mineral County High School cross-country team. He's a thirty-year-old administrator in the tribal housing office. Sometimes his knees hurt.

"It looks big," Lockwood said of the mountain. "Once you start up, it's not as high as you think it is, and it only takes thirty minutes to come down. When I was young, I was up there all the time." But the mountain has places Lockwood hasn't seen. He'll hike, not run, to them. He does enjoy jogging after work.

"I thought, 'I'm going to do some hills today,' " Lockwood said of an early evening workout. "I took my little dog. I thought, 'Man, we're not even in the hills yet and I'm dying. We're going home.' The dog looked at me like, 'Are we going home already?' I'm not as competitive as I used to be in running."

Lockwood, who has seen some of the world and earned a measure of fame, enjoys his life on the Walker River reservation. The community isn't the easiest place to make a home. The reservation is fairly remote, in Mineral County where economic times are tough. Not so long ago, tribal members could find employment down U.S. Highway 95 at the Hawthorne Army Ammunition Depot, but a lot of that work is gone.

Norma Crowley, a longtime Walker River resident, has retired as the tribe's employment rights director. She called the reservation's jobless situation "horrendous." In the old days, Walker River was a ranching community. The Paiutes raised cattle and grew alfalfa. They kept chickens and pigs. Crowley, who grew up on the reservation, remembers.

"The way the reservation was set up, those of age were given twenty-acre parcels," she said. "They were also given cattle. They had land. They were given seeds to plant. This was quite a thriving farming community. Everyone back then had a garden. Everyone had chickens and pigs."

Now, those are mostly memories. "You don't see that anymore," said Crowley, who blamed the decline on falling farm prices and increased costs. Now some of the lucky ones, like Lockwood, work for the tribe.

Others must seek jobs off the reservation. Walker River's location makes that difficult.

"So many of our people are unemployed," Crowley said. "Employment is almost non-existent. We are a rural community."

When Crowley was a child, the reservation had four stores. Her father, Walter Voorhees, owned one. Today, Walker River has just a single store. "It isn't prosperous," she said of the reservation.

In the face of all the difficulty, Verna Quartz has started a business. "Big Daddy," a hamburger shop, is the place where you can get something to eat on the reservation. A Big Daddy Burger costs $4.25. Make that $4.95 with fries. A twenty-one-ounce glass of fresh-squeezed lemonade to go with the burger costs $2.00. Every Wednesday, the special is Indian tacos.

"It's holding its own," Quartz said. "This is my second venture. I had a deli and made submarine sandwiches. That went over pretty well."

Big Daddy, which used to be a gas station, is small — with a kitchen and a counter for ordering. Seating is scarce. Most people leave with their burgers. On the other side of the wall, there's a weight room with an almost-new set of workout equipment. The view looks sort of weird, a weight room adjacent to a burger joint, until Quartz tells you the story.

The weights belonged to her son, Cody, who died of leukemia. The weight room is a sort of memorial to Cody. The place attracts a lot of reservation youngsters, many of them his friends.

"I thought the kids would really enjoy it," Quartz said. "It's one of those universal sets that you can do anything on."

Billie Rose Brown helps Quartz in the kitchen from 11:30 a.m. to 1:30 p.m. weekdays. "The rush at lunch gets crazy," Brown said. The community has no other place to

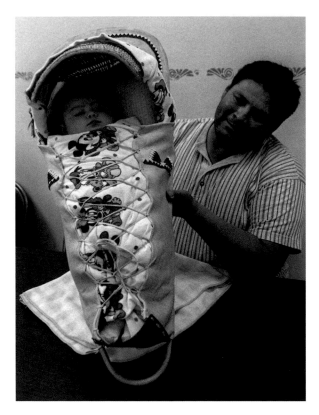

Four-month-old Cassius Quintero, snug in a traditional cradleboard made by his great-grandmother, is held by his father, Robert Quintero.

go for lunch.

Big Daddy is on the main road through Schurz, the tribal headquarters and the reservation's principal community. Schurz Elementary School also is there. The school, which includes students in kindergarten through eighth grade, is nearly brand new, having opened in 1998. Everyone, teachers and students, is proud of the school's computers.

"This is a poor county and in decline," said Principal Joel Hodes, who has been teaching reservation kids for twenty-three years, since coming to Walker River from Los Angeles in 1976. "But when it comes to technology, we are probably first or second in the state."

The Schurz computer lab is designed for twenty terminals, all with Internet access. Third-grader Jamie Lovelace doesn't care about any of that as she works at her computer.

"I'm typing about my dog," she said.

The children spend three days a week in computer class, and the other two days studying American Indian traditions.

"I find our kids are more computer

Painter, sculptor, muralist finds inspiration in two worlds

Melvin Brown

The land around the Walker River Paiute Reservation is rugged: the mountains, the desert and the rocks. Melvin Brown notices the rocks.

"I'm coming across all these neat rock formations," said the forty-eight-year-old painter and sculptor who was born and raised at Walker River. "I'm incorporating them into my paintings." Brown, who has been painting since he was eighteen, has a studio in Schurz. Nearby Black Mountain is one of his subjects.

"I was just a naturally born artist," said Brown, who studied ceramics at the Institute of American Indian Arts. "I had easier access to the right side of my brain."

His work includes traditional and non-traditional Indian art. He incorporated both in a mural he painted in 1989 on one of the old buildings in Schurz.

"I wanted to do something that had its foot in two worlds, to remind us of our beginnings and how Indians are perceived."

As a sculptor, Brown is just getting started. "Just a handful, ten at the most," he said of his work. "I've collected a lot of scrap pieces of metal. I'd like to get into metal casting."

Artist Melvin Brown painted this scene of the Black Mountains near Schurz.

Time to go home: A little girl picks up her school books from the Schurz Elementary School playground.

literate," said Jessica Lake, who teaches technology and tradition. Under the label of cultural studies, Lake's students learn Paiute lore, arts and crafts. One thing they don't learn much of is the Paiute language.

"I can't look at any of the students in here whose parents would actually know the language," she said. "They might know some words. I don't know much of the language, even though I was born and raised here."

Like many reservations in Nevada, Walker River is losing its native language, which isn't spoken extensively in homes or on school playgrounds. The tribe is trying to put together a language program for kids and adults.

"It's not going to be using a lot of written materials," said Cindy Benjamin, the tribe's education director. "Our language is not written. We don't want to get into having to develop a written language. The purpose is to get more people *speaking* Paiute." To start with, Benjamin wants to stress instruction for older tribal members who know some of the language, hoping to provide more teachers for the children.

"We have a number of people in the

In front of Schurz Elementary School, three boys practice yo-yo tricks while waiting for the bus.

community who understand the language but don't speak fluently," she said. "If we could focus our program on that group, they would become speakers much more quickly. We would have more teachers in the community."

Lew Lockwood, a former tribe vice chairman and John's father, doesn't believe in teaching the language and Paiute traditions in school or other classroom settings. Lockwood, who used to box professionally and spent many years traveling off the reservation, learned his language and lore at home.

"I used to listen to my grandma tell stories," he said. "They used to tell us in Paiute. The elders here now, very few of them can talk Paiute." The program Benjamin envisions could change that. "It should be taught by the parents on down the line, not in class," Lockwood said. "I don't believe it should be taught in public in general."

In one Schurz home, a tradition was handed down when Charlotte Dunnett taught daughter Charissa basket weaving. "Since I was about six, I've done it," said Charissa, now thirteen. "My mom had basket-weaving classes. I used to go and help." The Dunnetts specialize in miniature baskets, about the size of your thumb, which means more than just keeping a tradition alive.

"I want to try to do it full time, if I can get enough customers to support myself and my daughter," Charlotte Dunnett said. Her baskets are popular. In early 1999, she sold every one she had shortly after posting a small sign advertising them at tribal headquarters. Charissa recalled the time she lost one of her mother's tiny baskets.

"I got spanked bad," she said.

Lew Lockwood believes in discipline. One thing he wants to see at Walker River is more sports programs, including boxing, to occupy youngsters." If you've got the kids participating in athletic programs, the kids are more likely to stay in school," he said. "We have a high dropout rate."

Lockwood ran a boxing program on the reservation for twenty years, but Walker

Norma Crowley

River hasn't had organized boxing for a decade since then. "I tried to get it going again," he said. "It was harder and harder to get kids."

His son, John, was good enough to reach the U.S. Olympic Trials as an amateur boxer before joining the Marine Corps. After leaving the service, he fought a couple of times, then stopped.

"I had some real bad headaches," Lockwood said of the aftermath of a bout in northern California. "I said, 'I don't think I want to fight anymore.' I just stopped."

But the running continues, sort of. "Most of the time, I'll start from my house and go to the reservoir turnoff," he said. "That's six miles out and six miles back. I got this urge to run all the way to the reservoir. That's eight miles out and eight miles back.

"I made it out there, but I didn't make it back. I found a friend out there. I got a ride back. Your feet start hurting. Luckily, he was fishing."

No need to talk about it: everybody knows what to do

obody says anything. They don't have to. Everyone just knows. Someone will sing the opening song and bless the pine nuts on the Walker River Paiute Reservation. The name isn't on a list and isn't announced.

"It's an implied thing," said John Hicks, who was born on the reservation. "They know who that person is. We know who that person is. They know when they are supposed to be there. They just do."

Every September, the Walker River Paiutes celebrate their history and traditions with the Pine Nut Festival. The fun and games last three days, starting on a Friday and ending on Sunday. But the most important time is Saturday night, when the party stops for a while, usually about two hours.

"Come sundown is when we go into the blessing of the pine nuts," said Hicks. "We have everything shut down." Traditional Paiute songs are sung and the community joins in circle dancing, which is also traditional. "We have one singer per year to do the opening song. The actual blessing of the pine nuts happens. We have a designated person to do that."

Although the ceremony is supposed to last about two hours, it can take longer, depending upon the dancing and singing. "Normally, we have a bunch of round-dance singers from all over," he said. "We normally have them sing two round-dance songs apiece. If there are fifteen singers, we try to have them do two songs apiece. We go through all the singers."

Pine nuts are central to the Paiute way of life. While they aren't eaten regularly at dinner anymore, the nuts always have been an important tribal food. They go back a very long way, just as the tribe does. The Walker River Paiutes still follow the custom of harvesting and roasting pine nuts in the fall. The custom is one of the strongest links residents of Walker River have with their ancestors.

The annual festival, which is open to the public, has evolved to include much more, often drawing two or three thousand people to tribal headquarters in Schurz. They attend a pow-wow and see a rodeo, a queen contest, a parade and a car show. These are all relatively recent additions. Mostly, the festival is about the tribe getting together.

The Walker River flows swiftly over rocks near Schurz.

"It's a community-type thing," Hicks said. "Years ago, the elders danced and sang. They ate. It was kind of a get-together, I guess. It just happened. It became kind of a tradition of the tribe."

Actually, the activity starts in the spring when tribal members go out into the northern Nevada country looking for the largest concentrations of pine cones, the way their ancestors did. At that time, they also say a blessing.

"At the end of April or beginning of May, we go into the mountains and bless the ground that, hopefully, we will have an abundance of pine nuts," said Norma Crowley, who grew up at Walker River. "Anyone from the tribe can go. They walk in there, they look at the area and they bless the ground. They have a big meal."

They do something else that's equally important. "They sit and they talk, about the past, the present, the good times and the bad times," Crowley said. In the fall, shortly before the festival, tribal members return to the mountains and forests, this time to harvest the pine nuts.

"There is a lot of country down in the Hawthorne area," Hicks said of one of the tribe's traditional harvesting areas. "Sometimes we have to go farther out of Hawthorne, sometimes to Bridgeport, California. We can go two hundred miles." They return to the reservation with pine cones, which are roasted underground. Then, the nuts are removed.

"Sometimes we are blessed with good weather," Hicks said of the harvesting, which is done by hand. "Sometimes in the fall, we get a lot of wind. Sometimes we get a howling one."

But one thing stays the same: "It's an implied thing," Hicks said. "People know what they are supposed to do."

When crime victims call on Laurie Thom, she's there to help

Laurie Thom and her son, Dorsey Carl Thom, Jr., attend a community gathering in Schurz.

Laurie Thom loves basketball but remembers some of the worst times of her life trying to play the game in the high school gymnasiums of Southern California. Thom was in a war zone.

"It was awful," she said of her brief teenage time in the Orange County community of La Verne. "When I was playing basketball, we had to be escorted by armed guards. We used to have to get dressed in the locker room of our high school — take your towel, take your water bottle and that's all you take."

That was the easy part. "You get on a bus," she said, explaining the procedure for a cross-town trip. "One guard sits in back. The other guy sits in front. They get you as close to the gym door as possible. They get you in a circle and take you in. They could only ensure your safety during the game." Parents and fans of the visiting team weren't allowed to attend. "They couldn't ensure the safety of your parents going to the game," Thom said. "I told my mom I didn't want to play that way."

The family returned home, to the

Walker River Paiute Reservation, and Thom went down the road without guards to Yerington High School. She played basketball and softball. Her basketball team won two state championships and her softball team won three. She graduated in 1988.

"It was neat to look in the stands and see huge crowds," Thom said. "It was such a big difference."

Today, more than a decade later, she holds a unique position at Walker River. At twenty-eight, she's a leader in the tribe's crime victims program, which specializes in handling domestic violence cases. Thom, whose office in the tribal headquarters community of Schurz, is called out at all hours of the night, usually to be next on the scene after tribal police to deal with all sorts of bad situations and emotions — most often anguish and fear.

"We provide immediate crisis intervention," she said. "This is a program for all crime victims, but domestic violence is one of the highest. We need to address it." Thom knows firsthand what she is talking about: she was a victim.

"I went through seven years of marriage that was violent," she said. "It was the week after high school that I started dating him. I was twenty-one when I got married but I was still kind of young. I divorced him after he attempted to stab me. That was the last straw."

Thom remembers facing the situation alone. "I know what it means to go through the trial court system and testify," she said. "I went through that on my own. There was no advocate. I want to make sure other women don't have to go through it on their own."

Miranda Quintero works with Thom. "We serve the victims," she said, noting the work isn't easy, especially on the reservation where the families they deal with are usually familiar.

"People have told me it's the toughest job they've ever heard of," Thom said. "You are dealing with a family in crisis. Then you see them later. You're a trigger. They see you and it reminds them of what's going on. You can't take it personally."

Thom has re-married. Her husband, Dorsey, is an old Yerington High School classmate. "I should have stayed close to home to find a husband," she said. "We went to school together. He was really smart. I was intimidated by him."

When Thom goes out on a call in the middle of the night, Dorsey doesn't complain. "My husband understands completely," she said. "He knows he's going to get a call at three o'clock in the morning. He just says, 'It's for you. Drive safely and come home.' "

The new generation: Yerington High School senior Gina Dini tackles her homework at the Schurz community center.

There have been attracted to the Comstock range hundreds of gamblers of all grades, and men of all kinds who live by their wits.
    William Wright, The Big Bonanza

Nevada is a creature of the mining frontier.
    Russell R. Elliott, "Nevada's Mining Heritage:
    Blessing and Burden," East of Eden, West of Zion

Mining Towns

An abandoned building near Ruth at the old Kennecott Copper Mine

Austin

Austin's 19th-century Episcopal church

Quirky, independent folks find a different beat, off the beaten path

Mitch Contrell's bottles catch the late afternoon sun in the windows of his gem shop in downtown Austin.

IMPORTANT DATES

- **May 1862:** Silver discovered.
- **1863:** Thousands of miners arrive in the Reese River area. Miners set up camps, including Austin. Original International Hotel moved from Virginia City to Austin.
- **May 1863:** *Reese River Reveille* newspaper begins publication.
- **September 1863:** Austin wins election to become Lander County seat. First bank opens.
- **1871:** Lander County Courthouse built.
- **June 17, 1881:** Austin City Railway completed.
- **1887:** Major mining operations cease.
- **1897:** Stokes Castle built by mine owner Anson Phelps Stokes.
- **1919:** First election to move county seat from Austin to Battle Mountain fails.
- **1938:** Second attempt to move the county seat fails.
- **1953:** Third attempt to move the county seat fails.
- **September 1958:** Fire destroys portion of International Hotel.
- **1969:** MM&S Mining company opens.
- **Oct. 7, 1976:** New jail dedicated.
- **Aug. 26, 1977:** Fire destroys historic Austin Hotel.
- **May 1979:** Fourth attempt to move county seat succeeds.
- **1989:** New school opens.
- **1993:** Reese River Reveille ceases publication.

T ilman Jones rode a motorcycle into town in 1987 and never left. "I came in on a chopped Triumph," Jones said. "I was a long-haired stereotypical biker. They looked at me kind of strange." But people in Austin are used to guys like Jones – independent, a little quirky and looking for adventure.

Jones hands out business cards that read, "You have just met a biker. Difficult deeds done routinely." Some might call Jones and others who live in town misfits. That's not how Austin sees it. Jones isn't much different from people who've been showing up here for more than 100 years, starting when the place was a nineteenth century Nevada mining boomtown after the discovery of silver in 1862.

"They figured there was a value in having me out here," Jones said. "I haven't proved them wrong yet. It's a place where you can be different. It's accepted and allowed, sometimes even encouraged."

It's also a place where you're pretty much left alone. That's one of the reasons Jim Andersen showed up from northern California twenty-five years ago. Now he serves the town as a part-time justice of the peace. When

Andersen wrote a magazine article about Austin, the town saved it and used it to explain itself. He enjoys telling a story to illustrate the community's appeal.

It's about opening a restaurant.

"I walked over to the county courthouse," Andersen said. "I held my breath. I asked, 'What do you have to do to open a restaurant?' The girl looked at me kind of funny. She said, 'Hang out a sign, I guess.' At the time, it was the very essence of freedom, living here." There were few rules about restaurants, or anything else.

Some things have changed. Andersen no longer has the restaurant. Austin hasn't been a boomtown for a long time. There's little mining. The county seat was moved to Battle Mountain in 1979. Austin struggles to hang on, depending mostly on summer tourists traveling through town on U.S. Highway 50. There are more rules and regulations.

"We started enacting some laws, business laws," said Andersen, who worked in Austin as a deputy sheriff before becoming a judge, "but there's still a lot of freedom. You're not going to get away from regulations anymore. I suppose we have as few as anybody does." As a judge in a small town, Andersen is in a

peculiar position – enforcing the rules and regulations in cases where he almost always knows the plaintiffs and defendants.

"I found the thing that hurts friendships are small claims," Andersen said. "I know both parties. It's uncomfortable. Generally, it's somebody who rented a house from a local and didn't pay the rent for one reason or another, then just moved out. Or, somebody sold somebody a car and the engine blew, so they don't want to pay for it."

When the day's judging is done, Andersen goes home. "I want to put my feet up on the railing in the summer, tip a cold one and not have to listen to jackhammers," he said. "We don't have those. It's very quiet."

Austin is in the middle of wide open space. That's part of its appeal, but when you choose the place, as Jones did after he jumped on his Triumph and left his home in Fernley behind, you're giving up some things. "You're giving up shopping, dentists, doctors, haircuts, even pizza," said Andersen, who made the same decision Jones did. For all those things, a once-a-week trip to Fallon or once-a-month visit to Reno-Sparks has to do.

"It's just a good exchange for me," said Andersen, who says he simply isn't suited for city life. "I don't have what you have to have to stand in line. And always being in a press of people — that's not the way I want to live."

There's peace and quiet in Austin. There are also problems. Some of the town's historic buildings are falling down and there's nobody to occupy them. Businesses are leaving. The ones that remain operate mostly in summer. The future is uncertain.

"This community lives off the highway," said Pat Waits, who started a mountain bicycle business in town, hoping to take advantage of the area's reputation for good trail riding. "If it doesn't come off the highway, we're out." That means the few restaurants, gas stations and motels in Austin have only the summer season, from Memorial Day in May to Labor Day in September, to make a living for the year.

"People are surviving," Waits said. "Basically, that's what we're all doing, surviving." Austin frustrates Waits, a retired plumbing contractor from Las Vegas. "A lot of people just aren't interested," he said. "It's a difficult thing to get people to turn out for

Hot tub for a Montana dog, fifteen-year-old Aiko, is a pool at Spencer Hot Springs about twenty miles from Austin.

Lost in Austin: Two sides of the street

This excerpt from an article by longtime resident Jim Andersen has been reprinted by the Austin Chamber of Commerce.

Ninety percent of Austin lies on the hillsides to the north, and there's a reason for that — winter sunshine. If you live south of the highway, a hill blocks the sun, and you won't cast a shadow from November through February.

One Halloween I slipped and fell on a patch of ice near the IML Building, which is on the south side of the highway. I was carrying a stop sign at the time — nobody needs to know why — and it gouged a furrow in the ice.

The following St. Patrick's Day I slipped and fell again, and there beneath my elbow, puckered like the skin around an old war wound, was the scar left by the stop sign. Nearly five months had gone by, and yet I'd slipped on the same damn patch of ice. That summer I moved as high up the northern slopes as I could get.

All of the motels in Austin, incidentally, are located south of the highway. Vicky Jones owns the Lincoln Motel, and she finds the winters down there acceptable, but then Vicky is from Sweden. I

Jim Andersen

guess if you've lived near the Arctic Circle you may like it south of the highway.

That same sun-blocking hill is, however, the best place to go to get a good view of Austin. It's known as "A" Hill, because that's where the big white-washed rock "A" is located, and there's a road to the top angling up from the town park. It's a pretty good hike considering the elevation, but I wouldn't recommend driving up there unless your vehicle has large knobby tires and Yosemite Sam mudflaps.

AUSTIN

- Population in 1999: 380 (26 percent under 18, 41 percent 18-44, 27 percent 45-64, 6 percent 65 and older; 52 percent male, 48 percent female).
- Population in 1990: 566.
- Population in 2003: (projected) 323.
- Median household income: $24,242.
- Total retail sales in 1998: $1.567 million.
- Total retail sales in 2003: $1.715 million

- Claim to fame: Led the development of central and eastern Nevada after silver was discovered in 1862. At its peak in the 19th century, the population was 7,000.

- How it got its name: The legend is the town was named for Austin, Texas.

- Local legend: Reuel C. Gridley, owner of the Gridley Store, lost an election bet in 1864 and had to carry a 50-pound sack of flour the length of Austin, to the tune of "John Brown's Body." The sack was auctioned, with the proceeds going to relieve suffering caused by the Civil War. The sack was sold many times during the day, with each buyer returning it for resale. Other mining camps heard of the auction and had Gridley bring his sack for sale. The sack ended up raising $275,000 for Civil War relief. Austin remembers Gridley and the flour sack with its annual Gridley Days celebration in June.

This Austin garage proves that art is found in the strangest places.

things that would really help us."

Austin, like mining boom cousins Virginia City and Eureka, has historic buildings. Like Virginia City and Eureka, Austin is picturesque — or, at least, it used to be. Unlike Virginia City, Austin isn't packed with weekend tourists and, unlike Eureka, Austin hasn't been flush with cash from mining taxes to pay for restoration.

"Most of these buildings are in a condition that if you tried to go in and renovate them, if you tried to get them up to code, I don't think there's enough money to do it," Waits said. "We looked at a couple of these buildings. Economically, it's just not there."

Vicky Jones manages the International Hotel, a bar and restaurant that dates from 1863, when it was moved from Virginia City at the beginning of Austin's mining heyday. Vicky is married to Tilman Jones, the biker known as "TJ." They met the day he rode into Austin. Vicky, a native of Sweden and longtime Austin resident, had her truck break down right in front of Tilman's Triumph. "The town gets real protective of its citizens," Tilman Jones said. "When I first started dating her, I was pulled aside, literally, and told, 'You treat that woman right or we'll

dump you down a mine shaft.' They were dead serious."

Vicky Jones is one of Austin's survivors. "You make it in the summer and you put it away so you can pay your bills in winter, or you ain't going to make it," said Vicky, whose Swedish pancakes are a breakfast treat at the International. "Hopefully, it will be good this summer. It will depend on how the tourist trade is."

On a bulletin board inside the International, there's a notice offering a $2,500 reward "for information leading to the arrest and conviction of person or persons that shot a cow." In Austin, that's a crime wave.

"It's a nice place to raise kids. All these small communities are," said Paul Tremayne, who coaches boys' basketball at Austin High School. "It's just a nice place to be." Tremayne survives. In 1998-99, there were nine boys in grades nine through twelve. They all played basketball, losing in the first round of the state tournament.

"The community supports sports big time," said Matt Tremayne, son of the coach and a player on the team. "During the state tournament, we were joking about sneaking back into Austin and stealing everything

At the top of Austin Summit, two wild irises tangle in the wind.

Ray Salisbury has spent the past 30 years collecting license plates. He has nailed 300 of them to the trailer of Ray's Automotive in downtown Austin.

because nobody was here. Everyone was in Reno watching the game."

When Paul Tremayne first came to Austin from Boise, Idaho, the coach wasn't sure what he was getting into. "We got to Battle Mountain," Tremayne said. "My wife asked 'Where are we going?' We were going to be here two or three years."

Katrina Inchauspe, who graduated from high school in 1999, has been in the Austin area all her life. She lives on a ranch twenty-five miles outside of town. It's where she grew up. "I just know I'll be homesick when I leave," said Inchauspe, who plans to attend college in Idaho.

Another teenager, Neisha Fox, who spends the school year in Austin and the summer in Bakersfield, California, can't wait to get out of the rural Nevada town. "It's very boring," Fox said of Austin. "I like bigger cities."

Johnny Young, who, like Inchauspe, is a local ranch kid, isn't looking for New York or Los Angeles, but he probably won't stay in

Austin. "Maybe Reno," said Young. "With the exception of Katrina, a lot of kids don't want to stay. They think it's all rednecks. I think most of the kids want to take off."

Tilman Jones may know what the kids are talking about, but he's not going anywhere. "My sister came down for a visit from North Dakota," Jones said. "She'd been living in a pretty structured environment." Austin was a shock. "I said, 'Look, our day-to-day reality is stranger than most people's fantasy.' You have to have a slightly different approach to life to live in an isolated small town like this and not go stark raving crazy."

Is there a ghost haunting the Austin County Courthouse? Tammy Manzini says she heard footsteps upstairs early one morning.

In historic halls, ghostly treads still linger

T he ghost of the International Hotel doesn't like people climbing his stairs.

"We had a guy buy this place," said Tilman Jones, whose wife, Vicky, manages the historic International. "I guess the ghost didn't like him because he kept pushing him down the stairs." Jones pauses before finishing the tale about one of the International's former owners.

"He wasn't always sober," Jones said with a laugh. The International's "ghost" is named Tommy Wallace, a man who Vicky Jones said died of "natural causes" in one of the upstairs rooms in the early 1970s. Wallace, supposedly, has haunted the place ever since.

"There was a local guy a few years ago, he was bartending," Tilman Jones said. "There was just him and one other customer playing pool. The bartender was lining up his shot. This voice came out of the back by the fireplace. It said, 'You're going to miss.' He missed."

The International, moved from Virginia City to Austin in 1863, is no longer a hotel. The upstairs rooms are closed and the building operates as a bar and restaurant.

As a local landmark, the International is a likely place for tales of the supernatural, and there are plenty of ghost stories around Austin.

The old elementary school, built in 1929, has a tale of its own. "One of our principals hung himself in his office," said Val Andersen, a life-long Austin resident. "I loved the story as a kid growing up. My dad graduated from the same building and so did his grandmother. The story started way back then."

Now, Andersen says, the building creaks. "If you're in there at night, it does creak."

William Cox, a teacher at Austin High School, has been in the elementary building at night. "If you're up there past twelve o'clock walking around, the hair on the back of your neck does stand up," he said.

It wasn't creaking that Tammy Manzini heard in the old County Courthouse in Austin. It was footsteps. Manzini, who runs the county commission office in the court-house, constructed in 1871, tells this story: "I can attest to one time when myself and another woman actually heard somebody walking in the upstairs hallway, preparing

to go down the steps." Manzini said she heard the sounds after unlocking the front door to enter the building. "I couldn't figure out how anybody had gotten in before me. We were waiting for somebody to come down the stairs and nobody came."

Maybe it was the ghost of Richard Jennings, a man hanged from the courthouse balcony by a lynch mob years ago. "This is a true story," said Manzini. "The old jail used to be downstairs in the courthouse. At one point, a gentleman shot and killed another gentleman downtown. He was thrown in jail."

Jennings shot John A. Barrett, a popular local rancher, on December 12, 1881, in the bar of the International Hotel. Historical accounts confirm the story.

Jennings had arrived in town from Grass Valley, California, about a month before the incident.

"A lynch mob came up here in the middle of the night, took the prisoner and dragged him up here to the balcony and hung him," Manzini said. "I don't know whether the ghost that resides in the courthouse is the hung man."

At the International, employees just

Left: Vicky and T.J. (Tilman) Jones step out on the front porch of the International Hotel, one of Nevada's oldest buildings, moved from Virginia City in 1863.
Right: The historic town of Austin is built into a canyon along Highway 50 in central Nevada. St. Augustine's Catholic Church held its first service on Christmas Eve in 1866.

assume their ghost is Tommy Wallace.

"There's been a couple of times when Vicky said the ghost said 'hello' to her," Tilman Jones said. Vicky Jones confirms the story. She is often alone at the International early in the morning.

"I hear it so clear," she said. "I look around and nobody is here."

Austin: just trying to stay alive

Stokes Castle, once the summer home of Anson Phelps Stokes, was built of native granite in 1897. Stokes was an Eastern financier who built the Nevada Central Railroad from Battle Mountain to Austin.

Austin once was the heart of Nevada. But that was more than a century ago, when the town was full of miners digging for silver in the middle of the state. Today, Austin has an air of desperation about it. In many ways, it's a forgotten place, except to the people who live there.

"We're just trying to stay alive, to keep our heads above water," said Tammy Manzini, president of the Chamber of Commerce. The mining boom that made Austin one of the state's largest communities ended at the turn of the century. Since then, survival has been a struggle.

"If it weren't for the history of Austin, which was magnificent, would there be an Austin today?" state archivist Guy Rocha asked. "Probably not."

In 1862, silver was discovered and the subsequent rush to find it made Austin the center for the development of central and

U.S. 50 is the livelihood for Austin's economy.

eastern Nevada.

In 1979, the Lander County seat — which Austin won in the election of 1863 — was lost to Battle Mountain.

"Losing the county seat was really a shot in the heart," said Rocha, an expert on Nevada history. "In the nineteenth century Austin was a principal town in Nevada. What I see over time is an increasing isolation."

Austin is trying to hang on. It wants to be part of an economic development partnership among Lander, Eureka and White Pine counties — but that's in the planning stage. "We have nothing," Manzini said of jobs in Austin. "Hopefully, the other counties would help us as much as they could."

Since the county seat moved, Austin has lost population. In 1997 there were 420 people in Austin. In 1998, there were 380. There is a fear in town that the elementary school will be closed, with all students attending classes on the Austin High School campus.

"Right now, with things so depressed, it's hard to make a living here," said Beth Watts, who has lived in Austin off-and-on

Hundreds of abandoned shoes, boots and even a pink flamingo decorate an old cottonwood tree beside Highway 50 between Fallon and Austin.

for seventeen years. She is a waitress at the International Hotel bar and restaurant and says she likes the place despite the difficulties,

"I've always loved Austin," she said. "People here stick close together."

They hope for better times.

"We've been down before," said Joy Brandt, treasurer of the chamber of commerce. "Something usually happens and we come back."

Ely

East Ely Railroad Depot Museum

Isolation and memory bind ties of loyalty

A quartet of deer look up from the brush at the Ruth mine overlook outside of Ely.

IMPORTANT DATES
- **1867:** Gold discovered at Treasure Hill on Mount Hamilton.
- **1869:** White Pine County formed from portion of Lander County.
- **1878:** Selby Copper Mining & Smelting Co. founded on site of present City Hall; settlement is called Ely City.
- **1887:** Ely becomes White Pine County seat.
- **1899:** D.C. McDonald locates Ruth mine that touches off Ely-area copper boom. Story goes that McDonald named discovery for 3-year-old daughter Ruth.
- **Sept. 29, 1906:** Nevada Northern Railroad begins operations in Ely. More than 50 mining companies organized.
- **May 1907:** Ely incorporated.
- **Feb. 9, 1908:** Passenger service begins.
- **April 13, 1908:** First ore train.
- **July 15, 1929:** Opening of six-story Hotel Nevada, state's tallest building.
- **1933:** Nevada Consolidated Copper Corporation, owned by Kennecott, takes over most mining operations.
- **June 30, 1938:** Local passenger rail service discontinued.
- **1958:** Kennecott gains control of most mining operations.
- **September 1978:** Kennecott closes Ruth mines; ore trains stopped.
- **1983:** Kennecott donates steam engine and other Nevada Northern Railway properties to White Pine Historical Railroad Foundation.
- **1986:** Great Basin National Park established.
- **1987:** "Ghost Train of old Ely" begins operation as tourist attraction.
- **July 1995:** Broken Hill Proprietary Company Ltd. of Australia begins mining operations in Ely-Ruth area.
- **Aug. 16, 1999:** 90th anniversary of White Pine County Courthouse.

Businesses were boarded up, the big company was shut down and people rushed to leave town.

"It was unbelievable," Virginia Terry said of Ely as it was in the 1980s. "Every other house was for sale. It looked bad, it felt bad. When we had those cold gray days, it felt like we weren't going to make it at all."

Then something happened, and the Ely native knew her hometown would be OK. The something was a parade — a really big one — on July 4, 1987, as Ely celebrated its own and the nation's birthday. Ely always has a Fourth of July parade. That's when White Pine High School's class reunions take place.

But this was special: Ely's centennial. Hotel rooms were booked with former Ely and White Pine County residents returning home. Local merchants, the ones surviving the tough times, prepared to celebrate.

"When July 4th came, they had a huge parade," Terry said. "It went on for hours, it seemed like. They had beautiful floats. Each business put in a float. There was lots of entertainment after the parade. It was a real important time."

Kennecott, the giant mining company, had stopped digging for copper. From 1978 to 1983, Kennecott closed its operations — first the huge open pit in Ruth, then the smelter in McGill and finally the railroad through Ely. That devastated White Pine County. Overnight, Ely and the nearby mining communities ceased being what they had been for most of the 20th century — company towns.

"Kennecott was king and the workers were the subjects," said Ken Kliewer, who has been in town since 1974 and is publisher of the Ely Daily Times. "They had Kennecott houses heated with Kennecott heat." But on July 4, 1987, they only had themselves.

"That started making everything turn around," Terry said of the centennial celebration. "They saw we had a future. They saw other people who had grown up here, how this place was very important to them."

That's the way it always has been. Ely, the hub of eastern Nevada, goes through good times and bad, and the town survives. Mines open and close. People leave and come back. Even those who stay away celebrate the place. Every year, picnics are planned in Reno and Las Vegas for White Pine natives.

For 2000, the beginning of the new century, White Pine High School is planning a Fourth of July reunion for anyone still living who ever had graduated from the school. Graduates started booking hotel rooms a year ahead of time. Few other places in the state produce stronger ties between people and their community.

"They have a great love for this area," said Karen Rajala, coordinator of the White Pine County Economic Diversification Council. "They've been here through the tough times. There is great optimism and tenacity in this area."

That was evident when Kennecott left. "We pulled ourselves up," businessman Ken Curto said.

Some say isolation can breed loyalty. Ely is alone, not close to anything. No freeway, just two-lane U.S. Highway 50 connecting the place to the rest of the world. Reno is far away, as are Las Vegas and Salt Lake City.

"The thing is, Ely is the most geographically isolated community in the forty-eight states," said Lorraine Clark, president of the White Pine Chamber of Commerce. "Ely is 250 miles at least from any major city, 350 from Reno. When you're out here in the middle of nowhere, community becomes very important. You have to depend on each other. When you leave here, you still feel connected." Clark left and returned. When her high school class held a thirtieth reunion, July 4, 1999, she was there.

Many say the ties that bind come from shared history and experience. Most of the people who live or did live in the area probably can tell stories about how they worked for Kennecott, or their parents did, or their grandparents did. They lived in Ruth and worked in the pit, or McGill and worked in the smelter, or Ely and worked on the railroad.

"It's because of the nature of that industry," said Guy Rocha, state archivist and Nevada history expert. "It's that life, the shared experience. That was life in company towns for most of the 20th century. Many

An abandoned building casts its shadow on the old Kennecott Copper site.

people belonged to a union that was also a fraternity. They had union meetings."

You grew up together. You lived together. White Pine County was among the country's most diverse areas, especially for the size of its population. The county had many nationalities, most immigrants working in the mines. Their traditions survive. In March, every year, Greek Independence Day is celebrated in Ely.

"The families intermarried; you deal with ethnicity," Rocha said. "These people have a tremendous sense of heritage. I don't know of any community in Nevada that does reunions the way they do. There is something about the Ely connection. It's like going back to the homeland."

Some say it's the memories. "The master mechanic dressed up like he was going to church," said Darrel Hall, who worked

Reno refugee cranks out ridable art

Ray Fisher leans against a Harley-Davidson motorcycle he customized at Gone Wild, his Harley store in downtown Ely.

otorcycles are works of art, especially if you build them by hand, piece by piece, from the ground up. Just ask Ray Fisher.

"For people who build one bike for one person, one bike at a time, they are artists," said Fisher, who creates custom Harley-Davidson motorcycles in his Gone Wild bike shop on Aultman Street. "The others are manufacturers."

The forty-eight-year-old Ely native returned to his hometown to open Gone Wild on November 15, 1997, after operating an automotive machine shop in Reno for twenty years. Fisher's art isn't inexpensive. One of his finished works, displayed in the shop window awaiting customer pickup, cost

$21,000 — and took a year to create.

"The whole bike is special," said Kelly Marker, Fisher's partner at Gone Wild. "The sky is the limit, depending on what a customer wants. There will never be another motorcycle made exactly like this."

Most of Fisher's customers, about eighty percent of them, come from outside the area. He builds bikes for enthusiasts in California, Utah, Idaho and throughout Nevada.

"For us, advertising is real important," said Fisher, who promotes his shop in national motorcycle magazines. "They call us and come talk to us. It's a beautiful trip to Ely, but it's a long trip."

ELY

- Population in 1999: 9,961 (0-17, 25 percent; 18-44, 40 percent; 45-64, 23.5 percent; 65-plus, 11.5 percent; male, 58 percent; female, 42 percent).
- Population in 1990: 8,619.
- Population in 2003: (projected) 11,716.
- Retail sales in 1998: $63.338 million.
- Retail sales in 2003: (projected) $90.365 million.

- Claim to fame: Capital of eastern Nevada's mining country. White Pine County seat. Eastern gateway to U.S. 50 in Nevada.

- How it got its name: Named for Smith Ely, president of Selby Copper Mining & Smelting Co., which established refining operation in 1878 on site of present City Hall.

- Local legend: Rancher George N. Swallow organized "Operation Haylift" to feed starving livestock in winter of 1949, when one of the worst storms in history of the eastern Nevada made cattle impossible to reach by land. More than four million pounds of feed were air-dropped to livestock. Movie made in 1950s based on the event.

almost thirty years for the company railroad that hauled copper ore from Ruth to McGill through Ely. "There was a lot of prestige in being management. Each shop had a foreman and they dressed up."

Hall, once a mechanic for the copper railroad that ran around the clock, now is a consultant for what's left. The White Pine Historical Railroad Foundation operates trains from the old East Ely depot for increasing numbers of summer tourists.

"Where my mother lived, we can see her house from here," said Hall, standing in the rail yard. "Down at the end, in those trees, my mother and dad lived there. When they quit running the train, she couldn't sleep because there was no noise."

For Hall, the railroad was Ely. He remembers working on the old steam engines. "Terrible, horrible, miserable," Hall said, describing what it was like to repair the monsters. "Everything weighs a ton. Everything is hard to get at; everything is hard to loosen up. The bolts don't want to move."

Terry's father, Thomas O. Bath, was on the first train to arrive in Ely from the outside world in 1906. He managed a lumber company and the family continues in the same business. "You need a spirit of adventure," Terry said of living in White Pine County.

After Kennecott left, it took more than history, heritage, experience, spirit and a centennial celebration to turn Ely around. Some things happened, such as the opening of Great Basin National Park nearby and the construction of a maximum-security prison in Ely. Small businesses, such as Keith Carson's Murry Springs Bottling Company, have opened. Carson sells natural spring water from Ely to customers in Nevada, Utah, Idaho and Colorado.

"This spring has run for hundreds of years," said Carson, who also operates a

Eroded tailings from the abandoned Kennecott Copper Mine in Ruth, five miles west of Ely, are a backdrop for junipers.

R. Oden

Ely's Ghost Train

construction company. "It's not like mining or logging."

Some mining also came back, in the form of Broken Hill Proprietary Company, Ltd., an Australian outfit that began working at Ruth in 1996. But the 464-employee operation closed in 1999, initiating another tough time for Ely.

"People are getting scared," said Bridget Paris, a White Pine High School student whose family lives on a ranch. Kids can tell how the local economy is doing. When mineral prices are high, more students play on the school athletic teams and more people are in the stands watching them. When prices are down, the school has fewer players and spectators.

"It gets hard to cheer," said cheerleader Jasmine Danner.

Ely knows it can't depend on outside help when the mining stops. "We're looking at not having the mine," said Terry, who serves on a committee to expand home-based businesses. "We need to look at the window of opportunity to find other things. If we don't get other things, we'll be down the tubes again."

The town is counting on itself. "We're after former residents to come back when they retire or move their business back here," said Clark, who brought a desktop-publishing business with her when she returned to Ely. "That's one of our economic plans, to go out to former residents to get them to come back here."

One native, Ray Fisher, returned on his own after twenty years in Reno to open a custom motorcycle shop. That's the type of small business Ely is seeking.

"White Pine County is kind of cool," Fisher said. "If we can make a living, we'll be all right."

Hollywood stars such as Gary Cooper and Ingrid Bergman once had guest rooms at the Hotel Nevada in Ely.

Hope rises again for hotel that was once Nevada's tallest building

Bert Woywood never drinks at his own bar: "It doesn't taste the same," said Woywood, co-owner of the historic Hotel Nevada in downtown Ely. "It might be the same for a cook, I don't know. Your own food doesn't taste good, you go someplace else."

But that's tough for the longtime Las Vegas casino executive who took over the six-story Hotel Nevada in 1994. "I can't go anyplace else because I've eighty-sixed so many people out of here," he said with a laugh. "I go to another bar, I've got ten people staring at me."

So Woywood stays at his own place. He has worked hard to clean up the Hotel Nevada — opened in 1929 as the state's tallest building — and he has plenty to do. Community leaders are hoping the hotel will help with their continuing efforts to attract more business to downtown, now checkered with busy shops and vacant storefronts.

"There's a number of very fine buildings and very fine businesses," said Karen Rajala, coordinator for the White Pine County Economic Diversification Council. "We also have some pretty critical gaps in

services and some empty buildings."

The hotel has a long history, going back to the days when movie stars such as Gary Cooper and Ingrid Bergman spent the night on their way to Sun Valley, Idaho. They usually drove from Hollywood to Las Vegas, then north to Ely before reaching their famous resort destination.

"It's halfway between Las Vegas and Sun Valley," Woywood said of his red brick hotel. "In those days, every other business was a bar, so Ely was pretty wild. It was wild when I got here, but I cleaned it up a little bit." When Woywood came to town, the Hotel Nevada had a reputation for more than history.

"We had a band six nights a week and people would come in here bragging about getting into fights," he said. "We had an 86 list that was four pages long. Whenever somebody caused a fight, we kicked them out and didn't let them back in."

Despite the policy, he reports strong — if calmer — local business. He also counts on tourists attracted to the area by the Great Basin National Park and other destinations. Bands still perform at the Hotel Nevada, mostly on summer weekends.

An old photo from the Ely Historical Society shows a busy street crowded with cars outside the Hotel Nevada in the 1940s.

"I don't care for bands," said Woywood, who used to stay at the Hotel Nevada when he came from Las Vegas to White Pine County on fishing and hunting trips. "The customers are different. They're not gamblers. I don't want that."

What Woywood *does* want is a restoration of the hotel's past. Outside, on one wall, a huge mural of the hotel's symbol — a donkey character — highlights the Hotel Nevada. Stephanie Brueggeman, a former Woywood employee, restored the painting.

"We did it with my secretary," Woywood said. "She was an art teacher. We would put up scaffolding every afternoon. She would put on her shorts and start painting." Brueggeman is no longer at the Hotel Nevada, but her name is on the mural.

Inside the building, Woywood is filling the guest rooms with antique-style furniture and movie memorabilia. "I'm going to make a Clark Gable room, an Ingrid Bergman room," Woywood said. "We're going to have a room for each of these people. We'll ask our guests, 'Which celebrity room would you like to stay in tonight?' "

Another famous guest might not be honored with a room. "Pretty Boy" Floyd Nelson, notorious Depression-era gangster, once stayed at the Hotel Nevada. Woywood isn't sure if Nelson was on his way to Sun Valley when he spent the night. "Nobody asked him," Woywood said with a chuckle.

The state's ultimate entertainer, Wayne Newton, sang in the Hotel Nevada lounge. "That's where he learned to work an audience," Woywood said. "If he could work this audience, he could work anywhere."

Ely's main street is called by locals, "Gateway to the West."

Ely joins its neighbors to become a gateway

Ore cart

The long stretch of U.S. Highway 50 that twists and turns its way across the width of Nevada is advertised proudly as the "Loneliest Road in America," but it has stops along the way: Ely, Eureka and Austin. And don't forget Great Basin National Park and Baker.

Those communities have joined with an out-of-state neighbor, Delta, Utah, in an effort to get their 300-mile section of U.S. 50 designated a National Heritage Area by the federal government. If Congress approves, the route could be the first in the West with that designation.

From Delta to Austin, it could mean a higher profile, more tourism and improved economies, plus ten million dollars to upgrade and promote historic and other sites in the corridor. Ely, with plenty of its own history to market, joins with Great Basin National Park and Baker as the eastern gateway to U.S. 50 in Nevada.

"It's the route, the entire experience," said Ely's Lorraine Clark, White Pine Chamber of Commerce president and a member of the Great Basin Heritage Partnership. History is linked along U.S. 50 and follows much of the old Pony Express Trail.

It includes mining, ranching, old buildings, stories to tell and hotel rooms to fill.

"One of the fastest-growing segments of tourism is culture and history," Clark said. "People want to find out about their history. Each area on U.S. 50 has a unique bit to offer: the Ghost Train we have in Ely, the Eureka Opera House, copper mines, the mining camp in Austin."

The nation has sixteen heritage areas, most in the East and South but none west of the Mississippi River. Along with the U.S. 50 communities, a region in Montana is applying for heritage recognition. At stake, along with prestige, are federal funds — a million dollars a year over a ten-year period — to improve tourist facilities and historic sites.

"A million bucks would be nice," said Wally Cuchine, director of the Eureka Opera House. "It's an opportunity for all of us to promote ourselves as a single area. It ties us all together."

Clark, one of seventy-five people along the U.S. 50 route working on the project, figures it will take two or three years before Congress makes a decision. The local effort started in Baker and the Great

The world's biggest copper mine, near Ely, once put Ruth on the map.

Basin National Park in 1998 and continued during the summer of 1999 with a series of heritage partnership meetings in U.S. 50 communities, including Ely.

"One of the things we found was that we needed broader appeal than just the park," said Tonia Harvey, chairman of the partnership, who operates a gift shop and cafe in Great Basin National Park. "It makes a much larger destination for all of us."

Once a bustling mining town, Ruth lies quiet today.

Eureka

The nine-room Jackson House Hotel, built in 1877, and neighboring Eureka Opera House, 1880, are among the restored buildings attracting tourists.

This town holds its gems close to its heart

A Barbary sheep is one of 30 trophy animals watching over the groceries at Raine's Market in downtown Eureka.

B uying groceries in Raine's Market can be intimidating: You're not sure if you're going to eat what's in the store or if what's in the store is going to eat you. A Canadian timber wolf guards the Frosted Flakes, a Colorado black bear is opposite the Slim Fast and a mountain caribou from British Columbia looms over the Kleenex boxes.

The store on Eureka's main street is as much a hall for hunting trophies as it is a market to pick up tonight's dinner or tomorrow's breakfast. The animals aren't for sale. They're stuffed. In all, the store has twenty-seven trophy heads, five stretched skins, five sets of antlers and two mounted fish — including a Pacific tuna — amid the cereal, milk, eggs, bread and canned fruit juice at Raine's. Store owner Lee Raine did much of the shooting. Her state record mule deer from 1981 looks down on the checkout register.

Eureka displays lots of its history for tourists driving through on U.S. Highway 50, the "Loneliest Road in America." There's the old Opera House, the old hotel and the old Courthouse. Everywhere, visitors see stone buildings, most of them old.

"I just like the whole town," said Theresa Minoletti, who graduated from Eureka High School in 1999. "The way it sits in the hills, it's really pretty."

Civic leaders want tourists to feel the same way.

"That's what we have to sell in this community," Eureka Opera House Director Wally Cuchine said of his town's colorful past. "The reason we have such a good skyline is that the same families have owned these buildings for years and they take care of them. They are the family business."

In Eureka, you can see plenty from the outside, but it's inside where the town reveals itself. Take the Tommyknocker Studio, owned by artist Judi Klindt, who specializes in stained glass.

"You don't know?" Klindt almost shouted when asked what a Tommyknocker is. Then she explained: "They are related to gremlins and elves. They like to live in mines. They steal tools and lunches. They pay for their keep. They knock on mine timbers before a cave-in."

That's perfect for Klindt and for Eureka, which rose quickly in the late 1800s as a leading producer of silver and lead, then fell just as fast when the mines closed in a relatively short time. Today, a few new miners populate the area, along with descendants of old families, ranchers, farmers and some people escaping from wherever they came.

"People here are very open and forgiving," said Klindt, who came to Eureka from Southern California in 1971. "You can do just about anything you want to do as long as it does't hurt anybody. That's great in a small town."

Along with picturesque buildings and easygoing natives, Eureka offers something else to locals and visitors — isolation.

"A lot of people have the perception that technology never got here," Cuchine said. "I can draw groups of people to come here and have a conference at the Opera House who tell their friends, 'I can't plug in my computer. My cell phone won't work. I'm out of communication until I get back.'"

Little in Eureka looks high-tech. Inside Tommyknocker Studio, along with all the stained glass, there's an old bank vault built into the back wall.

"They said this side of town was built around that vault," Klindt said.

Raine's Market and the Tommyknocker aren't the only places with surprises on the other side of the front door. Try the Eureka County Courthouse, built in 1879-80 and restored in 1998. The outside is red stone with white trim. The inside houses the office of County Clerk/Treasurer Joan Shangle.

Appointed in 1963 and elected the next year, Shangle is Eureka County's longest-serving elected official. She doesn't say much, until you get her talking about what's inside the glass case on one side of her office. She pointed out the items one by one, starting

Built in 1880, the Colonnade Hotel is one of the oldest buildings in town.

with a 1916 calculator.

"You twist the handle," Shangle said, demonstrating the mechanical calculator's clicks and grinds. "There's $500 on one turn and five turns in all." She put down the calculator and picked up something else that looks just as old. "A lot of people have never seen this kind of pen holder," she said.

Also inside the case is a set of small volumes – law books. "These were saddlebag books," said Shangle. "They were law books the district judges used to put in their saddlebags to ride the circuit." She pointed to other items – a scale, paperweight and inkwell – all part of a desk set that belonged to her great-grandfather. On one wall is an old clock with the hands stuck at a quarter to three.

"It's because I haven't gotten onto a chair to wind it up," she said.

Shangle keeps the minutes of all County Commission meetings and court proceedings. She does it by hand, in perfect script. Her neat writing fills volumes of large ledgers; it's the county history.

"My computer is in the next room," Shangle said. Somehow, it wouldn't look right in her office. Across the street from the courthouse there's more

White leather wedding boots at the Eureka Sentinel Museum

Painter gets his impressions from Nevada's natural state

G ary Link has figured out what he wants to be.

"I'd like to be known as the Nevada impressionist painter," said 44-year-old Link, who is starting to find subjects in the central part of the state.

"It seems like it's moving in that direction."

Link, a onetime commercial artist in Chicago, teaches art at Eureka High School. He has been in the classroom nine years, but didn't get really serious about painting until after receiving his master's degree in art, then had a show of his work at the Eureka Opera House in 1999.

"I'd kind of been sleeping around with the art for eight or ten years," said Link, a native of North Dakota. I was so busy with the school and learning to teach. I decided to get my master's in painting. It just kind of galvanized me."

Link studied art during summer vacations at Northwestern State University in Louisiana. Now, during the school year, he teaches photography, silkscreening and beginning art and is advisor for the yearbook. A graduate of the Colorado Institute of Art, he got into teaching when advertisers stopped hiring artists in Chicago.

"I was kind of getting tired of commercial art," he said.

"It was the 1980s and there was a recession. I was getting laid off every couple years. I decided to get a teaching credential."

When the time came to get a teaching job, Eureka turned out to be an easy choice. "I was kind of looking around," Link said. "I had offers in Montana and Minnesota. This was the highest paying offer by about $10,000."

Artist Gary Link, a teacher at Eureka High School, paints the local landscape.

EUREKA
- Population of area in 1999: 1,057 (28 percent under 18; 18-44, 42 percent; 45-64, 22 percent; 65-plus, 8 percent; male, 55 percent; female, 45 percent).
- Population of area in 1990: 1,107.
- Population of area in (projected) 2003: 1,097.
- Median household income: $15,041.
- Retail sales in 1998: $6.728 million.
- Retail sales in 2003: (projected) $7.747 million.
- Claim to fame: A center of silver and lead mining in the late 1800s, the town was known as the "Pittsburgh of the West" because of the black smoke from 16 ore smelters. One of the best preserved of Nevada's historic mining towns.
- How it got its name: The legend is the town got its name when miners shouted "Eureka!" — meaning "I have found it." — upon discovering silver. Another story is that George Haskell, a resident when the town site was established, named the location "Napias," the Shoshone Indian word for silver, on Jan. 13, 1870. But the name was changed to Eureka two weeks later when the post office was established, with Haskell the postmaster.
- Local legend: Edna Covert Plummer, appointed Eureka County District Attorney in May 1918, the state's first female district attorney. She lost in the November general election. A pioneer for women's rights, she organized Farmers and Merchants National Bank.

Beau Buchanon, left, and Nick Etchegaray, both fifteen, practice steer-roping at the Eureka County Fairgrounds.

writing, but you'll need Cuchine to find it.

Inside the Opera House, behind the stage, there's a wall covered with signatures of singers and other artists who have performed in the historic building, starting with the Stutz Theatre Company on July 16, 1897. Built in 1880 on the ruins of one of Eureka's many fires, the Opera House was restored in 1993, with a grand reopening April 15, 1994. Country singer Eddie Rabbitt was the featured attraction. Rabbitt's name is on the wall. So is the name of Juice Newton, another popular singer, who appeared in 1997.

"We have all these entertainers come in," said Cuchine, a Montana native who first came to Eureka as an environmental scientist in 1981, "but people here listen to country and western music more than anything." Eureka receives three FM radio stations and two of them are country, but the Opera House wall also is autographed by the Ying Quartet, a classical group.

"We do twelve to eighteen major cultural events a year," said Cuchine, who became director of the Opera House and other county performance and recreation facilities in 1993. Recent Opera House performers include a Celtic harpist and acting companies from around the state. Audience members come from across northern Nevada to see events in the historic place.

"I've had up to 160 people for an ordinary cultural event," Cuchine said. "We typically do a major country-western act once a year."

Cuchine loves the Opera House, which he calls the "house." He'll show off the canvas curtain, installed in 1924 after the 1881 original burned.

"The original hand-painted curtain was a scene from Venice," Cuchine said. "In 1923 there was a stage fire and the curtain burned, as did part of the stage. As we go back, you'll see the wood, the trim from the curtain is still charred."

Sure enough, behind the curtain there is a small section of burned wood.

Along the top and sides of the 1924 curtain are painted advertisements from local businesses that paid for construction at the time. One ad reads:

"Kelly and Rebaleati Garage. We repair everything but a broken heart."

Now the house isn't just for concerts – it gets a lot of community use, too.

"We get to have all our dances in there," Minoletti said. "It's really neat having it in an

Cocoa-Puff, a five-week old baby llama, seems to smile back at thirteen-year-old Julie Etchegaray, who was training llamas for a 4-H project.

old building." Eureka kids as well as adults have a sense of town history.

"In the Great Depression, our bank was one of the few banks that stayed open," Nicholas Etchegaray said of Eureka's old Farmers and Merchants Bank that didn't close when a national bank holiday was declared in 1933.

Nicholas, his thirteen-year-old sister Julie and mother Laurel — descendants of Canadian and Basque settlers — live on a farm outside of town. "The kids are totally Eureka," Laurel Etchegaray said with a smile.

So are the folks inside the Jackson House, a restored 19th-century hotel.

That's where you'll likely meet Nancy Brewer, a graduate of New York's French Culinary Institute, now cooking in the middle of Nevada as chef of the hotel's restaurant.

"The big thing was, we didn't want to leave Eureka," said Nancy's husband, Rick, who manages the Jackson House and the newer Best Western Eureka Inn down the street. "We came to the conclusion we didn't want to be in a big city with our daughter."

With just nine rooms, the Jackson House opened in 1877. It was restored in 1981 and renovated in 1999. The restaurant, with

Brewer preparing just about everything to order, opened last year. If you want to eat well in Eureka, you'd better hope she continues to enjoy small-town living. Here's a tip: Brewer and her husband used to own a restaurant in Ely, the White Pine County seat. She believes Ely is too big.

Brewer has just one problem in Eureka. "I can't just run to the store if I forget something," she said of ordering food supplies. "I have to think far ahead. I use a gourmet company out of California."

A couple of blocks away from Brewer's kitchen is the Colonnade Hotel, built in 1880 as the meeting house for the Italian Benevolent Society.

Inside, seventy-eight-year-old Mary Jean LaBarry — a resident for more than fifty years — has been running the family-owned Colonnade as an old-fashioned hotel since 1973. Old-fashioned means the bathrooms are down the hall, not in the rooms.

LaBarry has a good story — a tale about the Colonnade, Prohibition, illegal whiskey and a tunnel: "There is an empty room in the Colonnade," said LaBarry, a French Basque. "They used that to make whiskey and they had a tunnel to the Eureka Hotel. They would bring whiskey. That was the time they couldn't have any whiskey. That's what they told me."

From the outside Eureka looks good, but inside is better. That's where you see the people and hear the stories.

Fire hats circa 1916

In seven cemeteries, history sleeps

D ie in Eureka and you've got a wide selection of resting places.

Cemeteries are everywhere. Wally Cuchine, director of the Eureka Opera House and an expert on local history, counts seven. If he's got some time, Cuchine will show you each one, whether or not you're shopping for a grave site.

"None are well kept up," Cuchine said, warning of the general condition of Eureka's cemeteries. Five are on the west side of town, which at various times was known as "Grave Yard Flat" and "Death Valley." There's the Catholic Cemetery, the Masonic Cemetery, the County Cemetery, the City Cemetery and the Odd Fellows Cemetery.

"You weren't allowed to bury anybody just anyplace in those days," Cuchine said of Eureka's cemetery tradition. In the Odd Fellows Cemetery, some of the headstones have photographs of the deceased.

"It's a big thing in Eureka and Ely to have photographs on tombstones," Cuchine said.

The more mysterious cemeteries are Jewish and Chinese. Little remains of those gravesites. "Some graves are unique and so old that no one remains as family to properly care for them," said Eureka historian Connie

Hicks. The Jewish Cemetery on the edge of town is overgrown with sagebrush.

"There's only about three headstones left," Cuchine said.

Despite their disrepair, the cemeteries are a big part of Eureka history.

"I think we should preserve the cemeteries," said fifteen-year-old Nicholas Etchegaray, descendant of Basque, Italian and Canadian settlers who arrived in the area more than 100 years ago. "In the future, people should know who lived here."

Eureka resident Allyn Niles agrees. "We do have a lot of cemeteries around here," he said. "There are quite a few people around who like to visit various cemeteries, especially older cemeteries. Some of the cemeteries around here are in a bad state. They should be brought up."

In Odd Fellows Cemetery, one of seven Eureka cemeteries, a gravestone is adorned with a photograph.

A lizard rests in the noontime sun on a fence in Eureka.

Even in rugged times, death did not discriminate between the aged and the very young.

The cemeteries are a result of Eureka's diverse ethnic roots. It was a booming mining town in the nineteenth century that attracted people from Europe and Asia. In 1875, more than two-thirds of the men in Eureka were from foreign countries. There were Irish and Cornish miners. There were Italians and Swiss-Italians, most of whom burned charcoal to fuel Eureka's giant smelters.

In 1879, one of Eureka's biggest and most controversial incidents took place – the Charcoal War. It was an attempt by the Italians and Swiss-Italians to get more money for their charcoal. The dispute ended on August 18, 1879, when a sheriff's posse shot and killed five charcoal burners.

"It was the Swiss-Italians saying to the smelter people, 'We want a little bit more money for our charcoal,'" Cuchine said. "The sheriff went out and literally murdered five charcoal burners."

For a Nevada mining town, there was also a large Jewish population in early Eureka. By 1879, there were about 113 Jews in the community, most from Russia and Poland. Jewish merchants owned Eureka's first general store, Nathan & Harrison.

Many Chinese who helped build the Central Pacific Railroad in Nevada ended up as cooks and laborers in Eureka. They were not always welcome.

On June 23, 1876, the Eureka Anti-Chinese League was formed to limit Chinese immigration into the state.

Eureka saved downtown just in time

Patty Peek moves chairs from the floor of the Eureka Opera House, the town's cultural arts center since its restoration in 1993.

istoric Eureka is looking its best. The Opera House has been restored and the courthouse repaired. The old hotel has been renovated and a new one built.

"Fortunately, it has been saved," Eureka County Recorder/Auditor Michael Rebaleati said of his hometown. Just in time: the prolonged slump in gold prices has cut the flow of cash the county used for most of this decade to pay more than $14.8 million for construction projects — the most expensive of which transformed downtown.

The county spent $3.8 million to restore the courthouse, a project completed in 1998, and $2.3 million to rebuild the Opera House, the restoration finished in 1993. The two buildings, both opened in 1880, are now town landmarks.

"It was going to be bulldozed, or it was going to be saved," Opera House Director Wally Cuchine said of the situation in 1990 when the county traded land to acquired the building from private owners. "The roof was going. Once the roof is gone, the building falls down." Today, the building is standing, with audiences coming from across the area to see regional and national performers.

"That was a good thing for Eureka, the restoration of the Opera House and the courthouse," said Theresa Minoletti, a seventeen-year-old lifelong Eureka resident. It probably couldn't happen today because the plunge in gold prices means a corresponding drop in the tax collected on net income from the county's mines. Instead of money to rebuild the town, the county is looking at budget cuts and a thirty percent decline in revenue.

Wally Cuchine, director of the Eureka Opera House, glances at a backstage wall where recent performers have signed their names and messages.

"It's pretty close to that," Rebaleati said. "We cut back. We haven't had layoffs." One big thing in the county's favor — no debt. The projects were paid for when the money was rolling in. "We're in a serious holding pattern," Rebaleati said.

Not everyone was pleased with all of the restoration. "The exorbitant amount of money spent was unnecessary," said Connie Hicks, an expert on local history who likes the

Restoration has revived historic buildings along Eureka's main street.

Opera House and courthouse, but not the new sidewalks. The county's spending led to private investment downtown. A dentist from Elko, Jeff Bartley, built the forty-two-room Best Western Eureka Inn, which opened in April 1998, and renovated the nine-room Jackson House, a hotel that dates back to 1877.

"It's a neat town," said Bartley, who travels to Eureka every other week to do dental work in the medical clinic the county built during the spending spree. "With the restoration that's taken place, it makes you feel safe making an investment. There are quite a few people doing little projects, restoring some of the old homes."

Rebuilding Eureka wasn't easy. A few nails got bent in the process. The Opera House needed a lot more work than originally was anticipated. "It started as a much smaller project," said Cuchine, who took over as director after the restoration. "They envisioned it being a little over a million dollars and it would take nine months. It cost over two million and took three years."

Recently restored, the historic Eureka Courthouse has stood on this corner since 1879.

McGill

Once owned by Kennecott Copper, these houses now are owned by new families or those who stayed behind when the mine closed.

Glory days forged a strong sense of self

Norman Linnell has been tending bar at the McGill Club for fifty-three years.

When the giant copper smelter that dominated McGill for most of this century closed in 1983, Norman Linnell finally got a day off.

"I worked seven days a week until Kennecott went down," said Linnell, who has been tending bar at the McGill Club almost nonstop since 1946. "Then I got the biggest break of my life: I work six days."

The McGill Club is historic. So is Linnell. The club opened in 1907. By 1999, the seventy-eight-year-old bartender had been pouring drinks for fifty-three years, more than half the bar's lifetime.

"Everybody around here says, 'Norman, if you ever quit here, this place is dead,'" Linnell said.

The McGill Club, with its wooden bar that's more than a hundred years old, and Linnell, a native born on Thanksgiving Day 1921, are among the last landmarks in a town that was once one of the state's most important and famous. McGill was a company town through and through, owned and operated by Kennecott.

Men such as Norman's father, Andrew, worked in the smelter and mill, which processed the copper ore hauled by train from Kennecott's huge open pit mine in nearby Ruth. They lived in company houses, paying Kennecott three dollars per bedroom per month.

McGill was, and still is, linked to Ruth and Ely, the "big city" twelve miles south on U.S. Highway 93. McGill was, and still is, distinct. When McGill residents talk about "downtown," they don't mean Ely. They mean their own shrinking commercial district where the club, a grocery store and post office are located.

Dan Braddock, a retired public works director who moved from northern California to McGill in 1996, learned about location in a hurry.

"I get in trouble when I say, 'I'm going to town,'" said Braddock, whose daughter, son-in-law and grandchildren live in McGill. "They say, 'Where?' I say, 'Ely.'" Wrong answer. "Ely is Ely," Braddock said. "McGill is McGill. Don't mix them up."

The glory days of McGill are long gone. Once it was a copper giant and the largest community in White Pine County with about 3,000 residents. Between 1978 and 1983, when Kennecott closed its mining and smelting operation in eastern Nevada, McGill was hurt

badly — but it didn't die.

Linnell, who can walk from the bar to the house where he grew up on Third Street, remained. So did the McGill Club. "At one time, I knew where everybody lived in town," said Linnell, who went to work at the bar when he returned home from World War II. "Today, I sure don't. When Kennecott went down, the younger people went other places to make a living. A lot of them moved to Elko, a lot moved to Reno, a lot moved to Las Vegas. That left a lot of empty houses."

More recently, some of the old smelter workers' houses have been occupied by employees of the state's maximum-security prison, built in White Pine County after Kennecott closed. Retired Kennecott workers still live in McGill, along with young miners employed by Broken Hill Proprietary Company, Ltd., an Australian outfit that dug copper around Ruth from 1996 to 1999. But that hasn't been enough to keep McGill from losing pieces of itself.

The movie theater is closed. So is the barbershop. The town used to have two bars; now it has one. Several grocery stores once served the community; only one remains. The drugstore has been turned into a museum.

"You can see all this stuff closing down little by little," said Linnell, who used to drink what he called a "Presbyterian" at the McGill Club — a half shot of whiskey, a splash of 7-Up and water. Linnell, who doesn't drink it anymore, recalls other tough times in McGill.

During the Great Depression, the Nevada Consolidated Copper Company offered his father and the other smelter workers a choice:

The rusty remains of a once-thriving copper industry serve as a reminder of the uncertain future of a company town.

many could be laid off or they all could take turns working.

"My dad worked fifteen days, then he'd be off forty-five to sixty days to give another fellow a chance to work in order to survive," Norman Linnell said. "They were a nice company to work for."

In those days, McGill was divided along lines of race and nationality. Many immigrants worked in the smelter, including Italians, Mexicans, Irish, Serbs and Croats. McGill had Greek Town, Japan Town and Austria Town. Norman Linnell is Scandinavian, equal parts Swedish and Norwegian. He mixed with everybody.

"I knew them all," he said. "I played with the Italians; I played with the Greeks."

Company bosses lived in what is still called "The Circle." Their homes had steam heat and were connected to the Kennecott power plant. Workers' homes were heated with coal. McGill's children liked going to the movie theater. But first they'd stop at the McGill Club.

"Practically all the kids were raised in here," Linnell said. "You sold ice cream, candy bars, chewing gum and all that stuff before the show." Inside the McGill Club, on a

"You lived in these company towns on company terms"

McGILL

- Population in 1999:
1,900
(0-17, 22 percent;
18-44, 43 percent;
45-64, 22 percent;
65-plus, 13 percent;
male, 61.5 percent;
female, 38.5 percent).
- Population in 1990:
1,258.
- Population in 2003:
(projected) 1,785.
- Median household
income in 1998:
$30,372.

- Claim to fame: One
of state's most
famous company
towns and location
of copper-ore
smelter until
Kennecott closed its
mining operations
in White Pine
County. At one time,
the county's largest
community.

- How it got its name:
The town was
originally a ranch
owned by William
N. McGill. Ranch
was purchased by
Nevada Consoli-
dated Copper Co.
for smelter site.

- Local legend:
Russell R. Elliott,
famous Nevada
historian and
professor at the
University of
Nevada, Reno,
grew up in McGill
and wrote a book,
*Growing up in a
Company Town*,
about his experi-
ence.

An excerpt from the book, Growing Up in a Company Town *by Russell R. Elliott, McGill native and Nevada historian. The former University of Nevada, Reno professor died March 15, 1998, at age eighty-five.*

Russell R. Elliott

The physical and social needs of the employees and their families were addressed by building the Clubhouse, opening a large outdoor swimming pool, encouraging athletics, and sponsoring dances, holiday celebrations, and other social events. All of these activities reflected the "welfare capitalism" that became widespread nationally in the 1920s.

By 1930, it was clear that individuals in the company towns of McGill and Ruth gave up much of their economic and local political autonomy as well as the direction of their social life in exchange for physical and economic security. You lived in these company towns on company terms, or not at all.

In addition to beautifying the area around the Circle, company officials encouraged the employees to plant lawns and trees, and to grow flower and vegetable gardens. The company supplied topsoil, fertilizer, lawn and garden seeds, fencing material, including posts and wire, and, of course, water.

The company also oiled most of the roads during this period and put in cement or blacktop sidewalks for pedestrians. By that time, however, the habit of walking in the middle of the road was too ingrained to break.

wall near the front door, are pictures of 145 town residents who served in World War II. They're all very young. One is Linnell.

"Every one of them was either drafted or enlisted from McGill," he said. "There's a lot of people up there."

Another is Bill Ireland, a famous McGill native and fixture in the intercollegiate athletic programs at both the University of Nevada, Reno — where he was head baseball coach — and the University of Nevada, Las Vegas, where he later became head football coach and athletic director.

"It had a built-in structure," Ireland said of the McGill in which he grew up. "It was a company town. It had some built-in discipline that you didn't have in Ely, Elko and Wells, that type of town. When we moved out into the state, we were disappointed that other towns didn't have the same thing."

McGill had something else that was unique — badger fights. "If we got a new person in town and he was kind of a bragger, they arranged for a badger fight," Ireland said. "This new person was designated to pull a badger out of a barrel. There were a couple hungry dogs on the outside waiting. They'd give the guy a big rope."

A crowd would gather on the main street to watch the action. "They'd yell, 'Are you ready?'" Ireland said. The new guy would grab the rope and run. At the other end — no badger. "It was a port-a-John," Ireland said. "He's pulling an outhouse down the street. Then, they'd all go down to the McGill Club and have a few drinks."

Across the street from the club is another of the town's survivors, Bradley's Market, which opened in the 1940s.

"My parents have been here forever," said Tiffany Larsen, whose mother and father own the store. "McGill has had its ups and downs, but it has managed to stay alive."

Larsen, like Linnell, grew up in McGill. But she doesn't live in the community anymore. She's in town while husband Jasen serves a tour in Alaska with the Army. Ruby Fullerton, a lifelong resident, visits with Larsen in the market. She remembers the company houses.

"Kennecott owned those homes," Fullerton said. "They used to furnish the most God-awful paint. My grandmother had a dark purple bathroom and a dark yellow kitchen." Larsen also remembers. "My parents had an orange house," she said.

In the front yard of his McGill home, retired Kennecott machinist Tom Lake, 82, weeds his flower garden beside a miniature wooden train.

They both remember the last big day in McGill, September 3, 1993, when the 750-foot smokestack from the copper plant was taken down.

"We had a lot of people watching in our yard," Larsen said. "People from everywhere came to see it."

Fullerton nodded her head.

"I never saw the town so busy," she said.

The smelter smokestack, a longtime McGill landmark, is gone, but the town has the swimming pool.

"Ely people think it's terrible to come over here," Fullerton said. "They gripe because they have to come over here to use it."

That's the McGill-Ely thing again. Sometimes, Fullerton goes to Ely — but not by choice. "My daughter lives over there and my sister too," she said. "But I wouldn't go if I didn't have to. I used to have to go over there when my daughter was in high school. For sports activities, it was a trip to Ely."

That seems like a long way from McGill.

With the demise of big-time mining, the rail depot reached the end of the line.

Drugstore captures a portrait of the past

The town of McGill sits along Highway 93, twelve miles north of Ely. Fields in the background, now used for grazing and growing hay, once were barren tailings from the Kennecott Copper mine. Reclamation began in 1987.

I f you want to look inside the historic McGill Drugstore, call Dan Braddock. He's got the keys.

"It only takes a couple of minutes for me to get down there," said Braddock, who lists his home telephone number on the drugstore's brochure. Braddock, who moved to McGill from northern California in 1996, has taken on the old drugstore as a personal project.

A lot of McGill's history is tied up in the place. The drugstore opened in 1908 and closed for good in the mid-1980s when the last operator, Elsa Culbert, simply locked the doors. All the store's inventory — toothpaste, cough syrup, hair spray, combs and shoe laces — remained on the shelves. Many items now inside were there in the 1940s, '50s, '60s and '70s.

"Tubes of Ipana toothpaste sit across the aisle from jars of Dippity-do, an industrial-strength styling gel used to hold a woman's hair in place several inches above the head," reads Braddock's drugstore pamphlet. You can't buy anything. The store is a museum, turned over by Elsa Culbert's sons — Michael, Daniel and Steven — to the White Pine Public Museum

in 1995. It comes complete with a seven-stool soda fountain. Sometimes, Braddock serves ice cream.

The store has no regular hours of operation. You make an appointment with the retired public works director. Braddock, whose grandfather was a pharmacist in Southern California, got his first look at the McGill Drugstore when he started making trips to town from the Sacramento area to visit his daughter, son-in-law and grandchildren.

"My wife and I said, 'My gosh, why isn't it a museum?'" Braddock said "You couldn't see through the windows, they were so filthy." When Braddock retired and moved to McGill for good, he joined the White Pine Museum's board and was made responsible for the drugstore.

"It became a passion," he said.

The drugstore was much more than just a place to buy tooth-paste — it was one of McGill's important social centers. During McGill's mining boom, when the Kennecott copper smelter operated around the clock, a variety of nationalities lived in the company town. The drugstore and post office were about the only locations where they all met outside work.

"It was one of the two places where all the ethnic people would associate," Braddock said.

The drugstore is also the place where historian Russell R. Elliott discovered Vinol. In his book, *Growing Up in a Company Town*, the McGill native wrote about a childhood illness:

"The suggested tonic was a patent medicine known as 'Vinol' that, I found out later, had a rather high percentage of alcohol. I liked the stuff and went through a number of bottles. Fortunately, before I became a child wino, I began putting on a little weight and eventually the cough disappeared.

"Some years later, I spotted a bottle of Vinol on the shelf at the McGill Drugstore and couldn't resist buying it. What a disappointment! It tasted awful."

Braddock said state officials will destroy all the old medicine, but the unique bottles will be saved for display. Now the drugstore has a new roof, thanks to a $10,000 state grant. But turning the building into a museum hasn't been easy.

"When I got there, they didn't have any

Inside the historic McGill Drugstore, time stands still.

water," said Braddock. "Nobody knew where the water came into the building.

"With my background in public works, I started digging. We got water."

Braddock won't sell you Vinol, but if you want to look around, just call.

School's blue ribbon stirs pride in McGill

What a great place to hide! First-grader Earl Cupples finds shelter inside a huge mining truck tire on the school playground.

Teachers at McGill Elementary School keep food in their classrooms for students who don't always get breakfast at home.

"Nobody's wealthy in McGill," said Margaret Thiel, who has taught first grade at the school for thirteen years. "We make sure the kids who are terribly at risk get their power bills paid. We have stuff in our rooms for anyone who hasn't had breakfast."

It hasn't always been easy to live in McGill, especially since 1983, when the copper mill and smelter closed after dominating what had been a thriving company town for most of this century. The big mining company, Kennecott, has been gone for more than a decade. McGill isn't what it used to be, one of the state's most famous and important towns, but the school remains a focus of the community. It could become more important than ever.

"It's kind of the hub," said Thiel, a teacher in the White Pine County School District for twenty-five years. "The parents are very concerned with their children and the school. There isn't very much else here. The school is about the only thing left."

That's why the school, ranked among the state's best, is a source of continuing pride.

McGill Elementary has carried the designation since 1993-94, when a federal panel christened it a Blue Ribbon School.

"We were the only school in Nevada that made it that year," said Virginia Terry, McGill Elementary principal at the time. "Not only was it good for the faculty, it was good for the community. They may not have had as good jobs or as many jobs as they wanted, but they had a good place for their kids to come."

Enrollment was 150 students in kindergarten through fifth grade in 1999. Thiel's first-grade class had fifteen.

"I remember when I first taught in the district, there were over 500 kids in McGill in 1976 when the mine was still running," Thiel said. With so much adversity to deal with in town, the school needed that Blue Ribbon award. It needed something good to happen.

"We had to meet many different requirements for the physical plant, the curriculum offerings and staff training," Terry said. "They came here and inspected."

Along with its Blue Ribbon honor, McGill Elementary received a flag. "I'm not sure where it is," Thiel said of the flag, "but we'll have that Blue Ribbon School designation forever."

Seth Graham checks the weather chart in his first grade classroom.

"What time is it?" first-grade teacher Margaret Thiel asks her class at McGill Elementary School.

Tuscarora

A scenic view of Tuscarora.

Visitors are welcome in Tuscarora but don't crowd the hometown folks

Tuscarora resident Elaine Parks and Mike Molette, a Los Angeles artist, work on a trail to the "glory hole," a deep lake on the edge of town left from mining exploration.

IMPORTANT DATES
- 1867: Gold discovered.
- 1871: Silver discovered.
- 1876: Grand Prize bonanza discovered.
- 1877: Population reached 4,000.
- 1878: Mining peaked with $1.2 million in bullion shipped for the year.
- 1880: Census showed 1,400 residents, with 10 mines and three mills.
- 1907: Financial difficulties ended attempt to revive large-scale mining activity.
- 1966: Tuscarora Retreat and Summer Pottery School established by Dennis Parks.
- 1969: Tuscarora received state historical marker.
- 1984: Elko County Commission rejected proposal to create historic district in Tuscarora.
- April 1989: Residents fought against open-pit mining by Denver-based company digging for gold.
- August 1989: Horizon Gold Corporation agreed to halt mine expansion.
- 1991: Governor Bob Miller signed agreement with Horizon Gold to block mining within town.

When you flip a switch in Tuscarora, chances are the lights will come on, but it wasn't always that way. Tuscarora got regular electricity in the 1970s. Before that, the town counted on a generator and the cranky guy who ran it.

"You couldn't depend on him," said Dennis Parks, Tuscarora's most renowned resident. "He would decide some days he didn't like you and he'd snip the wire."

That doesn't happen anymore. The locals are pretty friendly. Tell Jim Sanborn that you're in a hurry and he responds with a quick question: "Why?" In Tuscarora, one seldom has a reason to rush.

"Right now, it's about half past March," said Sanborn, a retired miner who moved to the isolation and history of Tuscarora in 1993. "We don't worry about time." Sanborn is one of an estimated twelve permanent residents in Tuscarora, or what's left of the town.

Stone buildings and other remnants of the nineteenth-century mining camp are mixed with a few houses built by newer residents and the mobile homes of seasonal visitors. It all sits at the foot of Mount Blitzen in the northwest corner of Independence Valley, fifty-two miles from Elko. The first forty-five miles are on pavement and the last seven on a gravel road. Tuscarora is a world away from neon Nevada.

"Well, look at it," said Parks, a world-famous ceramic artist, when asked why he settled in Tuscarora. "You're surrounded by mountains; it's very reassuring."

The 1966 arrival of Parks and his family started Tuscarora's modern life as a community for artists. The gold-and-silver boom went bust in the late 1800s. Today, Tuscarora is high-tech. "We have one fax in town," said Parks. "We have four computers in town."

When he came to town, Parks started a summer pottery school that has been operating ever since, boosting Tuscarora's population by a handful in July and August. The full-time residents of Tuscarora include Parks, wife Julie, and son Ben, also a ceramic artist. Then there's Ron Arthaud, a painter who showed up after living in France, California and New Mexico; and Gail Rappa, a jewelry maker and Arthaud's girlfriend. Sanborn isn't an artist. He's just a neighbor.

"We haven't got a stop sign here and it's downhill to the graveyard," Sanborn said. "It don't get no better than that."

Tuscarora once had a population of four

thousand. That was in 1877, when the town had mines, schools, saloons, hotels and two newspapers. Today, the modern residents try to make do with what remains. They buy inexpensive land, then restore or rebuild whatever house happens to be on the property.

"I came through here; I saw this old house," said Arthaud, who arrived in 1996 and bought a one-acre lot with two buildings for eight thousand dollars. "I was here for one night. I saw my house for five or ten minutes. Luckily, I had this romantic view of what I saw."

Named during its gold rush days for a Civil War ship, Tuscarora apparently has what painters such as Arthaud and potters such as Dennis Parks are seeking.

"You have no pollution. The air is clean," Parks said. "I'm an hour from the Elko airport. That commuter airplane gets me to Reno or Salt Lake City for a connection. You can live on very little money, which is nice."

People who find Tuscarora have their own reasons for staying. "For painting, I love this area," said Arthaud. "I'm from Minnesota where it's so green. Here, you have the desert colors." And the desert has other advantages, especially in Nevada. "You have the state income tax thing," Arthaud said. Nevada doesn't have one.

On his Tuscarora property, where he lived the first year without running water or electricity, Arthaud mixes building with painting. Some days, he paints the striking mountain-and-desert landscapes that surround Tuscarora. Other days, he digs the basement for his house.

Sanborn watched Arthaud and nicknamed the artist "lightning" because the newcomer never strikes in the same spot twice. "You'd see him painting one minute, then working on his house, then fixing something," Sanborn said with a smile. "You never know where he's going to be. But he's

Once a thriving mining town, Tuscarora serves today as a small art community nestled in the sagebrush mountains.

always working."

Tuscarora isn't primitive, at least by the standards of the people who live there. They have telephones, electricity, running water and television — a station from Reno and a couple from Boise, Idaho. Arthaud just had to wait until he had enough of a house to install utilities.

"It hadn't been lived in for fifty years," Arthaud said. "It was full of rats. I was going to live in a tent if I had to. I cleaned it out. There was a little kerosene heater and I had a little sink with a bucket under it."

Arthaud's property includes the town's old mining-era assay office, which is being turned into a studio for Gail Rappa's jewelry. When she's not creating earrings and bracelets, Rappa watches the visitors who come to town in summer.

Governors count on Tuscarora artists

TUSCARORA

- Population in 1999:
  12
  (10 percent under 18,
  40 percent 18-44,
  50 percent 45-64;
  60 percent male,
  40 percent female).
- Population in 1990:
  10.
- Population in 2003:
  (projected) 13.
- Median household
  income in 1998:
  $22,500.

- Claim to fame:
  Gold-and-silver
  mining boomtown
  in 19th century. Now
  a "living" ghost
  town and artist
  community with an
  art school.

- How it got its name:
  Named for U.S.S.
  Tuscarora, Union
  ship in the Civil War.

- Local legend:
  Dennis Parks, world-
  renowned potter, is
  Tuscarora's artist-in-
  residence and
  founder of the arts
  school.

The money comes in handy. Gail Rappa, a jewelry maker, gets some recognition for being selected to produce the pieces Governor Kenny Guinn wanted to use as awards to honor the state's top 1999 artists. More important to Rappa is the three thousand dollars she received for her work.

"Pay off VISA," said Ron Arthaud, Rappa's boyfriend, when asked where the cash would go. Or the dough could buy a lot of nails. Rappa and Arthaud, a painter, are building a house in Tuscarora. They're also renovating the old mining town's historic assay office for Rappa to use as a studio.

The couple came from New Mexico to live and work in Tuscarora. Rappa has been around and Tuscarora is her latest stop. Born in New York and raised in California, she went to Santa Fe, New Mexico, a world-famous art center, after high-school graduation to apprentice with professional jewelry makers. She studied at the Revere Academy of Jewelry Arts in San Francisco and was an artist-in-residence at the Mendocino Art Center in California for one year.

"It's a fun way of getting some exposure," Rappa said of the state art awards project, which also could lead to bigger things.

Another Tuscarora resident, ceramic artist Ben Parks, was commissioned to make the same awards several years ago. He crafted miniature clay cowboy boots, a big hit with then-Governor Bob Miller.

Later, when the State of Nevada was host for the 1997 National Conference of Governors, Miller asked Parks to make similar ce-

Gail Rappa, photographed by Ron Arthaud

ramic boots as gifts for President Bill Clinton and forty-nine state governors. Parks made enough boots for all the dignitaries who attended the conference.

Tuscarora may be tiny, but the work of its artists covers a lot of territory.

Custom jewelry created by Tuscarora artist Gail Rappa.

"There seems to be a couple of factions of people, " she said. "Either they come out here and scratch their heads and say, 'What do you guys do?' or they come out here and go, 'What a little bit of heaven; we aren't going to tell anyone about it.'"

Tuscarora has some part-time residents, according to the locals, who come for a few weeks each year to hunt or arrive in summer and leave when it gets cold. "You start to feel a certain resentment for the people who pop in and out," said Rappa, who came here from Santa Fe, New Mexico. "There is a certain pride you have. There is an attitude that we stick it out all winter."

It gets cold and it snows. But mostly the wind blows and blows and blows. "I was amazed; all the windows were just rattling," said Annette Dunklin, a friend of Arthaud and Rappa. "A bird was flying into the wind. It was flapping as hard as it could. It was going backwards. It landed in this tree. Then it got blown out of the tree."

When the winds are calm and the weather warm, visitors arrive in Tuscarora looking for a ghost town and its art work. Rappa and Arthaud have mixed feelings about those visitors. They're customers, but they also disrupt the town.

"They're kind of disappointed," Arthaud said of the tourists. "On maps, Tuscarora is advertised as a 'ghost town.' It's really not. We've had people wander through the yard picking stuff up. 'It's a ghost town.' No, it's not. It's where we live."

Arthaud struggles with the economics of tourism, even though it's on a small scale. He can sell paintings to the visitors, but he's not a businessman. Shipping his work to galleries in California and New Mexico is easier, he said. He's guaranteed half the sale price on all pieces. The galleries charge more for Arthaud's paintings than he would. So, if you visit Tuscarora, you probably can get a good deal.

"Usually, we're strapped for money, we're trying to get some quick money," Arthaud said of selling his work in Tuscarora. "It's hard. You want to sell your work. You want to sell it for a price they're comfortable with. I often just say, 'What will you feel comfortable paying?' If I can handle it, I just sell it."

As Tuscarora and its artists become better known, business opportunities may increase. That presents a dilemma. "We need to sell," Arthaud said. "At the same time, we came

here for the isolation.... There was a guy here writing a little tour book. Do we want to be in it? Do we not want to be in it? Do we want our telephone number in it?"

Those are tough questions in a community where one of the big attractions is escape from the outside world. In Tuscarora, people depend on themselves for just about everything. Neighbors can help, but that's usually a last resort.

"People stick to themselves; that's the common thing about people here," said Arthaud, who studied carpentry so he could build his own house. "They're friendly, but they do their own thing. They don't ask for help unless they really need it."

Tuscarora's brand of self-reliance is something Arthaud learned as he settled into

A gallery of rusty relics is scattered throughout the small community.

the community. He discovered that what were routine tasks in other places can become major undertakings in Tuscarora.

"You have to plan ahead here. You're fifty-two miles from Elko," he said. "It's such a challenge. You can't walk to the hardware store." Or the gas station. Or the supermarket. Tuscarora doesn't have those things. Most townspeople probably would tell you they don't need them.

"It's so small compared to the complaints most people have," said Rappa, comparing the difficulties of daily life in Tuscarora to problems in the outside world. Tuscarora has things that make it worth the trouble.

"There hasn't been a day when I walked out that there hasn't been a great horned owl or an eagle in the trees," said Dunklin, who lives in northern California. "I have to go back, but I'll visit here. It's kind of a sanctuary."

Tuscarora still life: an old teapot sitting in the afternoon sun

A world-famous potter founded an art colony in a former mining boomtown

Clay is shaped into a pot by the hands of Deborah Pittman, a student at the pottery school.

uscarora was discovered twice — first by miners who dug for gold and silver in the 1870s, then by Dennis Parks, who came in the 1960s to create and teach. He probably doesn't want the title, but Parks is Tuscarora's leading citizen as the twentieth century ends and the twenty-first century begins.

Parks, whose ceramic work is displayed in some of Europe's great museums, gave the crumbling old boomtown-gone-bust its modern identity as a remote enclave for artists in the high desert of northeastern Nevada when he opened the Tuscarora Retreat and Summer Pottery School in 1966. Every summer, students from around the world show up to live in a small nineteenth-century brothel-turned-hotel and to study with Dennis, his son Ben, Ben's wife Elaine and other artists.

Despite his international reputation, Dennis is as much a part of the regular Tuscarora community as the few retired people and miners who live side-by-side with the artists. "The cemetery is a great place to walk to," Dennis said as he guided a tour of Tuscarora. "It reminds you of your mortality."

He pointed out other landmarks: "That was a home that burned down. See that building? It was a brewery for a while. It also used to store dynamite."

Dennis and Ben work in studios they built themselves. Along with museum-quality pieces, the father and son make a variety of dishware and other items for sale. One of Ben's more unusual projects is a set of large containers patterned after the plastic bottles that hold soap and other household cleaning fluids.

"You know the potter tradition of making large vessels," Ben said. "It struck me as a quirky thing for them to do, to make really large pots. You go digging in Greece and Rome and you dig up these large pots. These are what we have, large soap containers. The ancient Romans had their urns. We have our plastic bottles."

Ben grew up in Tuscarora. He was two years old when his parents stopped here for the first time, in 1962, on their way from Washington, D.C. to northern California. They'd heard about the place from a friend and decided to take a look. The family paused in Tuscarora but kept on going to Pacific Grove, California, on Monterey Bay.

Dennis Parks discovered this ghost town and founded the Tuscarora Retreat and Summer Pottery School in 1966. Now the town has twelve permanent residents.

They ended up in Southern California, where Dennis studied and taught, but he never forgot Tuscarora.

"We kept coming back all the time," said Dennis, who finally decided to stay and open the school. Today, his son has taken over directing the summer art school.

"I feel pretty much like I was raised here," said Ben. "As a kid, I was just off in adventure land."

When Dennis came to town for good, he bought two houses and the building that had been a brothel, rooming house and hotel. "In the late sixties, I was able to buy all these buildings up here for a few thousand dollars," said Dennis, who has become protective of the town.

In the 1980s, Dennis helped the townspeople lead a battle against modern miners looking for leftover gold. Their protests resulted in a halt to blasting and digging near the town.

"The blasting, the trucks and the dust would come right through town," Dennis said. "Something had to be done. Things calmed down, then gold prices went down. They were much easier to fight on the way down."

Julie Parks, Dennis's wife, works in the town post office. "We get mail six days a week," Dennis said. "The mail is brought up from Elko. It's sorted here. What belongs to the locals goes into their mailboxes. The rest is taken on up to the ranches. We have good telephone service now."

And great pottery.

Dennis Parks, left, and his son, Ben, discuss the merits and disadvantages of gloves for pottery-makers.

With twelve permanent residents, Tuscarora is not a ghost town

Jim Sanborn unwraps fudge bars and Heidi, his German shepherd, looks hopeful.

Customers who buy ceramics, paintings and jewelry are welcome in Tuscarora, but the small group of artists who live in the historic northeastern Nevada mining town also fear that what is now a trickle of summer visitors could turn into a flood.

"It's always a mixed blessing, the publicity," said Gail Rappa, a jewelry maker. "It's why we're here, the quiet." Rappa has seen one famous artistic community turn into a popular tourist destination. That's one of the reasons why she left Santa Fe, New Mexico. "That's what was sort of hard about Santa Fe," she said. "Everybody wanted a piece of what was special about it. I don't see that happening here."

She's probably right. Rappa and her Tuscarora neighbors estimate their unique community has twelve permanent residents. That's right — twelve. You can meet all of them, if they're at home, in less than an hour.

Other people, mostly outsiders from Reno-Sparks and California, show up for a week or two during various hunting seasons or spend part of the summer in the "living" ghost town that boasted a popula-

tion of four thousand when everyone was showing up to dig gold and silver in the 1870s.

"Tuscarora." It sounds neat, just saying it. The name was given to the place by nineteenth-century miners to honor the *U.S.S. Tuscarora*, a Union ship in the Civil War. As with most Nevada mining camps, the boom in Tuscarora went bust after a few years of digging. Artists discovered the remote location in the 1960s. It's about an hour's drive northwest of Elko at the end of a dirt road.

Along with being quiet, Tuscarora is an inexpensive place to live. Painter Ron Arthaud paid $8,000 cash for a one-acre lot and what was left of two buildings, including the old assay office on the property. He is building a house and restoring the office.

"I was moving all around the West, trying to find a good place to live," Arthaud said.

Tuscarora is known for art mostly because Dennis Parks lives there. The world-famous ceramic artist founded a

A weathered bike leans against a weathered barn in Tuscarora.

summer school with a handful of students in 1966. The Tuscarora Retreat and Summer Pottery School attracts more students every year.

"It was a restlessness," said Parks, recalling what brought him to Tuscarora after traveling and working throughout Europe. "I decided to stop here and stay a while. I never found a place I liked as much."

Home-grown planter

Virginia City

C Street in Virginia City

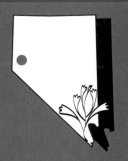

"Some people are meant to be here"

Richard Riggin of Port Norris, North Carolina, waits for his wife to finish shopping while a dog named Bear Girl naps on the wooden sidewalk.

Ben and Karen Wesner didn't quite fit in when they moved to Virginia City from Berkeley, California, in 1974. The couple looked as if they belonged on Telegraph Avenue, not the Comstock.

"We had the headbands," Ben Wesner said with a smile. "We all looked a bit from that era. Coming up here, there was a watchful eye on us."

Eventually, the Wesners were accepted, but not until Ben proved his manhood to the locals. Ben and Karen set about building a house. Their neighbor, old-time miner Jack Goode, observed the daily labor with approval. Finally, Goode came over to meet the Wesners and offer Ben a proposition: membership in the town, if he could meet the challenge.

"Jack lived right across the street from us," Karen said. "He would sit out on his lawn and watch. One day he came over and he said, 'I want Ben to do single jack.'"

Single-jack drilling is an old and difficult Comstock tradition. Take a hammer and pound a steel spike into a slab of stone. This is a physical feat, kept alive mostly by teams competing in local contests. All the old miners, including Goode, did it. He was asking Ben from Berkeley to do it. Karen remembered the conversation with Goode that served as a sort of welcome from Virginia City to the newcomers.

"He said, 'I've been watching you and how you work. You can do this. You've got a good arm,'" she recalled. Then Goode had to convince some of his pals to help teach this new guy from Berkeley the single-jack technique.

"This is a conservative area and here's this guy with long hair," Ben said. "They weren't sure if I could do it." But he did it.

"Ben had never seen it done," Karen said. "They said, 'Ben, here's what you do,' and he did it in ten minutes. It about killed him. They went in back of one of the mines with this big stone slab. That got respect." Gaining acceptance in Virginia City, the state's most historic town, is not that hard. You just have to be willing to sweat a little.

"That's my point," said Ben, a contractor and designer whose specialty has become the restoration of nineteenth-century Comstock buildings. "In those days, it was not who you were or what you had. It was the work ethic. That's what they looked at. This community has a lot of respect for hard work. I passed my test."

So have a lot of people, going all the way back to 1859, when the Comstock Lode was discovered and Virginia City was born. In seven years, miners dug five hundred million dollars' worth of gold and silver from under and around Virginia City. The wealth made Nevada a state, built San Francisco, paid for the Civil War and shaped the history of the West.

Men came and got rich — John Mackay, James Fair, James Flood and William O'Brien, who formed a mining partnership and became known as the Silver Kings. Others came and got famous. One young adventurer, a newspaper reporter, showed up as Samuel Clemens and left as Mark Twain.

Nobody's digging gold and silver, at least not like they used to, but Virginia City attracts people. Plenty of tourists visit, especially in summer. And folks like Ben and Karen come to stay. They're the ones who often see Virginia City as an escape from somewhere else, usually a place with too many people, too much noise and not enough community.

Fly is one of those people. He doesn't use a first name. He's just Fly, who operates Fly's Silver Dollar Saloon on C Street. Unlike many of Virginia City's bars, which cater to tourists and are hard to miss, Fly's can be hard to find, down a flight of stairs below street level. This is a local hangout.

"We can live up here and do what we want to do without any of the hassles created by most places where you'd work in a normal job atmosphere," said Fly, who has been in Virginia City six years.

"We can wear our hair; we can wear our clothes. We can act out who we want to be and we can do it every day. If we want to ride

Kansas City visitors Roger Fleener, left, and Gary Mineo laugh about eating fudge for breakfast in Virginia City.

horses, we can ride horses. We grow our beards and we wear our clothes because we can." In Virginia City, as long as you don't bother anybody or break any important laws, you can do pretty much as you please.

Fly has one of the town's most famous beards immortalized in "Virginia City Beards," a poster by local artist John Hunt, which includes four other bearded citizens dressed in old-miner Comstock fashion. Fly is second from the right on the poster.

"We have a very unusual town," Fly said. "We have a collection of the most talented musicians, painters and writers." One of them walks into Fly's. This is Hunt, the painter who is also one of the beards on the poster. He came to Virginia City from Sun Valley — not the one in Idaho, the one next to Reno.

"There are a bunch of characters up here who don't quite fit in," said Hunt, who counts himself among them. He's part of a long Virginia City tradition, one that dates back to Mark Twain. From its early days, the town has attracted creative people with imagination — a collection of writers, painters and poets looking for subjects.

"This was a fountain for story-telling," said Guy Rocha, state archivist and Nevada history expert. "It was a crucible for writers and journalists, these people like Twain. Since the 1930s, it has become sort of a Bohemian enclave."

Mike "Black Fish" Dyer is one of Hunt's subjects. The former Navy SEAL came to Virginia City after twenty-seven years in the service. "I wanted to retire close to California without being in it," said Dyer, a member of the Virginia City Gunfighters, a group that performs Old West re-enactments. "My granddad was an old Montana cowboy. I went back to my ranching roots."

Dyer lives in a house in town. He's got a horse and a wolf cub. Hunt's painting of Dyer is for sale at the Old Washoe Bar. That's where you can also find Dyer and Cal Phillips, who owns the saloon. This is where Virginia City's elite drank. The second floor was the Millionaire's Club of Washoe. Regular members included Mackay, Fair and Twain.

Saloons were — and still are — a big part of Virginia City's economic and social life. Fly said the town had a hundred and seven saloons during the mining boom. Today he counts seventeen, which make money in summer and survive in winter.

"If you break even in winter, you're happy," said Phillips, who came to Virginia City from Southern California five years ago. "But it's good fun."

Summer is when most of the tourists show up, but winter can be the time when Virginia City is, well, Virginia City — especially if the ground has a dusting of snow. The old wooden sidewalks mostly are deserted and the old brick buildings mainly are populated with the local characters.

"Up here in the winter, it's like a Robert Service poem," Hunt said of a poet who wrote about the Alaskan and Yukon wilderness. "It's the isolation."

Ben Wesner enjoys what's left of that feeling. "There was a time when the town turned back to us in winter," he said. "That's a nice time. It was slow up here. You'd go into town and see a lot of locals."

Ben helps preserve what's best in Virginia City. His restoration projects include the carriage house next to the Castle, one of the nineteenth-century mining mansions on B Street.

"We were able to salvage some," he said of construction work that took three and a half months. "We measured all the heights as best we could. We tore it down, then built it back. We put a foundation under it, which it didn't have before."

The carriage house and the Castle, like the Fourth Ward School and Piper's Opera House, are Comstock landmarks residents are in the process of saving.

"We're in as good a shape as we've been in since the 1940s," said Marshall Hansen, whose family maintains the Castle. "Up until the forties, a lot of things were torn down. I think we're headed in the right direction. A lot of individuals have done an excellent job."

Another Virginia City, away from the historic buildings and saloon characters, is where Cherie Nevin lives. "I like the smallness of it, knowing everybody," she said.

Mark Twain   R.Oden

- 1941: Virginia & Truckee Railroad line between Virginia City and Carson City abandoned.
- 1942: Federal order stops precious metal mining during World War II.
- 1960: Virginia City Camel Race revived.
- 1965: Saint Mary Louise Hospital, opened in 1876, redeveloped as arts center.
- 1976: Short Virginia & Truckee Railroad line re-established for tourists between Virginia City and Gold Hill.
- 1985: United Mining Corp. closes mine and milling operation.
- 1986: Fourth Ward School Board of Trustees organized to restore building.
- August 1995: Mine shaft collapses, creating a 2,700-foot-deep hole.
- May 2, 1999: Grand reopening of Piper's Opera House, first opened January 28, 1878.

Inside the Silver Dollar Saloon, Comstock characters Sweetwater John, left, and Fly (That's right, just Fly!) sign a poster called "Virginia City Beards."

Nevin, a senior at Virginia City High School, goes to class mostly with kids with whom she grew up. "My whole family is from here. My grandparents came at a very young age."

Her father, Mike, is the town fire chief. Her mother, Virginia, works at the post office. They graduated from the same high school their daughter attends.

Gary Fox is one of Nevin's classmates and also a Virginia City native.

"There are no secrets; you can't hide from anybody," said Fox, a basketball and baseball player who'd like to return to his high school as a teacher and coach. "With everybody in town, you have a connection."

Fly and his saloon customers feel that connection. They call Virginia City "the hill." When it's not snowing, Reno is a reasonably short drive down the hill, otherwise known as Geiger Grade, but for Fly, the city is a long way off.

"Most of us don't like to go off the hill," Fly said. "We hate going off the hill. You go down there, you have to deal with all that stuff."

As Fly talks, his bar fills up. They're all friends.

Cassidy Blanton, six, of Virginia City, holds a clump of freshly-sheared sheep wool she was given at Bartley Ranch during a sheep-shearing demonstration, part of a Junior Ranchers program. She is wearing what her dad calls her "Rat Hat," because rats had chewed holes in the brim while it hung in their garage the previous winter.

"Some people are meant to be here," Fly said. "They have to deal with something in their lives. This is where you do it. You have something you have to finish. It happens here."

Local color inspires ex-commercial artist

In his studio, artist John Hunt works on a watercolor of a Virginia City gunfighter.

John Hunt paints Virginia City. His subjects are the people who live in the historic town — folks such as Fly, Sweetwater John, Hippie John and Sierra Slim.

"I'm putting all the guys I know in it," Hunt said of one of his projects, a mural depicting Nevada history. "Fly's going to be the guide for the wagon train."

Hunt is among the growing group of artists and writers living and working in Virginia City. He's one of thirty in the Comstock Art Co-op, twelve of whom live in Virginia City. His work includes the "Gunfighter Series," a set of eleven pictures hanging in the Mark Twain Saloon, one of the town's many bars.

One of his most popular paintings, "Virginia City Beards," has been reproduced as a poster showing five of the town's men, including Fly and Hunt, sporting some of Virginia City's longest and bushiest beards.

Hunt, who grew up in Sun Valley outside Reno, came to Virginia City after spending time as a commercial artist in northern California. Before that, he spent four years in the Navy, and dropped out of the University of Nevada, Reno's art department because it was "teaching kids how not to make a living." Hunt, apparently, didn't learn that lesson.

"I did wine labels," Hunt said, "until I got burned out. I don't make as much money in Virginia City, but I'm a hell of a lot happier. I've got plenty of work and I'm turning people away."

Copy of "The Castle," a watercolor by Virginia City artist John Hunt.

In an old saloon, outcasts forged a new musical movement

Before anyone with flowers in their hair showed up on the corner of Haight and Ashbury in San Francisco, the first sounds of the psychedelic age were heard at the Red Dog Saloon.

"The movement started here June 1, 1965," reads a sign in the C Street bar in Virginia City. It all happened a long time ago — the band, light shows, crowds — and it all went by so fast. In two years it was over. By 1967, the Red Dog was closed and the whole wild scene had moved to San Francisco.

The Red Dog became a footnote in the history of the 1960s. The bar blended into the rest of C Street, like other Virginia City institutions, changing its name and function over the years — from bar to gift shop and back. You couldn't tell it was the place where a collection of outcast musicians from San Francisco called "the Charlatans" came together and turned everyone onto what would become the "San Francisco sound."

Now the Red Dog is back — with the name, bar, stage, posters and live music every Saturday night. The Charlatans are long gone. The new star is Marissa, a blues singer from — of course — San Francisco.

"She's the magic lady," said Mary Harris, who owns the Red Dog with husband Richard. "She's going to put us back where we're supposed to be."

Sometimes, telling where the Red Dog belongs is difficult. The longtime Comstock residents reopened the saloon in 1997. The music is modern, with a lot of northern Nevada acts, but in some ways, the Red Dog still lives in the '60s. The walls are adorned with posters from the era — celebrating such old San Francisco bands as the Chambers Brothers, Country Joe and the Fish, and Buffalo Springfield, and such old Bay-area institutions as the Avalon Ballroom, Berkeley Folk Music Festival and rock promoter Bill Graham.

"We love this place," said Mary, who first made plans with Richard to buy it when they sat at a table in the bar twenty-two years ago. "It's our heart."

The bar also is part of Virginia City, a town that's long attracted the adventurous and the unique. The Red Dog was the creation of three big-city fugitives taking refuge on the Comstock: Don Works, Chandler Laughlin and Mark Unovsky. Works, who owned a cabin in Silver City, had grown up in the Bay area. Laughlin was a Bay-area radio announcer. Unovsky was from Memphis, and he had money.

Their plan, according to Mary, was hatched on a snowy day in the cabin where Works lived. The three would open a saloon — with music. So they found the bar in Virginia City. The decor, food and sounds would come from someplace else.

"The Fox Theater was closing down in the Bay area at the time," Mary said. "They got the drapes. They imported a French cook from the Bay area. This was a real exclusive place at one time and it will be again." After the drapes and the cook came the music. "Mark told Chandler to find some musicians," Mary said. "They went over to the Bay Area and found The Charlatans."

The story goes that the San Francisco group was paid thirty-five dollars to get to Virginia City for a tryout. They made it, played and were hired.

In San Francisco, Mary said, The Charlatans had been

Solid brass 1913 cash register from the Mark Twain Saloon — the owner boasts, "It's Y2K compliant."

A silhouetted customer enters the Red Dog Saloon.

"What'll it be?" Richard Harris tends bar at the Red Dog Saloon.

the forerunners of hippies. In Virginia City, they became sort of psychedelic mountain men. "They changed their whole persona," she said. "They went from scraggly hippies and pretty much college kids to the gambler thing."

She has a picture of The Charlatans dressed in turn-of-the-century Wild West outfits, with vests, hats and guns. "There were a lot of shops here with old clothes and hats," she said. "They took up that costume of the

times, the Victorian era. Back in San Francisco, it became really cool to look like that, so all the thrift shops went crazy."

In Virginia City, the Red Dog and The Charlatans, who became the saloon's house band, attracted attention. "I'm sure it was quite a scene," Mary said. "A lot of the old-timers were mystified."

Richard listed other bands that joined the Charlatans at the Red Dog — an outfit called "The PH Factor," and another called "Big Brother and the Holding Company" — before Janis Joplin became the group's famous voice. For a time, the Red Dog was the 1960s music Mecca. After two summers, '65 and '66, it ended.

"Even though they got crowds in this little bar, it wasn't like being in the city," Richard said. "They were mostly city people. Mark was. He missed the city."

Virginia City wants to be "an experience"

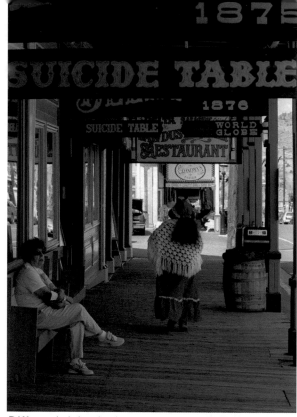

Different styles for two women on C Street. Which one is the visitor?

Virginia City is a tourist destination, but it's a brief stop for most visitors. They drive up Geiger Grade from Reno, stay a couple of hours, look around, maybe buy a drink and a souvenir, then turn around and come back. That's a pattern the historic mining town's business and community leaders want to change.

"That takes quite a shift," said Nolan Preece, who lives in Reno and owns an art gallery in Virginia City. "Make it a destination where they can have an experience. That's what so many towns like this are doing. Make it so they can spend two or three days instead of two or three hours."

Virginia City has plenty of history, including being where the Comstock Lode was discovered. But the town has only seventy-nine hotel and motel rooms.

"We get a million-and-a-half people through here a year," Preece said. "We want to make it a getaway. We're working toward that. I don't know how long it will take, but the history here is great. The history here is incredible."

A big part of the plan is the restoration of Virginia City's old buildings, such as Piper's Opera House, built in 1878 and reopened in

1999. The past includes the Virginia & Truckee Railroad, which once hauled the gold and silver out of town and one day might bring tourists back. Work was scheduled to resume in 2000 on rebuilding the old route between Virginia City and Carson City, but civic officials are blaming the Nevada Department of Transportation for a lack of progress on the line.

"NDOT is just not capable," Storey County Commissioner Chuck Haynes said. "I couldn't be more critical."

Since the completion of an initial phase in 1992, the restored Virginia & Truckee extends three miles from Virginia City to nearby Gold

Artist, teacher, actor and theater director Bill Beeson, head of the Virginia City Theater Muckers, stands inside the entrance to Piper's Opera House.

Hill. The next segment is a one-mile, six million-dollar stretch outside Gold Hill that must cross an abandoned mining pit.

"The pit is the problem," said NDOT spokesman Scott Magruder, noting that even if the railroad crossed the pit, it would still have about seventeen miles to go to reach Carson City. "There is still a lot of work to be done."

More track will take more money, which Magruder said could come from a combination of federal, state and local funding. Even if completion is a long way off, Haynes hopes the historic train carrying tourists from Carson City someday will spark construction of more visitor facilities in Virginia City.

"We are in a funny situation," he said. "Will the hotels bring the railroad or the railroad bring the hotels?"

A silent angel watches over crooked tombstones tilted by time.

Famous performers imported from New York and Europe once attracted crowds to Piper's Opera House in Virginia City. In the audience, wealthy silver barons and their bejeweled companions mingled with rough miners.

Building the long tangents of the Central Pacific across the Nevada desert was cold in winter, hot in summer and tedious at all times, but there were company towns along the way and saloons in generous multiplicity....
  Lucius Beebe, The Central Pacific & the Southern Pacific Railroads

Railroad Towns

A Union Pacific train, pulling grain cars, snakes its way eastbound out of the Sparks railroad yard.

Gerlach

Distance runner Gabe Herod practices after school on a dirt track near Gerlach High School.

Where the pavement ends

In a small oasis near Planet X, two Bogard boys check the pond for frogs

D ooby Lane is one of Nevada's strangest streets: the short stretch of dirt road in the desert near Gerlach doesn't lead anywhere. You don't follow it to get from one place to another. Instead, you walk down the path at the foot of Granite Mountain to marvel at the unique monument left behind by DuWayne "Dooby" Williams, the "Guru of Gerlach," who died in 1995.

One side of the lane is lined with flat rocks, arranged like tombstones, inscribed with bits of Dooby's life philosophy, names of friends, funny phrases and advice.

"The human race is like a watch, it takes all the parts to make it work," is written on one of Dooby's rocks.

"Nothing so small that you can't cut it in half. Nothing so large that you can't double it," is written on another.

Dooby also built small monuments and displays, all with rocks: a wedding chapel of sorts, a weather station of sorts and a television studio of sorts.

"He just put his philosophy on rocks," said Gerlach native Bonnie Crossley. "He was working on my rock when he died. I didn't get my rock."

Dooby Lane wouldn't suit a lot of places.

Getting that many flat rocks in Reno, Sparks or Carson City would be difficult. Getting somebody to give you a road to put them on probably would be impossible. But in Gerlach and the Black Rock Desert, it fits perfectly. Gerlach's longtime slogan is, "Where the pavement ends and the West begins."

State Route 447, all 107 miles to Reno, has had asphalt for years. The pavement even stretches north to Cedarville, California. But the outlook in Gerlach hasn't changed. This is an outpost, the last stop before the wilderness of Washoe County's far north — the stretch of mountains, sand and sagebrush that goes all the way to the Oregon border.

"You're on the edge," said Gerlach High School Principal Chris Smith. "You get a unique breed out here."

Dooby, who grew up in Gerlach and returned to build his road, was part of it. So is Bruno Selmi, the Italian with a thick old-country accent, who showed up in Gerlach with a couple of bucks in his pocket shortly after World War II.

Selmi spent four years working at the nearby gypsum plant in Empire, then opened a bar in Gerlach in 1950. He's the owner of Bruno's Country Club, the biggest business in the tiny town and the bar-restaurant where the hand-made ravioli is famous with longtime customers from Reno and Sparks who drive the 107 miles to eat it.

"You're supposed to fulfill obligations," said Selmi, standing behind his bar and talking about life. "People don't want to do that anymore." Selmi fulfills one of his obligations, handing Smith a $100 bill. The principal and the bartender had a bet on a school-bond issue. Selmi bet that it wouldn't pass; Smith bet that it would. "If you don't have it, don't spend it," Selmi said, explaining his philosophy about money.

Lena "Skeekie" Courtney, Selmi's daughter, has been working at the country club since she was a kid. She's behind the bar with Lina Lucchesi, her godmother. The country club is an extended family operation.

"We run this money-making S.O.B.," Courtney said of herself and Lucchesi. "Since I grew up, I've always had to work here. My dad believes in production." Courtney left Gerlach briefly, to work in Reno-Sparks, but returned to the country club — for a lot of reasons.

"Beautiful sunrises, beautiful sunsets," Courtney said, trying to describe the attraction of living on the edge. "It's the closest thing to

Chris Smith, principal of Gerlach High School, stops by Bruno's Country Club to give Bruno Selmi, who's pouring a drink for another customer, a school T-shirt for being the 1999 graduation speaker.

being on the moon you'll find."

That's the Black Rock Desert. With no cities on it or highways across it, Gerlach is the gateway. The desert draws an array of people looking for a variety of things — isolation, adventure, fun and, perhaps most of all, a place where they can do things they can't do anywhere else. Dooby built his lane. Hollywood folks made movies. A jet-propelled car from Great Britain set the supersonic land-speed world record.

"There's going to be a motorcycle coming from England, a jet motorcycle," said

This old railroad town attracts a certain type of person.

Potters put Planet X on the map

John and Rachel Bogard are Planet X Pottery. The artistic center in the middle of the desert outside Gerlach isn't a commune, cult or tribe of hippies left over from the 1960s. Planet X is where the Bogards live, on an old ranch John discovered in 1967. They leased it and finally bought it.

Inside Planet X, John Bogard creates pottery inspired by desert scenes. Below: Western motifs attract pottery collectors to Bogard's work.

"People assume it's a hippie commune out here," Rachel said. "There have been people who have come by and we have friends that visit. We generate ideas from other artists. A lot of what we do is the desert scene. All you have to do is look out the window."

In some ways, John and Rachel ARE from the sixties: they're from Berkeley, California. They're potters. Their work has become well known in northern Nevada, and not just because people are curious about Planet X.

"Just when you get sort of famous, when you can sell all your stuff, your body craps out," John, a potter for thirty years, said with a laugh. John and Rachel can sell their stuff. Their pottery is featured at craft fairs and shows in northern Nevada and northern California.

Their first pottery inspiration came from the West Coast. John lived and worked in Santa

Cruz, California, and Rachel went to college in northern California.

"There's a lot of people that work with clay who are in the mountains and on the coast," Rachel said. "We just got kind of burned out on it."

The Bogards don't spend all their time on the remote ranch. Sometimes they travel to San Francisco, or Paris.

"I spend quite a bit of time traveling because I enjoy it," Rachel said. "I go down to the Bay Area once a month, just to visit. I spend a lot more time now going to museums, going to different pottery stores, getting ideas."

GERLACH

- Population in 1999: 243 (29 percent under 18, 37 percent 18-44, 27 percent 45-64, 7 percent 65 and older; 55 percent male, 45 percent female).
- Population in 1990: 133.
- Population in 2003: (projected) 337.
- Median household income in 1990: $26,452.
- Median household income in 1998: $33,863.
- Total retail sales in 1998: $535,000.
- Total retail sales in 2003: (projected) $930,000.

- Claim to fame: Gerlach is gateway to the Black Rock Desert and the rest of the wide-open spaces of northwestern Nevada. World land-speed records have been set in desert, also the site of Burning Man Festival.

- How it got its name: Western Pacific Railroad created town site as division point and named it for local rancher Louis Gerlach. Some people in town pronounce it "Gerlock" and others say "Gerlack." Dave Green, a Gerlach native and former principal of Gerlach High School, said he pronounces it both ways.

- Local legend: Bruno Selmi, owner of Bruno's Country Club, came to town in 1950 and opened Capaccio Club, leasing building. He bought the place in 1952 and changed the name. Over the years, he added a motel, restaurant and gas station. His homemade ravioli is famous in northern Nevada.

Bev Osborn, who operates the Miners Club, one of Gerlach's five bars. "I've got a picture of it. It's supposed to go from zero to 500 miles per hour in ten seconds."

The Black Rock is a place to go fast — and a place to act strange. Every Labor Day weekend, thousands come for the Burning Man Festival. Many of them run naked. They create their own art. They burn a forty-foot wooden representation of a man who once, supposedly, stole the girlfriend of the festival's San Francisco-based organizer. Things happen on the Black Rock Desert that happen nowhere else on earth.

"Nobody knows why we like it so much, but I keep coming back," Crossley said of the desert's attraction. Outsiders, who come and go, look to the Black Rock for once-in-a-lifetime adventures or regular bizarre events, such as the annual Lucifer's Anvil Golf Tournament. Mostly, the people of Gerlach stay. If they leave, they return. Crossley lived in Columbus, Ohio, for eighteen years, then returned. "I couldn't wait to get back out here," she said.

Lloyd Mosley, whose parents owned a café, garage and grocery store when Gerlach was a thriving railroad stop, spent three months in Fernley at the south end of Route 447. That was long enough.

"There's nobody here that can give you any problems," Mosley said, standing outside one of the saloons that make up most of Gerlach's

Bill Stapleton helps manage the Texaco station.

downtown. "You just go out in the hills."

Gerlach isn't much to look at. You've got the bars, a post office, the school, a community center, a gas station, the Sheriff's Office and some houses, all surrounded by sand. A popular sign in the bars reads, "Hungry and out of work? Eat an environmentalist." This is the sagebrush West.

Residents bought the town from the Western Pacific Railroad in the 1970s; it cost $18,000. Officially, that's the total paid by homeowners for the ground under their houses; the railroad owned the land.

"We bought the water system; they gave us the town," Osborn said of the $18,000. "We bought the water system because the railroad was the one that had to keep up the water system and they didn't want to do that." Gerlach remains a railroad town, although passenger trains no longer stop there.

"One of my first trips to Reno was really exciting," Osborn said. "We caught a freight train and rode the caboose to Reno Junction. Then we had to catch another freight train from Reno Junction to Reno. That was quite a trip. They offered us coffee in that caboose. It was so strong you could stand your spoon up in it."

Dave Green has his own train story. "They

On Dooby Lane, the "Guru of Gerlach" built a rock monument to Elvis.

Not a UFO site in the desert, but the sign for Planet X Pottery near Gerlach

had a circus train when I was a little kid," he said. "They would run the circus train from as far as Wendover to Reno. It would stop at all the towns, pick up the kids and parents and take them to the circus."

Green is Gerlach's hometown boy. He grew up and went to high school here. He was principal of the high school for twenty-one years, then retired and was replaced by Smith, the winner of the barroom bet with Bruno Selmi. "It's a nice place to get a start, then it grows on you once you're here," Green said of what happened to Smith and other newcomers who decided to stay.

Green has played in the Lucifer's Anvil Golf Tournament, in which a piece of the desert near town is turned into a giant golf course. The sand is painted with greens and fairways. The paint is biodegradable, part of an effort to maintain the desert in its natural state.

"You'd be surprised how much fun it is," said Green, who bicycled between holes.

Equally larger-than-life croquet matches have been played on the Black Rock, which also is a place where scientists conduct experiments for the U.S. space program.

"We have people from NASA that come out here," Courtney said. "They say it's like riding

on the surface of the moon." For the second time, Courtney mentioned the moon while talking about the Black Rock. That's how remote it feels. That's what Courtney and Gerlach residents like, but they pay a price for isolation.

"It's a harsh area. You really have to want to be here," said Suzie Beck, who really wants to be there. "It takes you two hours to go grocery shopping in Reno. There are inconveniences that we choose to live with to be here."

John and Rachel Bogard made that choice when they came to the desert from Berkeley, California, and established Planet X Pottery on an old ranch outside of town. The Bogards are artists who draw inspiration from the Black Rock.

"It frees your mind; you're not so cluttered with the noises of city life," Rachel Bogard said. "Your mind goes blank out here because there is nothing bothering you. It's a very meditative experience here." But the Black Rock isn't for everyone.

"It takes the right kind of person who can live this kind of life and enjoy it," Rachel said. "A lot of my friends come up here just shocked. They say, 'How can you live out here? You're so far away from everything.' We wish we were farther."

Mike Stewart, right, owner and founder of Empire Farms, and farm manager Dan Moran inspect the garlic in a muddy field.

State-of-the-art Empire Farms started with an idea and one bale wagon

The professor at the University of Nevada, Reno who gave Mike Stewart an "A" on a paper in agriculture economics probably didn't know what he was starting.

"The project was to do a cost analysis of operating a bale wagon," said Stewart, founder and owner of Empire Farms outside Gerlach.

Sounds pretty dull, unless you're a farmer or want to be one. Stewart wanted to be a farmer. He didn't live on a farm; but he had grown up in Yerington, surrounded by farm country. He was eighteen when that classroom assignment gave him an idea.

"When I came home at midterm, I asked my dad to co-sign a loan to buy my first bale wagon," Stewart said. "That's the first machine I purchased."

Stewart was young, but he had it figured out. He'd do business with farmers in Lyon County, hauling their bales of hay from the fields and stacking them in each of the alfalfa growers' storage yards. The job is something the farmers could do themselves, but it took a special machine, the bale wagon.

While writing his college paper, Stewart decided that he could do the task on a mass-production basis at a lower cost per bale than individual farmers who had to buy their own machinery.

"A lot of the farmers had older machines that weren't as efficient," he said. "They contracted it out to me. I could use the machine on ten or fifteen different farms. I had better economy of scale than one farmer using a machine."

The plan worked. By the time Stewart graduated from UNR, he had three bale wagons and a thriving business. Now forty-two, he is still a farmer, which is all he ever wanted to be.

"He walks like a farmer; he thinks like a farmer," said Patty Hanneman, Stewart's administrative assistant since 1982. "He likes to think things over."

That thinking has paid off. The low-key Stewart, who raised and sold sheep when he was a student at Yerington High School, has created an agriculture-energy conglomerate. Based in northern Washoe County, the business ships twenty-two million pounds of garlic seed to growers annually and sells 35,000 megawatts of geothermal power per year to Sierra Pacific Power Company. He also operates a garlic-and-onion dehydration plant on the farm. Along with garlic and power, Stewart grows onions, alfalfa, wheat and other grains on fields in Nevada and California.

"With me, the thing that is most fun is the building, the doing and the challenge," said Stewart, who bought Empire Farms in the San Emidio Valley in 1982. "The dollars are one thing, but the challenge and fun of getting it done are more important."

When Stewart came to the desert south of Gerlach with Hanneman, he didn't find much. "There were just a couple of old broken-down tractors, some junk cars and two fields of hay," said Stewart, who has to be coaxed to talk about himself and what he has done. "The rest was basically abandoned."

At first, Stewart and Hanneman worked out of a mobile home. Farm papers were kept in a box. "You know those boot boxes with handles?" Hanneman asked. "We could carry all the payroll, everything that had to do with this farm we had in that box."

Again, as he had done in college with that paper on bale wagons, Stewart figured something out: he'd never make it growing alfalfa.

"I learned you couldn't just have alfalfa for a crop and keep pumping water on it," Stewart said. "There wasn't enough margin in it. I was looking for alternative things I could do to make the farm more profitable, to at least pay the mortgage." That led to garlic and power. Stewart saw steam coming out of the ground when he bought the property. He figured it had geothermal potential.

"He's got some kind of sixth sense to things," said Hanneman, who went to work for Stewart in Yerington when he owned the state's largest farm-supply business. "He stood up there and saw steam coming out and said, 'I'll bet there's geothermal over there.' He didn't know a thing about geothermal when we started, but I think he could write a book now."

Handmade adobe bricks are stacked in the sun, ready for use in farm buildings such as the laundry, shown at left.

The same probably goes for garlic. Stewart opens a thick binder filled with his notes divided into three categories: farming, energy and "other stuff." He flips to one page with a chemical formula for garlic.

"I had to have my director of research explain this to me several times," Stewart said with a grin. "There's *alliin* and *allinase*. They combine together to make *allicin*." That's what makes garlic healthy. Stewart got into garlic after reading about a scientist at University of California, Davis, who'd developed disease-free garlic seed. Stewart met the scientist, Dennis Hall, and once again figured something out.

"The business opportunity I saw was selling virus-free garlic seed from an isolated growing area up here in the high desert," said Stewart, who sells seed to California garlic growers. "You have a cold winter. You plant garlic in the fall and harvest in July. You plant here in the high desert, the garlic is not only virus-free, it's acclimated to the cold."

Stewart has it figured out.

"El Pollo Grande," a lost emu, was found wandering in the hills near the geothermal plant at Empire Farms outside Gerlach.

Words to the wise: just one in the collection along Dooby Lane

Who owns the Black Rock?

Bud Conley of Gerlach fears the federal government wants to kick him off the Black Rock Desert: "They want to keep people out of there. Before too long, they're going to have it so you have to be in an elite group to be out there. You won't be able to walk out there."

Conley and his neighbors, whose town is the gateway to the Black Rock, are used to running, riding and walking in the desert. They've grown up with the Black Rock as their back yard, but now environmentalists and government officials are concerned that increased use will harm or destroy the Black Rock.

Gerlach native Lena "Skeekie" Courtney calls the desert "the closest thing to being on the moon you'll find." But in recent years it has become a stage for such events as the Burning Man Festival, which attracts 10,000 to 15,000 visitors every Labor Day weekend.

"Basically, what you're starting to see are impacts of increased use on a fragile environment," said Les Boni of the Bureau of Land Management, whose Winnemucca office supervises the Black Rock. "An awful lot of recreationalists are coming up here

and starting to use the desert."

For years the area has been popular with hunters, off-road vehicle drivers and motorcycle riders. The desert is also a place for driving at supersonic speeds in jet-propelled cars, for wind sailing, camping and just looking.

"The other side is you have recreationalists who want to come out here and enjoy it as the emigrants saw it and experienced it," Boni said. "You have issues to address in preserving the various views; affording opportunities to use it for recreation, Burning Man, the land-speed record or RVs."

The BLM continues to work on a plan Boni hopes will satisfy everybody. His office had developed proposals that include setting a limit on "user days" each year, with one person on the desert for one day being a user day.

But Boni said the public opposes such restrictions and also dislikes another suggestion — designating the entire Black Rock desert as an environmentally sensitive area, subject to increased federal management. Desert users, Boni said, might favor the special designation for a smaller part of the desert.

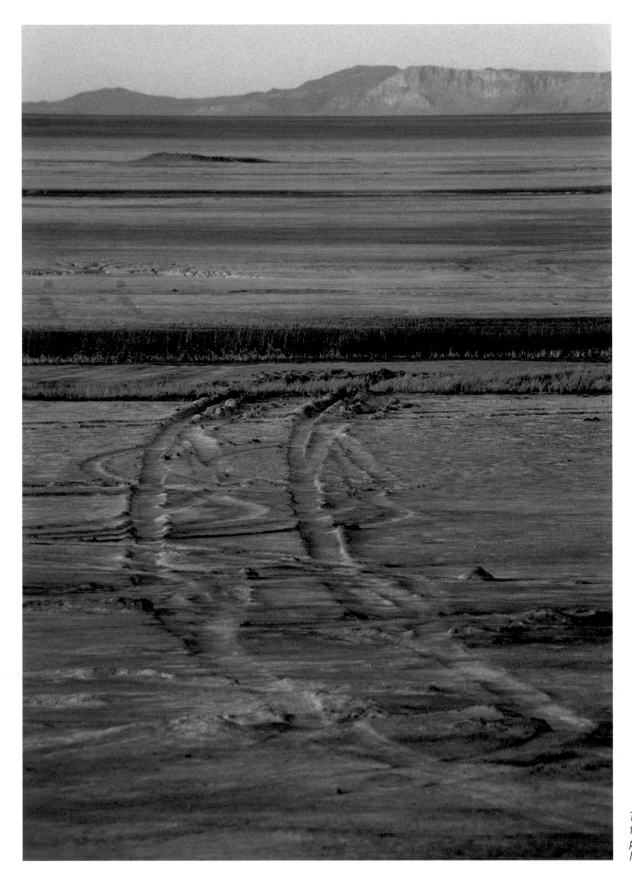

Tire tracks mark a path toward the roadless playa of the Black Rock Desert.

"There is a feeling that it's just too large," Boni said of the BLM's original proposal. A revised proposal will be subject to citizen review. Boni said the BLM does not plan to close the desert, but access could be limited.

"That's what we're trying to hash out," he said. "There is a really strong love for this area. Everybody, while there for different reasons, has that in common."

Hawthorne

Toward the looming mountains, a motorist heads west along a street in Hawthorne.

The town faces tough times with its usual tough spirit

Hawthorne High School senior Brandon Rather, left, planned to join the Navy. Fellow senior Jerry Bryant was heading to the University of Nevada, Reno.

IMPORTANT DATES

- April 14, 1881: Lots sold by Carson & Colorado Railroad for a town. Buyers got free train transportation to the site.
- 1883: Legislature votes to move seat of Esmeralda County to Hawthorne.
- 1905: Railroad moves from west to east side of Walker Lake and terminus switched from Hawthorne to Mina.
- 1907: Esmeralda County seat moved from Hawthorne to Goldfield.
- 1911: Legislature splits Esmeralda County and Hawthorne becomes seat of Mineral County.
- April 16, 1921: Road completed along west side of Walker Lake, most of it blasted out of solid granite, to link Hawthorne with Yerington.
- 1926: Fire destroys much of downtown business district.
- 1930: U.S. Naval Ammunition Depot established.
- 1940: Depot expands with the approach of World War II.
- 1944: During war years, population reaches 13,000.
- June 25, 1946: Hawthorne obtains legal authorization to incorporate as a city.
- 1950: Population declines to 1,861.
- Jan. 17, 1956: Hawthorne votes to end city government and return to status as unincorporated town.
- 1977: Department of Defense directs Navy to turn the ammunition depot over to the Army.
- Dec. 1, 1980: Depot turned over to private contractor.
- 1994: Mineral County High School girls' basketball team wins first of five straight state titles.

J erry Bryant didn't have much choice. He was graduating from Mineral County High School and he needed a part-time job to save money for college. Work was scarce in Hawthorne, so Bryant planned to move to Reno.

"I've got to go as quick as I can to raise money over the summer," said Bryant, who would follow a trail out of town traveled by many of Hawthorne's teenagers. "They leave as soon as they can to get some money." Times have been difficult in Hawthorne, a tough town fighting for its economic survival.

"You think about the millennium, here's a community that's unsure of its future," said state archivist and historian Guy Rocha. "Hawthorne's not a ghost town, but it's verging on ghost-town status. That's been Hawthorne's struggle forever."

Start with the Hawthorne Army Ammunition Depot, the world's largest ammunition storage facility which covers two hundred twenty square miles of high desert around the town limits. Since it opened in 1930, the depot has been Hawthorne's reliable producer of jobs and money. Generations of the town's young men and women went to work at the depot. They bought homes and raised fami-

lies. They counted on steady paychecks. But not anymore.

"They're killing the community," Eugene Dillard, acting director of the Mineral County Economic Development Authority, said of the base. The depot's work force, which numbers about 800, has been cut — and more layoffs are expected.

"They've laid off close to fifty people since December," said Dillard, whose wife, Carol, works at the depot. "It's projected they're going to lay off another sixty-five. It's been rumored that they may have to lay off another hundred or hundred and fifty."

For a small town, that could be devastating.

"Everybody talks. It can be at the bar, it can be at the bowling alley, it could be at the pizza place," said Tiny Cardenas, a Hawthorne native who is a civilian executive at the base with thirty-seven years of government service. "I've got a lot of friends here. I've got family here. They're sweating bullets."

But Hawthorne isn't giving up. It never does. Community leaders, including Dillard, are hopeful a California-based manufacturing company, Delta Star, will build a plant in

Now at the Mineral County Museum, this 1930 Model A Ford, originally a "two-seater" touring car, was modified by the Navy into this small truck and used by the electric shops as their runabout.

Hawthorne. "It's looking better," Dillard said of the ongoing negotiations with Delta Star, which makes electric transformers.

Plans call for construction to begin on a manufacturing facility, with 350 people working at the plant by 2005. Dillard also is trying to get companies that sell components to Delta Star to relocate to Hawthorne. But none of that is helping Hawthorne, which Dillard might ask the state to classify as a depressed area in order to speed up economic-development assistance. Uncertainty about the future nearly forced Dillard, who's trying to boost Hawthorne's economy, to join Bryant and others in seeking work elsewhere.

"This is probably about the worst, this year," said the Hawthorne native who was looking for another job outside town in case his wife lost hers — and with it, the family's all-important health benefits. "I have an interview in Fallon. I don't want to leave."

He won't. Instead of moving out of town, Dillard planned to quit his temporary development post to manage a new truck stop — some good economic news — opening on Route 95 at the edge of town.

People in Hawthorne have been through difficult times before. If it's not the railroad

pulling up tracks and moving, the mines are closing or the base is cutting back. Good times come and go. So do bad times. That has been a Hawthorne pattern almost since the town's founding in 1881.

"It's just the way they planned this town when they set it up," said Bryant, whose father and stepmother work at the depot. "The way they planned it, it wasn't a long-lasting kind of thing. They based this town on mining and, at the time, war. With the ammo depot, it's all leftovers now. Technology has advanced. We're stuck with leftover technology nobody wants."

Hawthorne's first crisis came in 1905 when the railroad moved, with its biggest boom taking place during World War II when workers flooded into the depot and pushed the area's population to 13,000.

"Hawthorne has had as many downs as ups," Rocha said. "Hawthorne's not alone, but it's more acute." Since World War II, the town's economy has run on a pretty basic cycle — when there's fighting, business is good; when nobody's shooting, things slow down.

"It's not totally new," Cardenas said. "Anytime you have a Bosnia or Vietnam,

Playing-card miniature captures demolished club

Don Banfield

Artist Don Banfield discovered the historic Hawthorne Club just in time. The casino and longtime community landmark was torn down several years ago, but not before Banfield photographed the place.

Banfield, sixty-two, who moved to Hawthorne from Southern California, used his photos to paint a miniature picture of the old club on the front of a playing card.

"I think I did it on the three of diamonds," said Banfield, who usually paints on a large canvas. "To do a miniature was a stretch for me and I really enjoyed it."

Banfield's painting was part of a traveling exhibit of fifty-two miniature works of art, all done on playing cards. The miniatures represent a fifty-two-card deck. Banfield was among the winners in a statewide competition. Artists from many Nevada communities submitted entries.

"I like (Hawthorne)," said Banfield, who teaches art at the Western Nevada Community College branch campus in town. "It's a place without a lot of hustle, but I can get anywhere I want to go."

Banfield is renowned for his images of the sign at the north end of Hawthorne.

HAWTHORNE

- Population in 1999:
  5,537
  (27 percent under 18;
  36 percent 18-44;
  23 percent 45-64;
  14 percent 65 and
  older;
  50.3 percent female,
  49.7 percent male).
- Population in 1990:
  5,196.
- Population in 2004:
  (projected) 5,371.
- Median household
  income: $33,281.
- Total retail sales:
  $24.138 million.

- Claim to fame:
  Southern gateway
  to Walker Lake and
  seat of Mineral
  County.

- How it got its
  name: Town, which
  organized April 14,
  1881 as terminus
  for Carson &
  Colorado Railroad,
  was named for
  Judge W. A.
  Hawthorne, an
  early Nevada
  pioneer and friend
  of the railroad's
  president.

- Local legend: Fred
  B. Balzar, state
  senator, then
  governor
  (1927-34).

that's the business we're in. You're going to see those upward spikes. When those kind of things aren't going on, you're down in that valley. You can never expect it to level off."

The first job Cardenas had out of high school was at the depot. The year was 1965, during the Vietnam era, and Cardenas worked ten to twelve hours a day, seven days a week on the ammunition line.

Rows of storage huts are spread across 147,000 acres of the Hawthorne Army Ammunition Depot.

"Some of the lines were running two shifts and some of the lines were three shifts," Cardenas said. "It was unreal. We were drawing people from all the outside areas, anywhere we could get people to man the lines." The job was basic — filling bombs with TNT.

"We were explosive loading 500-pound bombs and 250-pound bombs," he said. "We were taking molten explosive and putting it into steel casings. There were fifty-pound boxes with raw explosive. You put it into the hopper and measured it out. It went on a conveyor belt."

But bombs no longer are made in Hawthorne. The depot is used for storage, which requires fewer people. "We're just not having as much movement as we're accustomed to," Cardenas said.

The depot is an eerie place with 147,000 acres of bunkers and buildings. Few people are seen and hardly a sound is heard. The landscape is harsh, except for an area of stately brick buildings, lawns and large trees. When the depot had a large military presence, officers lived on the base. Called "Kings Row," some local theories said it was designed to resemble the campus of the U.S. Naval Academy in Annapolis, Maryland,

This bit of philosophy at the entrance to the Hawthorne Army Ammunition Depot was changed a few hours later to read, "Have a good weekend."

since the Navy was running the depot and many of the officers were academy graduates. One day in 1999, a sign at the base gate read, "In the middle of difficulty lies opportunity." Later the same day, the sign was changed to read, "Have a good weekend."

Despite the cutbacks, Cardenas said the depot isn't likely to close. It is operated for the military by a private company, but the facility's contract was almost up and the federal government was looking for new bids.

"Being that the contract is (almost) up, the Army isn't furnishing us with a lot of projects, which is forcing (the depot) to cut its work force," Dillard said of reduced activity at the base. The town shows signs of decay. Across the street from Dillard's office, a car dealership has closed. In another part of town, the movie theater is closed. Down the street from Dillard, Bob Tompkins runs an outdoor recreation equipment shop that has seen business fall off with the drop at the depot.

"Hawthorne is pretty depressed right now," said Tompkins, a retired deputy sheriff who guides fishing trips at nearby Walker Lake. "You've got the base situation and there's nothing else going. The mines all shut down three or four years ago. The economy is pretty poor. A lot of us are hanging on. It's the situation we're all in. There's not too much in the wind."

Jack McCloskey hates all the attention focused on Hawthorne's problems. He dislikes the pictures of closed buildings and other images of the town's troubles. "It's not a dying town," the former local newspaper publisher said with irritation at the question. "It's not a dying town. I keep repeating that."

The old courthouse is shut, but a new one is open. The hospital is up to date, as is the library. The town has new houses. Burton Packard is the ammo depot fire chief and he's not worried about his job.

"We may not be working for (the same contractor)," said Packard, who has been employed at the base since 1980. "But we'll be working for somebody."

McCloskey, who has retired, thinks Hawthorne will survive as a retirement community. "I'd say 50 percent of the people here you could classify as retired," he said. "That's what's holding the town together."

That's also what's wrong, according to Rocha. "Hawthorne just keeps getting older," he said. "Hawthorne exports its young people. The mayor of Carson City is from Hawthorne."

Tompkins said Hawthorne's best chance for a future might be with recreation and tourism. "The fish have really come back," he said of Walker Lake, the area's biggest outdoor attraction. "They used to be three-and-a-half pounds. Now we have lots of fives and sixes. I have one in the freezer that's nine pounds, eight ounces — a real healthy fish. They are trying to allocate a certain amount of water each year into the lake just to sustain the fishery."

At the same time, Hawthorne tries to sustain itself. "We're sitting here in the central part of the state with nothing but open land," McCloskey said. "We're not a dying town."

Just the same, Brandon Rather, another student at Mineral County High, isn't staying. "I'm leaving for the Navy," Rather said. "I'm out of here. Hawthorne really doesn't have anything for me. What's the point of staying? You've got to get out."

The Army Depot is at the crossroads of Hawthorne's future.

High school sports rally residents and offer kids hope

Mineral High School basketball player Kim Dement looks thoughtful when she talks about future plans.

When Ashlee Orndorff and Kim Dement are on the basketball court, they don't think about Hawthorne's tough times. The same goes for Keith Lawson and Darrel Rocquemore. In a town where many of the adults are fighting for their economic lives, the kids are heroes.

"When you're out there playing, that's when you can have fun and concentrate," Orndorff said. "Everybody is having fun and cheering for our team."

Yes, they are. Orndorff is the star of the Mineral County High School girls' basketball team, winners of five straight Class 3A state championships before losing in the semifinals of the 1999 tournament. Mineral County is a small school, with just 238 students, but its girls' basketball program, arguably, has been the state's best — on any level.

"The girls have been a real positive image," said David Gelmstedt, who has coached them since 1984. "The community itself has been on a downward slide. Economically, the town has been in a depression. The community itself has really identified with the success of the girls."

In 1999, Mineral County's boys shared the attention. They made their second straight trip to the state tournament, losing in the semifinals after winning seventeen regular-season games.

The town's grownups might be losing their jobs at the Hawthorne Army Ammunition Depot as the work force is cut at the world's largest ammunition storage facility, but they show up for basketball games.

"When you go to rural Nevada, in the smaller towns we have to rally around positive things," said Emmett Statzer, who was in his second season as boys' coach. "One of the things we have that's positive is our youth."

Statzer came to Hawthorne from Montana three years ago and coached the Mineral County High boys' track team. "A lot of the (track) kids went out for basketball for me," Statzer said. "In small towns, coaching is a necessity. If you've got a guy who wants to come in and coach, you coach a little bit of everything."

The girls in Hawthorne, with Gelmstedt coaching, have been winning for a long time. They started the 1998-1999 season with six state championships in fourteen years.

"We've been blessed with a lot of talent and dedicated people, people who take an

With her essentials, a backpack and a basketball, a Mineral High School student waits for a ride home.

interest," Hawthorne native Orndorff said as she tried to explain the sustained success.

Kim Dement, who came to Hawthorne from Oklahoma with her parents when she was a fifth-grader, offered another theory: "There's not much else to do in this town."

Coaches from big-time colleges with scholarship offers in hand are finding their way to far-off Hawthorne to watch Orndorff and the Mineral County girls. The trip is long, starting with an airplane flight to Reno, followed by a three-hour rental car drive across the desert to town.

"We've had the Oregon coach," Gelmstedt said. "Duke and Kentucky were in Fernley (to watch Mineral County). Oregon State and Arizona were coming. They ask how far the airport is (from Hawthorne). Then they want to know why we can't play closer to the airport."

Sometimes getting a look at Gelmstedt's team is tough — no matter how far you've come. When Duke and Kentucky showed up in Fernley, bad weather closed the road and Mineral County couldn't make it. The same thing happened to Oregon State and Arizona. That time, the road was closed and Mineral County's opponent couldn't make

it. So there was no game to watch.

Gelmstedt expects Duke, Kentucky and the rest will be back. He also figures Hawthorne's tough times motivate his players. "It actually helps our kids focus a little more because they see it as a way out," he said.

But the town's troubles eventually might catch up to basketball. Because of a drop in enrollment, Mineral County High was reclassified as a 2A school, one step down the state's athletic ladder, for the 2000-2001 season. Also, Gelmstedt's team might be starting to suffer from a lack of numbers.

"In the past, we had up to twelve strong players; we had a strong bench," Gelmstedt said. "This year our bench isn't as strong. We're missing those seventh, eighth and ninth players."

Along with the team, the school's enrollment dip could hurt Gelmstedt himself. He wants to move into school administration, eventually becoming a principal. That might be tough at Mineral County High School.

"Before, I was the youngest person on the staff," Gelmstedt said. "Now I'm moving into that upper division. I'm finishing my administrative credential. The enrollment is shrinking."

Walker Lake is the key to Hawthorne's future

Retired deputy sheriff Bob Tompkins leads fishing trips to nearby Walker Lake from Hawthorne, where he owns a sporting goods store.

The fish are fat in Walker Lake. That's good for nearby Hawthorne, where residents struggling in tough times hope fishing and other recreation will boost the local economy. When the big ones are biting, fishermen flock to Walker Lake.

They spend money at Bob Tompkins' outdoor equipment store. Sometimes they stay a night or two at the El Capitan Resort Casino in Hawthorne. The town needs all of that business, especially with the cutbacks at the Hawthorne Army Ammunition Depot — the town's longtime source of employment and paychecks.

"If we don't have Walker Lake, we're going to sink one of these days," Hawthorne resident Lana Treharne said. "With all the layoffs they've had out at the base, we can't guarantee we're always going to have the base. We've got to do something about tourism."

But nobody guarantees that Walker Lake and its trout will remain healthy. Four straight years of higher-than-average winter snow in the Sierra have filled the lake with water from spring runoff and vastly improved living conditions for fish, but it all could evaporate in the next drought.

"If we go into another drought, the lake evaporates about four feet a year," said Chris Drake, fish biologist for the state's Division of Wildlife. "If we go into another drought, we're right back where we started four years ago." Walker Lake nearly died in the early 1990s, during the last drought.

"We were a couple of years away from not being able to put fish in there," division spokesman Chris Healy said. Since that drought, Walker Lake has risen thirteen feet. At its deepest spot, the lake is 105 to 108 feet. Every year, one quarter of a million trout are planted in Walker Lake. Right now conditions are almost perfect, said Drake, who hopes the depth will increase another fifteen feet.

One major problem looms: Walker Lake doesn't have a permanent water source. The Walker River, which flows into the lake, has more users than water. A court battle is shaping up over water rights involving Lyon County ranchers, the Walker River Paiute Tribe and Hawthorne-area recreation interests.

"We're short of water as it is," said David Fulstone II, a rancher and member of the Lyon County Commission. "The farm-

The shoreline of Walker Lake, near Hawthorne, attracts welcome tourists.

crs, the tribe and [Hawthorne] all want more water."

Louis Thompson, head of a group trying to secure water for Walker Lake, estimates fishing and related activities account for twenty-five to forty percent of the economic action in Hawthorne and the rest of Mineral County.

"With a county as poor as Mineral, it would be devastating to the county if you lost the lake," said Thompson, chairman of the Walker Lake Working Group. "We're hurting now. The county couldn't stand to lose that."

Sparks

An eastbound Union Pacific train pulls into Rail City.

Gaming glitter, railroad roots

When Myneer Walker Jr., left, and his father, right, have lunch at the Coney Island in Sparks, ceramic artist Dayna Galletti greets her old friend with a kiss. Galletti helps out in the kitchen twice a week at her family's bar-restaurant.

Orsie Graves looked at his father's hands and decided he'd never work for the railroad. The hands were dirty. The fingers were smashed.

"He didn't have a fingernail left," said the retired Sparks High School teacher and coach. "Somebody was always swinging a sledgehammer. He had little tiny nails on each finger."

Like many Sparks men in the first half of the 20th century, Graves' dad, Orsie Sr., worked for the Southern Pacific Railroad. He, like most of those men, didn't have a nice job. He wasn't an engineer or conductor. He was a master mechanic in the huge repair roundhouse that dominated the rail yard on the south side of what is now Victorian Avenue.

Every day, he went to work in the roundhouse, repairing the giant steam engines that Southern Pacific used to pull its trains over the Sierra. Sometimes, he would forget to take his lunch, so his son would bring it.

"They used to have a whistle when it was noontime," the son said. "My mom would say, 'Take this down to your dad' and I'd run on down. You could walk up

and down the sidewalks. Everyone knew everyone else. You'd just walk into the roundhouse. I'd say, 'Where's my dad?' and he'd be down in the repair pit. To me, it was a horrible job, but it put bread on the table."

Now the roundhouse is gone. The biggest building in Sparks is John Ascuaga's Nugget, one of northern Nevada's largest hotel-casinos. But Sparks was never much of a gambling town, not like neighboring Reno. The Rail City was a working town where the biggest public event was the annual Labor Day parade — a town where men like Orsie Graves Sr. made a living with their muscles.

"It was pretty protected and pretty provincial," said Tom Swart, eighty-six, who, like many high school kids in Sparks, went to the railroad for his first job. "I didn't realize that until later. As for the parents, very few women worked. Mothers, I mean. Kids got pretty close supervision compared to today. There was *esprit de corps* among Sparks residents."

Carl Shelly was one of those kids. He was born the same day Sparks was chartered as a city — March 15, 1905. Shelly grew up to be a councilman and Washoe

County commissioner and served three terms in the Nevada Legislature, but first he worked for the railroad.

"When I was going through high school, I worked in the back shop as a machinist's helper," Shelly said. "I was in the roundhouse as a supply man. I worked in the freight and passenger department as an agent and all the rest of that stuff."

So did seventy-seven-year-old Tom Balmain. "I worked two months as an outside helper, putting sand and water in tanks. I worked for free because there were a lot of people looking for work," he remembered. "Then I got promoted to cellar packer. You had to put a big grease block on the axles. Those engines at that time came in hot. There was a big piece of metal that clamped on the axle."

The work was hard and dirty. "A pair of overalls would last you two weeks,"

Balmain said. Anybody from Sparks in a certain age group probably can tell similar stories.

"There was no place else to go," Shelly said of the railroad. "It was a one-industry town."

Everybody lived close to B Street, the main drag that's now Victorian Avenue. "The house I lived in was a little stone house behind a bar," former Sparks Fire Chief Bill Farr said of growing up during Prohibition. "The bootleggers would come to my house and in the closet where you hung your coats, they'd slide a door open. They'd run the booze through a tube all the way to the Owl Bar. When the bar burned down, there were still some bottles of booze up in those tubes."

Sparks doesn't have bootleggers today, but the community does have some modern railroaders, such as Dan Lee, a day-shift

Union Pacific engineer Dave Horn of Sparks pauses in the early morning sunshine before boarding an eastbound engine in the Sparks yard.

yard master for Union Pacific, which runs twelve to fourteen trains a day through the city. The roundhouse and steam engines have disappeared, but Sparks is still a big spot on Union Pacific's Oakland, California, to Chicago line.

"We switch 750 to 800 cars a day here," said Richard Green Jr., manager of terminal operations. "This is a major crew-change point."

Lee, who is responsible for keeping trains on the right tracks, sees it all from his control tower. Since 1978, as one of 450 railroad workers in Sparks, Lee has had a perfect 360-degree view of the area's growth from his perch high above the Truckee Meadows." You're coordinating all the moves," he said. "Transportation means moving. The whole game is to keep everyone moving."

Lee has seen a lot of growth in Reno and Sparks during the past twenty-two years. "I watched the Nugget and the Reno Hilton get built," he said. "I watched downtown Reno casinos spring up. It's wild when you watch it on a day-to-day basis."

One of the builders, Ascuaga, who came from Idaho in 1955, remembers when everything first changed in Sparks. The railroad switched from steam to diesel locomotives and closed the roundhouse in 1956.

"They thought it was the end of Sparks," said Ascuaga, who started in the city as manager of a sixty-stool coffee shop with fifty slot machines on the north side of B Street. "They didn't need the roundhouse and all the maintenance here."

Overnight, it seemed, Sparks stopped being a railroad town. "They closed down in one day, just like that," Farr said. "All the railroad men were out of work. Thank God for a guy named Dick Graves."

Graves, no relation to Orsie, was Ascuaga's boss. The two guys from Idaho

John Ascuaga

Union Pacific steam locomotive No. 844, nicknamed "The Challenger," chugs into the Sparks railroad yard from Winnemucca.

opened small Nugget casinos in Yerington, Carson City and Reno, but their jackpot came in Sparks. They knew their business, but to look at them, Graves and Ascuaga were an odd couple as they searched for a casino site in Sparks.

"Dick was about six-foot-eight and I'm five-four," Ascuaga said with a smile. "We'd walk up and down the street trying to find a location." They settled on a spot and opened the coffee shop.

If the railroad defined Sparks in the first half of the 20th century, the Nugget has defined it in the second. The Nugget opened on Saint Patrick's Day, March 17, 1955.

"Mr. Peterson owned a drug store down the street, which is now our personnel department," Ascuaga said. "There was a sporting goods store down the street, the Block S."

Two years later, Graves and Ascuaga transformed downtown Sparks when they moved their Nugget across the street to its present location. Two years after that, Graves sold the casino to Ascuaga.

"That was the first business, other than the railroad, ever to move on that side of the street," Farr said.

At its height, the railroad employed about 1,300 people in Sparks. The Nugget, the city's most prominent landmark with two hotel towers, now has approximately 3,000 workers.

"Nobody could believe Mr. Graves was going to build a place that large," Ascuaga said of crossing B Street. "They said it would be a good place to store onions and potatoes."

Most of the things Graves and Ascuaga tried worked — except for one. "We went to Chicago and happened to see the Playboy Club," Ascuaga said with a chuckle. "It was unbelievable how successful they were. The Playboy Club — we were going to do it here. Then we realized we didn't have the source of employees to fit the requirements of being a Playboy bunny."

Ascuaga enjoys recalling the Sparks he saw when he first showed up from Idaho. He eats lunch in one of those little places that remains, the Coney Island bar and restaurant built in 1935 that sits at the Sparks-Reno boundary at the west end of Prater Way.

"Oh, my God, old Big John!" Ascuaga said at the mention of the Coney Island's owner, John Galletti. "Jerry! Nette! I was down there the other day." Gerald and Annette are Galletti's brother and sister. Son Greg runs the place, opened by Galletti's father, Ralph. The place is named for an amusement park of the same name — complete with a lake and beer garden — that operated across the street shortly after the turn of the century.

Every Tuesday at Coney Island, the lunch special is spaghetti with roast beef. Every Thursday, it's corned beef and cabbage. Nothing has changed since shortly after World War II. The place used to sell beer to go for 10 cents a pound. You brought your own container. They filled it and weighed it. You can't buy beer by the pound anymore. But you still can eat spaghetti.

"It's the passing parade," Gerald Galletti said. "All the old-timers come in. You sit here long enough, you'll see everybody."

Dan Lee, day-shift yard master for the Union Pacific, works two phones at once in the Sparks yard control tower.

Watercolors lead artist to happy surprises

Judy Harkness Dettre likes rocks. "I'm sort of known as the rock lady," said Dettre, a Sparks watercolor artist who finds rocks interesting subjects for paintings. "Sometimes I have lots of rocks

Judy Dettre

at home. I'll throw a pile on the table and go to work with that."

The sixty-seven-year-old, who had

one of her paintings chosen for the Healing Arts Festival at Washoe Medical Center, is a member of the Sierra Watercolor Society and Nevada Artists Association.

"I really love watercolor," said Dettre. "It's fast. The other thing I like about it, it's a medium that lends itself to surprises. You can slather water all over the paper and put paint on it. You get happy surprises. You can wad the paper all up and go from there. "I'm doing all these paintings of rocks. They're more like design elements."

Dettre spent most of her life teaching, but earned a degree in fine arts from the University of Nevada, Las Vegas before taking early retirement from her campus education job.

"I started rocks when I first started watercolor," Dettre said. "It's a pretty simple composition. I thought I could work on the color and things like that."

"Yellow Days" is the title of this watercolor by Sparks artist Judith Harkness Dettre, "the rock lady."

Sunset casts a warm glow on the hills east of the Sparks Marina.

Floods and factories doomed Glendale

Don't look for Glendale. You probably won't find it. The old town and most of the farmland that surrounded it is buried under the vast industrial warehouse district in present-day Sparks. But if you stop at Sparks Blacksmith & Welding Inc. on South Stanford Way, Russell Miller might tell you about Glendale — the town that grew up along the Truckee River long before Sparks existed.

The small stretch of Stanford that curves between South McCarran Boulevard and East Greg Street was Glendale's main drag. Now, it's where Miller operates his metal-fabricating business. Miller likes local history. When he decided to locate the company on Stanford Way, he made sure to learn about Glendale.

"It was a license to steal," Miller said of the toll crossing two men established in 1857 near the Truckee River's present-day McCarran overpass. "Those poor people coming across in covered wagons. Every time they crossed the river, they had to pay a toll."

The crossing, a rope-operated barge, was owned jointly by George F. Stone and Charles C. Gates. "Toward the end of their togetherness, one of them was getting bigger than the other, as people do," Miller said of the business partners turned rivals. "They cut the rope right in two in the middle of the river."

The settlement of Glendale grew from the crossing in the early 1860s. "This place was a viable town; there was a hardware store," Miller said. "They came across the river, then they had a series of buildings. They had the Glendale Hotel."

There was no Sparks, no B Street, no railroad. That all came later. "Glendale was the first post office," Miller said. "They figured everything would revolve around them. They figured they were going to be the county seat." But the Truckee River proved too much for Glendale.

"There was flood after flood," Miller said. "Everybody left." The railroad bypassed Glendale. Sparks developed. About the only thing left of Glendale is the historical marker on Miller's property. The Glendale School was moved from the site to Victorian Avenue, where people could see it.

"It was a wise decision," Miller said of the move. "It's not on the original site, but nobody comes out here."

The old Sparks roundhouse

From his vantage point on the Reno side of the Truckee, Brother Matthew Cunningham, chancellor of the Catholic Diocese of Reno, watched the warehouses replace open space on the Sparks side.

"That was a huge big marsh," said Cunningham, who lived at the Brothers of the Holy Rosary residence near the old Glendale site from 1963 to 1977. "Talk about wetlands, that was a major wetlands in the valley that was allowed to be turned into a major industrial area."

Before there were factories, there were farmers. "They raised vegetables for the local markets," Cunningham said. But most of the farms disappeared and few traces of Glendale remain.

"There was a lot of discussion about preserving that area," Cunningham said of the Glendale site. "They didn't do it. I was there when they filled in the marsh and built the warehouses. It was horrendous. That was truly a wetland and it disappeared in short order. In those days, nobody said much about it. They would never let that happen now."

A roundhouse was a circular building with a turntable in the center, used for storing and repairing locomotives. The Sparks roundhouse, built in 1905, once dominated the rail yard on the south side of what today is Victorian Avenue.

The Glendale School

The Sparks redevelopment district was the state's first

On a sweltering July afternoon, kids cool off in a downtown Sparks fountain.

om Young's business plan for his Great Basin Brewing Company in downtown Sparks is fairly simple: "There's a lot of thirsty people here," said Young, who opened the brewery, bar and restaurant in 1993.

Great Basin is a successful part of the redevelopment district, established as the state's first in 1977 to revitalize the city center. Redevelopment is one of two city projects bridging the twentieth and twenty-first centuries. The other is the marina taking shape on the east side, next to Interstate 80.

The thirty-year district life ends in 2007. Former Mayor Bruce Breslow figures work on the marina will go past that: "That's the true millennium project, the marina."

Sparks already had a big hole in the ground — the gravel pit. It became a lake overnight in the 1997 floods. The manmade stuff followed, with landscaping and boat facilities.

In the redevelopment district, work on a new city plaza was completed in the summer of 1999. Business owners such as Young and residents such as Susan Hill hope for more than just the brewery to attract people

downtown.

"I think the other challenge we have is retail stores," Hill said. "I don't think Sparks has enough retail."

But the city has movie theaters. In 1998, the fourteen screen Century Sparks complex opened — a big part of redevelopment and something Young was counting on to boost foot traffic for the Great Basin Brewing Company.

"It has had some impact," he said. "We

Neon lights on the Sparks Century 14 Theater brighten Victorian Square.

Ripe cherries at the farmers' market tempt three-year-old Jorge Allegra.

have a lot more people coming in Saturdays during the day, before the movie and after the movie."

Redevelopment, said Young, has been tougher in Sparks than in other communities because of geography. Downtown consists mostly of Victorian Avenue, a single long street with most businesses on the north side.

"At one time, it was one of the few cities in the nation with this type of situation," Young said. "It's taken longer to develop. These projects are complex. Downtowns are changing. They're getting a rebirth."

What downtown lacks, he said, are businesses with a lot of 8:00 a.m.-to-5:00 p.m. workers who take regular lunches and create foot traffic. "We call them 'daytime traffic generators.' They're office complexes. The Meadowood Mall area in Reno has that. The theater complex will start to define a center in Sparks."

Breslow agrees: "The hardest things to redevelop are downtowns. What we're competing against are the restaurants going up in South Reno. It's going to take a while."

Wadsworth

Cowboys wrestle a reluctant steer in a cloud of dust during branding at the Smoke Creek Ranch.

The quiet, small town was once a busy railroad center

A suspension bridge over the Truckee River

T he best place to cross the Truckee River is the footbridge in Betty Keife's back yard. When the bridge was damaged badly in the New Year's flood of 1997, Keife passed around a petition for Washoe County to fix it and got 822 signatures from people who live, or used to live, in Wadsworth. The foot bridge was fixed.

In the old railroad town that lost its rail and a lot of its town at the turn of the century, the wooden cable-suspension bridge is a landmark, but it can be hard to find. Driving around Wadsworth won't do it. You've got to get out of your car where the stately old high school sits abandoned and walk down Bridge Street — what else — to the banks of the Truckee. You reach the foot of Bridge Street and — there's the bridge. On the other side is Keife's back yard: walk across.

"You know kids, you've got to make it swing, that's all there is to it," Keife said with a laugh. Yes, you do, even if you're a grownup.

"That bridge has been there for I don't know how long," said Joe Mortensen, a local ranch manager who grew up in the area. "When I was a kid, we used to walk down to the bridge. When I got married, my wife and I used to go down there." The bridge was, in many ways, the heart of Wadsworth.

"This was the road that went across to go to town," said Keife, who used to be Wadsworth's postmaster. "In the Central Pacific days, that was the main deal." Wadsworth was the center of things in those days. There was a roundhouse for the railroad, hotels, restaurants, stores and a busy main street. But the railroad packed up and moved to Sparks in 1904, leaving one town and creating a new one.

The bridge remains. Eventually Interstate 80 bypassed Wadsworth, taking the traffic with it. Wadsworth became a place to drive past, but the bridge remains.

Keife arrived in the early 1960s with husband Paul. Wadsworth and their place on the river was, at first, a weekend retreat from Reno-Sparks. Later, it became a full-time home.

If you want to find the railroad in Wadsworth, look in Betty Keife's back yard. She's got a red caboose, a 1910 model from the Western Pacific Railroad, hooked to an 1890 passenger car. Now divorced, Keife lived in the cars when she first moved permanently to Wadsworth in 1975. Later, she felt cramped

Betty Keife's back yard

and moved into a double-wide mobile home. Today, the railroad cars are unique decorations in the back yard.

She and her former husband found the caboose on a railroad siding in Gerlach when their car broke down on a road trip. They had to have it. "We got stuck in Gerlach," she said. "We had to call into Reno to get the part and had to stay overnight. When we saw this caboose down on the siding, we went over and asked if we could see it. There was a little padlock on it. An old railroader had been living in it."

The two decided to do the same thing. But first they had to buy the caboose from the railroad and get it back to Wadsworth. "We had this property here," she said. "At the time, the tracks went from Gerlach to Wadsworth. We thought we'd just stick it onto the end of the train and have them pull it to Wadsworth."

That was before they found out about insurance and other complications. They ended up buying the caboose for about nine hundred dollars, then paid a house mover twice that much to tow it to Wadsworth. Later, the old passenger car was found near Sutcliffe on the Pyramid Lake Paiute Reserva-

tion and was hauled back to Wadsworth and hooked to the caboose.

They created a home, building a bathroom, bedroom and kitchen into the passenger car. The caboose, with a wood stove, was the living room.

Today, Keife seldom goes inside the train. When she does, she mostly finds cobwebs, closets full of clothes and some interesting artifacts. On the kitchen counter rests a meat and bread slicing machine made July 12, 1881. The blade is sharp.

"Here is where I spent most of my time," she said, pointing to the kitchen table. "Sitting here, eating there and watching TV." From the window, you can see the rest of the Keife museum outside, including a wooden barn moved from

After a morning of fishing in the Truckee River, Marian Zorger dries out her shoes. She and her husband retired from Mountain View, California, to this trailer in Wadsworth.

She believes in the "camera goddess" and recognizing the right moment

WADSWORTH

- Population in 1999: 1,169
(29 percent under 18, 36 percent 18-44, 17 percent 45-64, 18 percent 65 and older; 51 percent male, 49 percent female).
- Population in 1990: 640.
- Population in 2003: (projected) 1,626.
- Median household income in 1990: $16,172.
- Median household income in 1998: $20,833.
- Total retail sales in 1998: $5.017 million.
- Total retail sales in (projected) 2003: $8.727 million.

- Claim to fame: Major railroad town in northern Nevada in 1800s, until Southern Pacific Railroad moved repair and other facilities to Sparks in 1904.

- How it got its name: Central Pacific Railroad named site for James Samuel Wadsworth, Union Army general killed in Civil War.

- Local legend: Helen Marye Thomas, who gave her S Bar S Ranch near Wadsworth to the University of Nevada, Reno, in 1967, was a wealthy socialite who threw lavish parties at the ranch for several hundred guests at a time, including Hedy Lamarr and other Hollywood stars. Thomas died in 1970.

T he light in the desert is perfect for Vivian Olds and her camera.

"I'm totally hooked on the desert," said Olds, who teaches third and fourth grades at Fernley Elementary School. "As soon as I hit the desert, I picked up a camera. The light is wonderful."

Olds, who has lived in Wadsworth

Wadsworth artist Vivian Olds likes to paint Pyramid Lake from her own photographs, like this one she displays at home.

for ten years, photographs the land around her, especially at Pyramid Lake where her ancestors settled when they came to Nevada.

"My grandmother was a homesteader out there in the early 1900s," said the Quincy, California, native. Olds was a teacher and vice principal at Pyramid Lake High School before taking a job at Fernley Elementary, where she has taught for twelve years.

"You have to be there at the right moment and things happen," she said of her photo philosophy. "I believe in the camera

goddess." Her home in Wadsworth is an art gallery, Desert Light Art, where she features the work of painter Carlos Warner, who splits time between northern Nevada and San Diego, and potter Eric Woods, who has a studio in San Diego.

"It's a creative place," Olds said of northern Nevada and the desert. "The atmosphere of living near Pyramid Lake lends itself to an enormous amount of creativity. A lot of creative people come through here."

Sparks. Inside the barn there is a complete nineteenth century blacksmith shop, moved piece by piece from Dayton.

"You start collecting," Keife said of the barn, which was going to be the family garage. "You just bring something in and add it. Pretty soon, you can't get the car in."

Around Keife's home are farm wagons and old mining machinery. "That ran the Tonopah mine," Keife said of one large engine. "It ran everything inside." Near the mine machine sits the most bizarre item in the collection, a sixty-foot lathe from a San Francisco shipyard, once used to make masts for sailing ships.

"We were going to use it to make a flagpole," Keife said. "You don't make table legs on this." Or much of anything else. "I'll sell it to you cheap," she said with a grin.

Few landmarks are left in Wadsworth. The high school closed in 1951. The old downtown mostly is abandoned. Over the years, fires destroyed a lot of buildings. The handful left are closed. Much of present-day Wadsworth is on the Paiute reservation, including a modern subdivision for tribal housing. The new center of town is the Natchez Elementary School, part of the Washoe County School district, named for Paiute Chief Natchez.

"We try to make it a community school, as much as we can," said Janet Davis. "It is the center. A lot of things go on here."

Davis is a tribal member from Nixon, the reservation headquarters north on State Route 447. She was once a student at Natchez. Now she works there as a community liaison between the tribe and school. She talks as she fills balloons from a helium tank for the day's kindergarten graduation, one of Wadsworth's special events.

"I help in the classroom sometimes," she said. "If the kids get sick, I take them home. If parents need to come in for a conference, I go pick them up if they don't have a ride. Teachers

Aria Sumpter of Wadsworth watches children on the playground at Natchez Elementary School

have a hard time contacting parents."

The school serves a wide area, not just Wadsworth. It is the reservation's only elementary school with an enrollment of about 140 children, mostly Paiutes from the reservation, along with some non-Indians from Wadsworth.

Kindergarten teacher Pat Cox had twenty-four children graduating from her 1999 class. "It's a little family," Cox said of Natchez, where she has taught since 1981. "Most elementary schools in Reno-Sparks have a thousand students."

Another little family in the Wadsworth area lives on the S Bar S Ranch, where University of Nevada, Reno agriculture students learn to feed cattle, drive a tractor, cut hay and fix fences. The 288-acre ranch, once a party haven for Hollywood celebrities, is operated by UNR as a real-life classroom for a handful of students at a time, during the fall and spring semesters and all summer.

"We're finally getting around to repairing it again," Mortensen said of a shed where his

Kindergarten graduates Leanna Mix, left, and Chrissie Dick wait to perform for parents and friends at Natchez Elementary School in Wadsworth.

three summer students, all women, are repairing the metal roof. Mortensen has managed the S Bar S for twenty-one years. Along with running the ranch, he is also the teacher. He spends a lot of time listening. "I have to hear about all the girlfriends and boyfriends," he said with a smile.

The ranch belonged to Helen Marye Thomas, a wealthy eastern socialite, who gave the S Bar S to the university before she died in 1970. Students eat and study in the main ranch house. They stay in cottages once occupied by party guests. The kids have a good time.

"I'm having so much fun," said Katy Stevens, a freshman from Carson City. "I learned how to drive a backhoe."

Eshel Carrion, a sophomore from Eureka, grew up on a ranch. She's on familiar ground and living a familiar routine. "We get up at six o'clock and have breakfast," Carrion said. "At seven, we start work. We feed the animals. That takes about an hour. Then it's whatever Joe tells us to do. Katy and I went and dug a ditch. Joe and Enid went to spray weeds."

Enid Coulston, a junior from Capitola, California, lived next to the Pacific Ocean. When Coulston got to the S Bar S, she jumped into the Truckee River. "They're both cold," she said. "I didn't realize the Truckee was so cold. I didn't have any feeling in my toes."

She could ask Marian Zorger about the river. Zorger and husband Myron retired from the San Francisco Bay area and live on another part of the Truckee, in a mobile home in the Big Bend Ranch trailer park near the river.

Like the bridge, the park is a part of Wadsworth that's hard to find, hidden from I-80 and other roads. Residents raise their own vegetables in a community garden. Usually, their only visitor is the neighborhood coyote.

"She's our pet, she's courting the dog next door," said Zorger, who spends a lot of time at the river. "The other day, I caught a seventeen-inch rainbow trout …. I saw baby ducks, too."

A coyote trots across a field near Big Bend Ranch.

Wadsworth 157

Stan Ceresola of Wadsworth works with a crew of six men to brand cattle at Smoke Creek Ranch.

Wadsworth cowboys prefer the old way of branding cattle

Stan Ceresola belongs on the back of a horse. The longtime Wadsworth cowboy wouldn't look right anywhere else. Picture him behind a desk. Forget it. Wearing a tie? No way. A suit? You're kidding.

Ceresola's "office" is a dusty corral with a lot of noisy, nervous cattle waiting to be branded. Sitting on his horse, Ceresola talks above the racket.

"If you get good ropers, it's pretty easy," he said. "These guys are good ropers." But Ceresola is the best.

"You got to watch Stan," said Edward DeChambeau, part of Ceresola's six-man branding crew. "He just goes in there real quiet, gets her done fast and easy."

This is old-fashioned branding at the Smoke Creek Ranch north of the Pyramid Lake Paiute Reservation, a hundred miles from Reno with half the drive on a dirt road. The Ranch is not Ceresola's, but belongs to somebody he knows. He's helping out.

This is where you experience sagebrush Nevada at its most raw. It's cowboys and cattle. The sun is hot, the smell strong, the dust thick and the tradition rich. The branding is done with hot irons and a wood fire,

When Edward DeChambeau isn't cowboying in northern Nevada, he mines gold in Alaska.

with ropes and horses, the classic picture of the West.

"We just rope them by the hind legs and drag them to the fire," said Gene Curtis, another of Ceresola's cowboys. One by one, the cows are branded, vaccinated and castrated, with testicles tossed into a red Chase & Sanborn coffee can. None of this appears to bother the cows. Bottles of vaccination serum are stored in one picnic cooler. Beer is kept in another.

The cattle cluster at one end of the corral and cowboys ride among them slowly, picking them off one at a time. The cows don't scatter or try to escape.

"They do if you ride in fast," DeChambeau said.

One concession is made to modern technology: "We started the branding fire with propane," Ceresola said with a chuckle.

Sid Kochamp of Nixon helps with the branding at the Smoke Creek Ranch north of Pyramid Lake.

Curtis, DeChambeau and the others are branding cattle because they like it. They really have no other good reason.

"You've got to want to do it," said Ceresola, who belongs to a family that has ranched in the Wadsworth area since the turn of the century. "It doesn't pay that well. They usually make from fifty to a hundred dollars a day, depending on the ranch."

For twenty-year-old DeChambeau, who splits time between being a cowboy in northern Nevada and a gold miner in Alaska, branding is fun. "I was born and raised on a horse," said the Smith Valley resident. "It's just kind of a hobby. In the summer, I drill up in Alaska. I just kind of play around in the winter."

Traditional branding lets cowboys have a good time. "Sometimes, I get so darned dirty that when I get home, I've got to wash them three times," DeChambeau said of his cowboy clothes.

The cowboys have other, more practical reasons, for branding the old way. Some ranches don't have chutes and other facilities needed to run cattle through a modern mass-production branding line. On those ranches, it's the old way or no way.

"It's just faster to do it this way," said Ceresola, who brands his own cattle traditionally.

Randy Ownbey knows about branding. Originally from Kansas, the career cowboy's address is a post office box in Gerlach. Ownbey's basic rule of branding is simple: "The hotter it is, the less pain it causes," he said of the irons and the cows. "I've burned myself enough times to know." Ownbey estimated the temperature of the branding irons: "Less than red hot — but not much."

Seventy-year-old Gordon Frazier used to brand with Ceresola's grandfather. Today, he's branding with Ceresola. "He was a little squeaker," Frazier said of Stan Ceresola in the old days. A retired state highway worker, Frazier doesn't have to brand cattle for a living, but he does it anyway.

"I can't stay home," he said. "You get old staying home."

Joe Mortensen, manager of S Bar S Ranch in Wadsworth, lives on the ranch with agriculture students.

The Paiutes are reclaiming their tribal land

The railroad has been gone for a long time and, sometime soon in the twenty-first century, the rest of old Wadsworth could disappear too. The Pyramid Lake Paiute Indians are reclaiming it as part of a federal government program that began in 1990 and likely will continue until all of the town is within tribal boundaries,

"When you think about the future of Wadsworth, that's our largest community," said Norman Harry, chairman of the Pyramid Lake Paiutes. When Harry looks at Wadsworth he sees land for an industrial park and other commercial development to boost his tribe's economy.

Wadsworth sits next to Interstate 80,

twenty-seven miles east of Reno-Sparks. What used to be the small downtown is abandoned, mostly, except for the post office and a few homes. The Pyramid Lake reservation's largest tribal housing development is in Wadsworth, across the street from the Natchez Elementary School that serves Paiute children and a few others.

"Our primary source of revenue is going to have to be along the I-80 corridor," Harry said of future development. "It's location, location, location. There are all sorts of possibilities."

The government has been buying Wadsworth-area ranches, paying for them with cash from other federal land sales in the state, and

Paiute cradleboard

Enid Coulston, a University of Nevada, Reno junior from Capitola, California, works on the roof of a shed at the S Bar S Ranch in Wadsworth.

placing the property in trust for the tribe. This is an effort to restore the reservation's boundaries to what they were before the railroad came through and established the town in 1868.

The sales aren't forced, but longtime ranchers are taking the money and leaving. Some said they have little choice. "I see it changing completely," said Steve Ceresola, whose family has ranched near Wadsworth since 1910. "As the older families die off or move out, it's going to be all reservation. You're on the reservation." Ceresola figures his family will sell its ranch. "Eventually, the government will buy it," he said.

Harry said there are no plans to buy the S Bar S Ranch, owned and operated by the University of Nevada, Reno as a working classroom for agriculture students.

Portions of the town already are within the reservation. Harry said the next step, after the ranchers sell, is to buy remaining

Wadsworth property. But residents who don't want to leave won't be pushed out, said Aaron Peskin, the tribe's advisor on the land program. What's left of Wadsworth is at the southern end of the reservation.

Land ownership in the area has been in question for more than a century. In 1865, the federal government ordered ten miles of tribal land reserved for the railroad. Nine years later, President Ulysses S. Grant restored the original reservation boundary. In 1916, another government decision was issued that seemed to contradict Grant's.

"I just cringe every time I think about moving from there," said Linda McKnight, who lives on the Ceresola ranch. "It will be a whole different way of life, but I'll adjust."

While ranchers are as varied a breed of women and men as could be imagined, as a general rule they share a conviction that they are engaged in an activity that has both lasting social and economic value; more important, they believe that they are engaged in something innately virtuous. While that surety may not make converts, it does constitute a powerful conviction that overcomes considerable economic hardship and produces a feeling of camaraderie that is not easily broken. It also makes ranching that most incongruous of activities: something both individually rewarding and communally significant.
    Paul Starrs, Let the Cowboy Ride

Farming and Ranching

Mark Gomes of Kansas hangs onto a buckskin named Manzanita Moonshine during the bareback bronc riding event at the Reno Rodeo.

Fallon

Two Navy pibts climb into the cockpit of this F-14
Tomcat in preparation for flight.

Developers and the military are changing the face of a rural town.

Fallon rancher Virgil Getto, a retired Nevada State Assemblyman, likes to drive his favorite piece of farm machinery, a front loader.

As a child growing up in Fallon, Virgil Getto hated hearing his mother, Deslina, speak Italian in public: "I was ashamed. When she stood on the street speaking Italian to another lady, I'd kick her in the shins. I wanted her to speak English."

Getto's attitude has changed.

"Now I'm proud of it," said the prosperous seventy-five year-old Lahontan Valley farmer who served in the Nevada Legislature for twenty-four years. "I'm proud of my heritage."

His parents came to Fallon with almost nothing. His father, Andrew, came first in 1907 and then Deslina in 1923. "Dad heard about the water that was going to be available," Getto said. "He used horses and explosives to clear trees out."

Andrew cleared land for a farm by hand. Then the family created a life. The Gettos were self-sufficient. They produced their own food and clothes, raised turkeys and chickens, made salami and wine, cured ham, and grew potatoes, alfalfa and other grain. Virgil went to school in homemade clothes. Deslina sewed his shirts from flour sacks.

"My mom was a good seamstress," Getto said. "She made me shirts. She cut my hair."

Many descendants of original Fallon residents could tell similar stories. Brought by the promise of land, their parents or grandparents showed up and helped turn the Lahontan Valley into the state's most famous patch of farmland, the self-proclaimed "Oasis of Nevada." Thousands of acres of green fields, surrounded by sand, were cultivated by Virgil's parents and people like them.

"It was a wonderful opportunity for people who were hard-pressed," Getto said. "They had a great deal of ambition and came here to develop something."

All of it was made possible by the federal government's historic social experiment at the turn of the century — the Newlands Reclamation Project, named for Nevada Congressman and Senator Francis G. Newlands. The project, Uncle Sam's first under the National Reclamation Act of 1902, resulted in a system of dams and canals that brought water to the desert around Fallon. Settlers followed the water, a way of life that has lasted through the 20th century.

"It was part of an era when the federal government began to play a role in the lives of people," said Guy Rocha, state archivist and expert on Nevada history. "People came

IMPORTANT DATES

- 1894: Jim Richards builds general store; area is called "Jim Town."
- 1896: Mike and Eliza Fallon establish post office on their ranch.
- 1902: Federal Reclamation Act becomes law. Fallon family sells property to state Sen. Warren W. Williams and leaves valley.
- 1903: Work begins on Newlands Reclamation Project.
- 1904: Churchill County seat moves from Stillwater to Fallon.
- 1907: Speed limit set at 6 mph for automobiles and horses in town.
- 1908: Fallon incorporates.
- May 14, 1910: Fire destroys much of downtown Fallon.
- 1913: Lahontan Dam completed.
- 1921: Local farmers organize Churchill County Cantaloupe Growers Association and adopt "Hearts-of-Gold" trademark.
- Dec. 31, 1926: Truckee-Carson Irrigation District takes over management of Newlands Reclamation Project from federal government.
- 1930: Maine Street paved.
- 1942: Military airfield built.
- June 10, 1944: Naval Auxiliary Air Station Fallon commissioned.
- 1948: Stillwater Wildlife Management Area formed. Fallon Chamber of Commerce first uses phrase, "Oasis of Nevada."
- July 12, 1953: Parking meters installed on Maine Street.

An American black-necked stilt looks for breakfast in a marsh near Fallon.

about their land. "This farm, my father actually built it. I'll show you how he took hills and leveled them. It takes a certain type of individual to farm. You have to have an attachment to the land and the cattle. You can't be an individual who can just walk away and forget it."

Getto hasn't forgotten. He works some of his land and leases part of it to others. He has developed some acres, turning them from alfalfa to houses. Rocha predicts the same thing will happen on more farmland, that Fallon will change from a farm town into a military-residential community tied to the nearby U.S. Naval Air Station and the growing number of retirees settling in the area.

"Fallon is changing," said Rocha. "I'm arguing it's not an agricultural community in the way it was. It's a military town and a retirement town. Any place that has to change finds it difficult to change. It's not going to be the same in the 21st century."

The Navy base, which is a big deal for Fallon and has been for a long time, is home to TOPGUN, the Navy's famous and elite advanced-training program for jet-fighter pilots. Fallon is a patriotic place. The Navy has status.

"We're very supportive of the military and the nation," said Mayor Ken Tedford. "The Navy today is a huge operation for us." The mayor calls critics of the military "objectors" and has little patience with people who protest the noise made by supersonic jets over Fallon and the Navy's use of the desert for practice bombing ranges. He finds critics who don't live in the area especially irritating. "I don't know of many people in this valley who aren't supporters of the Navy," Tedford said.

As many of those folks watch the jets flying over their alfalfa, they still consider Fallon a farm town. "I hope it is a farm town.

from all over. It was a chance for the yeoman farmer to get a start. Come get your land and start a new life."

Now that era may be ending, or at least changing significantly. Rocha said, and Getto acknowledged, that Fallon won't be the farm town in the 21st century that it has been in the 20th. Fallon is being forced to give up water to the nearby Pyramid Lake Paiute Indian Tribe and the growing metropolitan area of Reno-Sparks. Federal and state legislation to settle disputes over Truckee River water mean fewer farms around Fallon.

Getto doesn't like it, but he's willing to live with it. "It's like giving up your home that you built with your hands," said Getto, explaining how he and his neighbors feel

A young Holstein calf, about five days old, tries to eat some alfalfa at Callaway Dairy in Fallon.

My prayer is it will continue to be a farm town," said Bunny Corkill, whose family settled in the area in 1861. "I like farm towns." But Corkill, who has a ranch outside of town, isn't completely happy. She suggested a drive around the outskirts of Fallon to show the sources of her discontent.

The journey followed Pasture Road and Corkill Lane, home to many farms and ranches. Corkill frowned when she saw agricultural land that's been returned to its original sagebrush-and-sand state because the owners had sold their water rights and moved away.

"I don't think I need to tell you what happens to farm land when they sell the water off of it," Corkill said, nodding in the direction of the barren ground. "I rest my case. What you see is what you get. Three years ago, it was alfalfa fields. You decide."

When Corkill was growing up, the farmers and their families didn't live in Fallon. Instead, they were residents of such places as Beach, Union, Harmon, Island, St. Clair and Lone Tree. Those were districts, seventeen of them, each with its own little school, church and country community.

"A lot of them had organizations of women," said Corkill, whose family lived in the Beach District. "There were the Northern Homemakers and organizations like that. They met once a month. They raised money for the schools. It was also time to quilt and visit with friends."

Fallon had two newspapers, the *Eagle* and the *Standard.* They carried reports written by correspondents from each district. "They wrote every week and told what was going on in their district," Corkill said. "It was a very comforting way to communicate. It was the village network. It was a very nice way for local people to keep track of each other."

Recalling the districts reminded her of another old Fallon story, about riding the school bus. "When I was a kid, the oldest kid — preferably a boy who rode the bus the farthest out — he drove," Corkill said. "The biggest, oldest, strongest girl, she was the conductor. If you said anything bad, she'd kick you off the bus. Kids are such wimps now. If you didn't play the game and shut up, you walked."

Carl Dodge's family developed the Island Ranch, for which the Island District was

The Lariat Motel on West Williams Street displays its patriotism along with a bright neon sign.

named. The former state senator wants farming to continue in Fallon on a large enough scale to keep the oasis green. "That's the perception," he said. "It's a beautiful perception. I hope, in planning, people will keep that in mind."

So does Virgil Getto, who still lives on the same land his father settled. "The pressure is for subdividing," he said of the decision farmers are making to develop. "The use will go where the money is. My neighbor is quite a farmer, but he is starting a subdivision with four hundred homes. He still has the farming end, but that nice farm will be homes. It will be a slow process, but he has already started building. There are subdivisions all around."

Even Getto's land has a subdivision with eleven new homes. "This may all be subdivided some day," he said. And the transition from farm to suburb isn't without problems. An example is the irrigation ditch that brings water to his fields. It runs through a residential area.

"Toys end up in the ditch," said Getto. "They come down to my fields. It's kind of a

headache. Some people don't understand." That includes some people who planted trees on the bank of the irrigation ditch. "They prune the trees and the branches go right in my irrigation ditch," he said. "They threw them all in my irrigation ditch. They didn't know the water comes down. When I started irrigating, I went up to look and I said, 'Oh, my God, I've got to get these limbs out of there.'"

Part of his property is a dairy, and that means problems for the suburbanites. Cows and residential neighborhoods don't always mix. "We have to do something with our manure," Getto said. "Sometimes it doesn't smell so good."

Now Getto has retired. The dairy is leased to another operator. He and wife Pat like to watch the cows from their living room window, but they don't have to worry about them. Getto still farms 180 acres, and he tends a garden, mostly for enjoyment.

"My wife can't understand it. I love to garden," he said. "I love to see those plants grow."

The barbershop smell of memory

This is an excerpt from an unpublished book about growing up in Fallon by George Earnhart, a retired state government employee who lives in Carson City but was born and raised in Fallon:

I relished my pilgrimages to the Forum Barber Shop, located on Maine Street between the bakery and the Horseshoe Club, for my monthly croppings.

It was a delightful experience to have Uncle Lloyd pamper me by gently and expertly trimming and combing my hair while conversing with me via the mirror. Without exception, after he finished the clipping, he routinely dusted my neck softly with talc adhering to his extraordinary long-bristled brush. Once the remnants of the haircut were dispensed with, he treated my hair and scalp with the fragrant liquid from a large, narrow-necked bottle of Jervis Hair Tonic for the final combing.

These excursions to the barbershop never lost their appeal for several reasons — indeed I could almost write the comfortable scenario in advance of my arrival. As I opened the door my nose was assailed by the pleasant aromas of Bay Rum, Lucky Tiger, Wildroot and Jervis, all concoctions expressly prepared for the hair and freshly shaven face.

Once inside the three-chair shop, the owner who presided over the first chair next to the ornate brass cash register ini-

George Earnhart

tially greeted me. I would select a seat from among the chairs placed in a row along the mirrored wall, pick up a dated copy of a dog-eared magazine, and make a mental estimate of how long I might have to wait.

As patrons were served in order of their arrival, I would bide my time by scanning magazines or eavesdropping on conversations. I declined the tentative offers of "Next?" until Uncle Lloyd was available. When he was ready for me, he invited me to sit in his throne-like, white porcelain chair and warmly greeted me as he deftly placed a striped white cape over me.

The barbershop was strictly a male domain, bordering upon a social institution where men and boys could gather and speak freely, and any topic was fair game with no subjects censored. You could speak as frankly and explicitly as desired without receiving as much as a raised eyebrow.

Runway at the NAS Fallon

TOPGUN is more than a movie

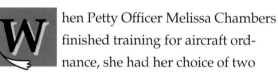When Petty Officer Melissa Chambers finished training for aircraft ordnance, she had her choice of two assignments: One was at a base in California; the other was TOPGUN at the Naval Air Station in Fallon. Chambers selected TOPGUN — the easy pick.

You know the movie. Tom Cruise stars as the slick naval aviator. In the Navy, pilots aren't pilots, they're aviators. The movie is more than a decade old, but it still makes the Navy look good, even sexy. So, what did the native Virginian find when she got to the Naval Air Station in Fallon?

"Definitely, there's no Tom Cruise here," said Chambers, one of the enlisted personnel who maintain weapons — the bombs, missiles and guns for TOPGUN. Instead, she found Navy Captain John Worthington. At the time, he was deputy commander of the Naval Strike and Air Warfare Center, the bureaucracy that includes TOPGUN and the other advanced jet-fighter training programs at NAS Fallon. Worthington, who joined the Navy as a sailor in 1967, followed some good advice and attended the Naval Academy Prep School. He studied and kept taking the Scholastic Aptitude Test until he scored high enough to qualify for the Naval Academy at Annapolis, Maryland. He became an officer, learned to fly, and then started moving up the chain of command.

After all that, the forty-nine-year-old is just a kid at heart — and proud of it. "If you're an aviator, you can stay young forever," said Worthington who flies high and fast with a lot of young hotshots in their twenties and thirties. "I love the same music. If you go out to my car stereo, Pearl Jam is blaring in there. You don't have to grow up."

Worthington, who transferred later from Fallon to a new assignment, is known in the Navy as "Jocko," his call sign. Anyone called "Jocko" by adults can't feel *too* old. All the pilots — sorry, aviators — at NAS Fallon have call signs: "Streak," "Punchy," and "Mongo," among many others.

Streak is Navy Lieutenant. John Scudi, a TOPGUN instructor. "It starts off with always having wanted to do it when you were a kid," Scudi said. "We come in like knights on chargers. It's pretty cool."

Everyone appears to agree on that. There's no other thrill quite like it. "No question about it, "said Worthington. "I do that every time I take off. You're on after-burners. You're climbing out. You get about 9,000 feet over the field, you look back over your right shoulder to the field and you say, 'Damn, this is neat!'"

Air Force Captain William Carter, on special assignment as an instructor at the warfare center, knows the same feeling. "We flew at night," Carter said. "The moon was out, there were really nice stars. When we hit the after-burners when we took off, you could see the other guy's flame shooting out. I think everybody gets that emotion. The other night, we got it."

But this is serious business. A day at TOPGUN can start with a 4:00 a.m. wakeup, followed by a 5:45 a.m. pre-flight briefing, when the good guys and bad guys go over the day's planned ACM — air combat maneuvers — or dogfighting.

"All the fighters and bandits get together; then we break up," said Air Force Major Dave Keddington, on special assignment as a TOPGUN instructor. "The bandits go into their briefing and talk about how they're going to challenge us. We talk about our tactics."

In the TOPGUN dogfights, the bandits always outnumber the fighters, usually two to one. "We always train outnumbered," Keddington said, noting that only about sixty minutes in a twelve-hour day are spent in the air. "We usually walk to the aircraft about fifty minutes before actual takeoff; it takes fifty minutes to get your stuff on and get the jets cranked up. Today we got up about eight o'clock. The mission was for about an hour. We fought from eight to nine, two full engagements. We got back on the deck about nine-thirty."

The rest of a long day is spent studying what happened. Videotapes are broken down, examined and discussed for hours. "The fighters get together and talk about what they saw, the bandits get together and talk about what they saw," Keddington explained. "Then

On the tarmac at NAS Fallon, aircraft ordnance worker Keith Riffle from Grafton, West Virginia, removes weapons rails from an F-14.

Navy Captain John "Jocko" Worthington served as deputy commander of the Naval Strike and Air Warfare Center at NAS Fallon.

we get together in a room and see all the computer-generated stuff. Who shot who. Who died. That takes us until noon. None of the learning has started yet."

Then they have more sessions, more discussions, more questions and more answers. "We look at each guy's radar tape," Keddington said. "Then I'll get to talk." The idea is to teach the students — all experienced fighter pilots — to be instructors, all with one thing in mind.

"We find those dogfighting skills are important," Keddington said of close-range air combat. "About seventy percent of our kills happen in an arena where we say, 'Everything is going to hell in a handbasket.' It's not where you have this nice controlled long-range intercept. You're in the target area; guys are getting shot, you can't see your wingman, you look over your shoulder and it's an enemy. Things happen."

Petty Officer Chambers was right: NAS Fallon has no Tom Cruise — and this is no movie.

A town wants to define itself

On his miniature pony, three-year-old Isiah Christy rides in the National Indian Rodeo Association Stampede and Pioneer Days parade in downtown Fallon, led by his aunt, Corrine Lewis.

Virgil Getto is a longtime Fallon farmer who is sure an era is ending: "I can see the handwriting on the wall. It's going to shrink down."

Getto, whose father started farming in the Lahontan Valley in 1907, figures that with legislation giving more Truckee River water to the nearby Pyramid Lake Paiute Indian Tribe, farm land eventually could be cut almost in half, from about 60,000 acres to 35,000 or 40,000.

Fallon will continue to farm and probably keep calling itself the "Oasis of Nevada." But it won't be the way it has been for most of this century, when irrigation resulting from the historic National Reclamation of Act of 1902 turned the desert green.

"Fallon, in its way, is part of a much bigger picture," state historian Guy Rocha said. "It's the urbanization of the American West."

The change isn't welcome in Fallon. Mayor Ken Tedford protests that the federal government, not the local community, is dictating Fallon's future. After all, it was a government program, the Newlands Reclamation Project in the early 1900s, which resulted in the dams and canals key to Fallon's growth. Now, the government is making different decisions.

"Every community should be able to define itself," Tedford said. "If the local officials who are elected by the people make that decision, the community is making a choice. The other way, the federal government is making a decision for you."

The water that helped create Fallon is being used elsewhere — by the Pyramid Lake tribe and in Reno-Sparks, a metropolitan area that barely existed when the Newlands Project first irrigated the fields that now belong to Getto.

"We don't mind the Truckee Meadows having their growth," Churchill County Commission Chairman Jim Regan said. "But don't try to screw us over."

"Changing conditions are dictating new policies," Rocha said. "The engineers said reclamation would work out. Now, 100 years later, the feds aren't with Fallon anymore. The policy has changed. The world has changed."

Fernley, another town built by reclamation, is turning its back on agriculture in favor of industry. Rocha predicts Fernley will surpass Fallon as the leading town in west central Nevada. "There is very little sentiment in Fernley to keep the farms going," said Rocha. "In Fallon, they don't want to let go."

Fallon isn't dying. Farming remains, as does Naval Air Station Fallon, the base that local economists estimate accounts for thirty percent of Churchill County employment.

"We know it's going to change," Regan said of Fallon's future. "But that should be a change we decide."

Petroglyphs on a boulder near Grimes Point, east of Fallon, are judged to be 500 to 2,000 years old.

Between Grimes Point and Sand Mountain, dark rocks spell out names on the whitewashed playa along Highway 50.

Gardnerville

Marie Lekumberry, center, visits with customers Charlyn Sarkis, left, and Liz McGeein during lunch at JT Basque Bar and Dining Room in Gardnerville.

Successive generations are the keepers of Basque taste and tradition

Walk into the past through the front door of the JT Basque Bar & Dining Room in Gardnerville.

Whenever Luke Neddenriep walks into the JT Basque Bar & Dining Room, he can remember his first meal in a restaurant. "I was a little guy," said Neddenriep, eighty-two, a lifelong Gardnerville resident. "My dad ordered steak. I hated gristle and fat on a steak. I liked meat, but not the fat. I cut all that off. Before we left, he said, 'You know, we have to pay for that fat whether you eat it or not, so you better eat it.' I ate the whole damn works."

That was a long time ago. But the century-old building housing the JT remains a Gardnerville landmark where a town's memories linger. Neddenriep still can walk to the JT from where he lives.

"I forced it down," Neddenriep said of the dinner. He figures he cleaned his plate on a day sometime in the mid-1920s. The JT wasn't the JT when Neddenriep was a fussy kid, but rather was Rahbeck's Gardnerville Hotel. Now names don't matter. People have been eating and drinking in the white, wooden, two-story building since it was moved from the Virginia City area to Gardnerville about 1896.

"No, actually, before that," said J.B.

Lekumberry, who owns and operates the JT Basque Bar & Dining Room with sister Marie. "There is a picture of it here in 1896. It sat in Genoa for a year."

Genoa? That bit of information starts a debate between sister and brother. "Do we know that for sure?" Marie asked of the building's supposed stop in Nevada's historic heart on its way to Gardnerville. J.B. isn't sure, but he likes the story.

"That's what the historic folks say," J.B. said with a grin. "It sounds good." One thing is certain, said Marie: "It's always been an eating place and saloon."

For years, those eating places and saloons, owned mostly by Basques such as the Lekumberrys, have given Gardnerville much of its character. Across the street from the JT, the Overland Hotel, another Basque bar-restaurant — built in 1902 — carries on a unique local tradition. Every year, on the first Friday in June, the Carson Valley Nut Club meets and eats at the Overland.

"They have a bunch of drinks and they have dinner," said local author and historian Ray Smith, a club member. "Dinner is always mountain oysters." More specifically, the oysters come from sheep. "There are no officers, there are no minutes and there are no bylaws," Smith said of the men-only club of mostly longtime ranchers and their kids. "It started around the mid-1930s. It's a get-together. A bunch of ranchers in the early days thought it would be a good idea to get together and have dinner. Very few people know about it."

Elvira Cenoz, sixty-seven, the Spanish Basque who runs the Overland, has a problem. "You don't have too many sheep," Cenoz said with a laugh. "Every year the club is growing. There are two or three generations of families in it. But the sheep aren't growing."

Carson Valley is, with its subdivisions filled mainly with retirees, Lake Tahoe casino workers or state government employees in Carson City. "There was no suburban experience," Marie Lekumberry said. "Now it's all suburban."

The JT and Overland are links with the past. "It might have evolved, but that core of what a Basque restaurant was about still exists here," said J.B. Lekumberry. "It's not like we're just a dinner house. It's very much a social place."

Gardnerville's Basque establishments also come with reputations. "All your old restaurants were here, all your old bootleggers were here," said Neddenriep with a chuckle. "A lot of bootleg whiskey went from here to Reno. They couldn't drink it all here." Neddenriep's family operated the general store in Gardnerville for sixty-nine years.

Illegal booze was a popular Carson Valley product during Prohibition from 1920 to 1933. "The Carson Valley was considered one of the most flagrant bootlegging areas in the country," Smith said. "Every little canyon had a still. It was remote, but relatively close to population centers."

Regardless of legalities, whiskey from the stills was needed to stay in business,

Dollar bills decorate the ceiling in JT Basque Bar & Dining Room in Gardnerville.

On Gardnerville's main street, U.S. Highway 395, the vacant East Fork Hotel shows its age.

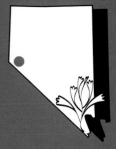

Fourth of July in Gardnerville

Raymond M. Smith is a longtime Carson Valley resident and author of books on the area. The excerpt about a turn-of-the-century Fourth of July is from Untold Tales of Carson, Eagle and Smith Valleys, Nevada.

Raymond M. Smith

By dusk almost everyone was thoroughly into the celebration — some with copious liquid libations, and all were again ready for the famous "Parade of the Horribles."

This distinctive Nevada affair was a traditional 4th of July highlight and almost every early day Nevada community boasted such a group. Formally they were known as the "Ancient Medieval and Modern Order of Horribles." They were usually circumspect and honored citizens of the community, but on this occasion, they were masked, usually "well-oiled" and unrepressed in action, clothing and attitude. Their own unique and highly individualistic parade was always the humorous highlight of the day.

The Horrible Parade gathering began at 5 p.m., announced by a tremendous clamor, the results of homemade cannons and black powder. This was the signal for the members and their paraphernalia to gather at one end of town for some sort of loose assemblage into a "parade formation." This was accompanied by much revelry, shouted imprecations, banging pots and other noise inducing instruments and general good fellowship. Sometimes a rousing chorus of "America the Beautiful" sung in German, or perhaps Paiute, was rendered as a proper first course. At any rate, the booming cannon was a signal for all the other celebrants to gather along Main Street from one end of Gardnerville to the other (three blocks) to watch the proceedings.

At the head of the procession was always the Grand Marshal, usually waving the "grand banner" of the society. This was usually a ragged grain sack attached to a sheep hook. The Marshal was suitably "guarded" by the formidable "flying artillery" — two large stovepipes mounted on manure spreaders, which intermittently belched salvos of black smoke and thunderous noise. The artillerymen manning these weapons were splendidly uniformed, each contrived from their wearer's imagination and what was available in their barnyards. These included bedpan helmets, assorted rags and the like.

said Marie Lekumberry, who has heard stories of that rough era. "There were some sheepherders making whiskey," she said. "People were just helping each other out. If you wanted to keep your (restaurant) open, you had to sell some liquor."

Jean Lekumberry, Marie and J.B.'s father, came to Carson Valley from the French Basque country in 1947 to herd sheep. He also cut hay at area farms and saved his money. On April 1, 1960, Jean and brother Pete bought the JT. When Jean died in 1993, Marie and J.B. took over the place and have been running it ever since.

The restaurant's initials don't stand for anyone in the Lekumberry family. JT is for Jaunsaras and Trounday, the restaurant's first Basque owners, who bought the place in 1954. "Confusing, isn't it?" J.B. asked with a laugh.

J.B. and Marie were raised to run the JT. "It's our home," said Marie, who studied and taught at the University of Nevada, Reno, but returned to the JT when Jean died. "We grew up here. That bar, that was like our living room. There is a real attachment. It's more than just a business."

J.B., thirty-four, and Marie, thirty-eight, never had a choice. "We were really raised by our dad to take this place over," said J.B., who oversees the kitchen. "We got the full concentration of Catholic Basque. You don't ever abandon the home. You might leave, but you never abandon it."

Owning the JT makes Marie and J.B. keepers of some Gardnerville history. They've restored the restaurant-bar, complete with a second-story balcony in front, using a 1910 photo as a blueprint.

"When we were little, old-timers would tell our dad, 'You know what this was when it was in Virginia City, don't you Jean?'" Marie said. "They used to say it was a cathouse. It's part legend." So is the Christmas Eve party, which started as a gathering

Elvira Cenoz, who runs the Overland Hotel, greets old friend Dotty Haman in the hotel's Basque dining room.

of family and friends at the JT. Today, it's a rock 'n' roll bash for the whole town.

"Everyone would stop by after midnight mass," J.B. said of the party's innocent beginnings. "When everyone hit twenty-one (years old), it turned into a party. Now it starts at eight or nine. Mass isn't a factor." But Christmas wouldn't be Christmas in Gardnerville without the JT. "It's all college kids coming home," said J.B. "Now we have somebody checking ID at the front door and you have Stevie Ray Vaughan screaming on the jukebox."

That is music to J.B.'s ears. Traditions are modified, but continue. Running the JT in its modern form lets J.B. keep a big part of himself in Gardnerville's past.

"I'm spoiled," he said. "I come to work where I was born and raised. Everyone comes to me. It's a consistent place. It's not eroding. All the old-timers still come here on Wednesdays for lunch."

The Overland Hotel's neon sign beckons locals and passing travelers.

History and traffic meet downtown

The first step being taken in downtown renovation in Gardnerville is to develop a public park and a parking lot close to the main street. It's the centerpiece for restoration.

"It's the village green," Town Manager Diane Pettitt said.

The park will be on the site of the town's former baseball field and rodeo grounds. Planning for park development started several years ago when the nearby Chichester Ranch was sold and turned into a subdivision. Now the town has regained control of the parkland after leasing it to Douglas County. Along with the park and parking lot, town planners want some side streets in the area and, they hope, commercial development.

"The Town Advisory Board is working very hard to put in a public parking lot down at the old rodeo grounds," said board member Tom Cook. "We should have something going on that before too long. You can't have business (downtown) if you don't have someplace to park."

Gardnerville's main downtown street is U.S. 395, where traffic flows heavy and fast. "We want to make it more people-friendly," Pettitt said. "We have a traffic signal there, so you can get across (the street) without getting yourself killed." But the area isn't designed for walking.

"Minden and Gardnerville have both been in this dilemma for thirty-five years," Cook said of Douglas County's side-by-side communities. "There's no place to park. Some people would love to go to these little stores. I think we'll get it solved but it costs money."

Gardnerville has a designated historical district along a stretch of U.S. 395 that starts near the Carson Valley Museum and includes downtown's distinctive cluster of Basque restaurants.

"We don't call it 'historic,'" Pettitt said. "It's the downtown vision plan." A vacant lot in the area soon will be filled with a hotel-casino. "It looks quite attractive," he said.

Across the street, one of Gardnerville's oldest structures, the JT Basque Bar & Dining Room, has been renovated by co-owners J.B. and Marie Lekumberry. Inside the restaurant are black-and-white photographs of the Lekumberry family, including J.B. and Marie's father, Jean, who came to Carson Valley from French Basque country in 1947 to herd sheep.

Bowhunter Larry Whitsitt removes arrows from his target during bow-and-arrow practice for the upcoming deer season.

Left: At the annual Kids' Fishing Derby in
Gardnerville, Jim Toles of Reno shows his three-
year-old daughter, Emily, how to handle a fishing
pole.
Above: Sam Suenaga of the Carson City Fly
Fishing Club prepares a pole for a contestant in
the Kids' Fishing Derby.

"Those kids at the JT have done a wonderful job," Cook said. "They have really improved the place."

Another successful restoration project in Gardnerville is the Carson Valley Museum and Cultural Center, which used to be the old Douglas High, built in 1916.

"It had become a white elephant," said Gardnerville resident Terri Hickey. "There was talk of leveling the old building for additional parking space."

The museum opened on August 19, 1995.

Hickey wants to see the downtown redeveloped along the lines of Victorian Avenue in Sparks. But U.S. 395 traffic makes pedestrian planning difficult. That's why residents and government officials have campaigned for years for a bypass to get all vehicles heading north and south out of

Gardnerville and Minden.

"Getting the bypass around town is the most important thing we can be looking at," Cook said. "More people are traveling U.S. 395. It's getting to be more of a main highway. They're coming up through here. We can't have it all funneling through the main drag of town."

Cook wants to see Douglas County designate redevelopment money for downtown. But a redevelopment district — which is different from a historical area — hasn't been created for downtown.

"The town hasn't formally asked the county to designate a redevelopment area," said John Doughty, county planning and economic development manager. North Carson Valley has a redevelopment district, and Doughty said something similar could be done in Gardnerville. "Creating a redevelopment district doesn't mean doing historic preservation," he said. "It's to use tax money from the district for improvements. It's going to take some time."

Swaps, luck built saddle collection

Welcome to the attic of Milos "Sharkey" Begovich. The wooden door at the top of the stairs squeaks loudly when opened. Inside is a cramped world of mementos and memories that Begovich can't find room for in the rest of his Sharkey's Nugget Casino, a downtown landmark on U.S. 395. Hundreds of saddles hang from the attic ceiling.

"There is so much history to some of these saddles," said the seventy-two year-old, who speaks in a gravelly boom. "A saddle is just a piece of leather. It all depends on whose butt sat on that piece of leather."

Begovich, who opened Sharkey's on January 1, 1971, paused to touch one of the saddles and tell its tale. The saddle isn't famous, but it has a story. They all do.

"I bought this saddle here from a local lady," said Begovich. "It was first prize in a trail ride in Santa Barbara. She'd never been on a horse. She said, 'I've got six more of them and this is the worst one I've got.'" Begovich turned and pointed to a pair of spurs mounted on a wooden plaque. They're more famous than the woman's saddle. "Those are the spurs John Wayne wore in the movie *Rio Bravo*," Begovich said.

"Sharkey"

Milos "Sharkey" Begovich collects portraits of famous Native American chiefs and hangs them on the walls of his Gardnerville casino.

Above: A bench outside Sharkey's spells out the rules.
Right: In a corner of the attic at Sharkey's, along with hundreds of saddles, a pair of John Wayne's spurs is "not for sale."

Downstairs in the main bar, a large glass case holds eighty-six of the casino's most famous saddles, including one owned by Wayne. Sharkey's is more than a casino — it's a museum, maybe one of northern Nevada's best.

"I never started collecting saddles until I came to Gardnerville," said Begovich, recalling the story of the first saddle. "I was in the bus station one day and this old cowboy comes in. He was going to another job. He threw his saddle down." Begovich looked at the saddle, which had started life as first prize in a Gillette, Wyoming, rodeo, July 4, 1909. "I said to the guy, 'What would it take to get that saddle from you?' He said, 'All it would take is a saddle that fits me. This one doesn't.' So, there was a saddle shop here at the time and I said 'We'll go in that saddle shop and see if they've got one that will fit you.' He went in there and he was happy. He found a saddle

that would fit him. I traded him."

The mass of mementos at Sharkey's contains a lot more than saddles. The walls of one dining room are covered with circus posters. Another is filled with more than 100 paintings of Indian chiefs, recognized by experts as one of the best such collections in the country.

"I had them painted one at a time by a guy who lived in Sparks," Begovich said of the artist who painted the chiefs in the 1970s from black-and-white photographs in books. "He was from China. He was just looking for something to make (money), to eat with."

Born of Serbian parents in California, Begovich was nicknamed as a child for heavyweight boxing champion Jack Sharkey, also a Serbian. In Gardnerville, he is an institution. Yearly, he celebrates "Serbian Christmas" according to the Serbian Orthodox calendar, in early January, with a free feast of roast goat, pig and other delicacies. Several thousand people show up to eat.

"He's a character," longtime Carson Valley resident and author Raymond M. Smith said.

For years, Begovich observed July 4 with an outdoor fight card known as the Cow Pasture Boxing Festival. His casino collection contains an array of posters and pictures from bouts both famous and obscure. Begovich has the gloves from a 1906 lightweight title fight in Goldfield between Joe Gans and Battling Nelson that lasted forty-two rounds before Gans won on a foul.

"I never worked at doing this," Begovich said of the collection. "What I happened to come across one way or another, I brought it (to the casino) and hung it up. Now I've had to cram everything into a little bit of space."

Sharkey's Nugget has been restored and renovated since an October 28, 1995, fire burned part of the roof. The collection was saved from the fire. One of the items in the downstairs bar is an authentic poster from Abraham Lincoln's presidential campaign. The upstairs banquet room has a bell sitting on a platform.

"The bell-making capital of the U.S. is Sandusky, Ohio," said Begovich, recalling the story of the bell. "An old guy was going back to visit somebody and he says, 'What do you want me to bring you from Sandusky?' I said, 'Bring me a bell.' He had a little pickup and he said, 'I wore out my back tires hauling that bell here.' So, I had to buy him a set of back tires, which wasn't a bad deal."

A mailbox on Centerville Road, just outside Gardnerville, suggests a horse-lover in the neighborhood.

Lockwood

R. Oden

In Lagomarsino Canyon are the remains of a stone house, built at the turn of the century — reputedly a bootlegger's rendezvous.

Split by the river, joined by a love of the land

Domenic Peri settled on a ranch near Lockwood in 1918. Now eighty-two, he lives in Reno but sometimes explores Lagomarsino Canyon with his three dogs.

IMPORTANT DATES

- Late 1800s: Lagomarsino family begins ranching in what would become Lockwood.
- 1916: Carl Lockwood buys Lagomarsino Ranch.
- 1917: Louis M. Lagomarsino dies.
- 1918: Constantino Peri moves from Dayton and establishes ranch.
- 1925: School opens, a shack erected over potato cellar.
- 1931: Schoolhouse built.
- 1951: One-room schoolhouse closes when enrollment drops to two students.
- 1967: Joe Conforte takes over Mustang Ranch brothel in nearby Mustang.
- 1971: Storey County passes ordinance clarifying status of Mustang Ranch as legal brothel.
- 1984: Gravel pit approved.
- 1985: Construction begins on Rainbow Bend subdivision.
- 1991: Hillside Elementary School opens.
- Jan. 1, 1997: New Year's flood results in removal of mobile home park from north side of the Truckee River.
- Jan. 7, 1998: Explosion at Sierra Chemical in Kean Canyon results in four deaths.

Domenic Peri stops his old pickup truck, steps down from the cab, lets three dogs jump out, looks around an isolated stretch of Lagomarsino Canyon and takes a deep breath.

Inhale, exhale. "Ahhhh!" Peri exclaims with a big grin. "Smell the air up here, the juniper trees; you can smell the aroma."

This is only a few miles from the Lockwood exit on Interstate 80, but the spot seems isolated. The pavement has been left behind. The road has become a dirt trail. No trucks are headed for the garbage dump or gravel pit. They're nearby, but can't be heard or seen.

Peri is home again. Now eighty-two, he lives in Reno, but he remembers when he used to ride horses in this canyon as a youngster. He looks across the canyon at the remains of a stone house built at the turn of the century. It's littered with the remains of modern society – broken bottles and other trash. The house wasn't Peri's, but he knows its story.

"The stone house was erected by a fellow named Bill Goodburn," said Peri, whose own family settled on a ranch in the Lockwood area in 1918. "He's buried there. It was a bootlegger's rendezvous. He was supposed to be mining. These fellows were supposed to be digging for gold. They weren't. They were making the hard stuff." Peri laughs and continues.

"I remember Goodburn," he said. "He had a horse and a buggy. He built another little log cabin. They also had a tunnel in the basement that went back into the hills. They made corn whiskey in there."

Bootlegging, apparently, was a tradition in the canyon.

The flood fuels the Lockwood-Rainbow debate

Wild horses roam through Lagomarsino Canyon near Lockwood.

The area surrounding Lockwood is known mostly for the dump, where Reno and Sparks residents take their garbage, and the Mustang Ranch, a legal brothel where people paid for other services before it closed in 1999.

"We have a freeway, a dump and a house of ill repute," Lockwood-area resident Susan Kershaw said with a chuckle. "That's our community."

That's true — but only to a point. First, the Mustang Ranch wasn't in the middle of Lockwood, but rather in Mustang, one exit farther east on the freeway.

"Do you know how Mustang got its name?" asked Peri. "This was way back in the early '30s. This fellow named Arnold started a service station over there. He made it out of stone. I was there. He was talking to my dad one day.

"Across the river there was a trail of horses coming down to the river to drink. Arnold says, 'I have to find a name for this station.' He says, looking at the horses, 'Why don't we name it Mustang?'"

More than the brothel, the freeway and the dump — located near the mouth of Lagomarsino Canyon — the Lockwood area is dominated by the Truckee River. The waterway splits the community in half, geographically and psychologically. To the south is the area's modern development —

Teacher inspires kids with an eye for art

Vincent van Gogh's painting of a vase full of flowers is OK, but David Tennis looks to more modern subjects for his art.

"I can draw Spiderman exactly," said the Hillside Elementary sixth-grader. "I really draw a lot." So does classmate Brenton Breeze. "He's really good," Brenton said of David's work. "I draw the Silver Surfer."

David and Brenton are two of the ten students in teacher Lynn Sumlin's class where art is just one of the subjects, but art is taken seriously.

For one assignment, the kids copied van Gogh's vase of flowers. Every year, Sumlin gives her class a picture of a van Gogh picture to reproduce.

"With older children, I work on more in-depth projects," Sumlin said of her sixth-graders. "Reproducing the great masters is not a five-minute project."

Along with van Gogh, the kids drew another vase with flowers. It was a live subject, removed from the desk of the school secretary long enough for Sumlin's artists to study it.

"You have to look at shapes and study the flowers," Brenton said. "You have to look for details." It was the same for the van Gogh reproduction in which David noticed something he thought was important.

"The cracks in the vase," he said. "There were cracks."

Pastel interpretations of a painting by Vincent van Gogh were done by Lockwood sixth-graders Brenton Breeze, top, and David Tennis.

David Tennis and Brenton Breeze

A herd of wild horses crosses the road to drink from a creek near the Lockwood dump. As many as fifty horses have been counted in Lagomarsino Canyon in a single afternoon.

the Rainbow Bend subdivision of about three hundred homes. Many of the residents commute to and from jobs in Reno and Sparks, about a five-minute drive.

Rainbow Bend is in Storey County. On the north side of the river is Washoe County, the site of Lockwood's combination bar/convenience store.

That also is where a cluster of mobile homes was located, wedged between the river and the freeway, until the New Year's flood of 1997 destroyed most of them. Rainbow Bend residents are quick to point out that the flood engulfed the opposite river bank, not theirs.

"We are really an unincorporated area of Storey County; this is Rainbow," said Linda Hoy, an executive for the subdivision developer. "It didn't get said very well during the flood. They said, 'Lockwood flooded.' Everybody thought they meant Rainbow Bend. We kept saying, 'Tell them Rainbow Bend didn't flood.'"

Blackie Simons has lived in the area since 1965. His mobile home is on the Storey County side of the river near Rainbow Bend, and he laughs about the Lockwood-Rainbow debate. "People over in Rainbow Bend, they don't like it, but they're in Lockwood too," Simons said. "I say, 'Where is Rainbow Bend? It's in Lockwood. Then, you live in Lockwood, don't you?'"

Even more than the geography and the dump, residents are concerned with the constant truck traffic coming off the freeway and through their community. "It's a huge problem," said Sandra Frost, a Rainbow Bend resident. "I was almost hit. Something is going to happen." But people seem to like living in the area. The community is in the country, reasonably quiet and close enough to Reno and Sparks.

"We have a little son right now and we don't want that," said Colleen Conley, who moved with her husband and son to the area after a shooting took place in their Reno neighborhood. "We have the security. We're all homeowners."

Conley lives on one side of the river, in Rainbow Bend, and works on the other, at the Lockwood Store and Bar. She has taken time to learn the area's history and can tell you about Carl Lockwood, the old-time rancher for whom the community was named.

The area's original ranch is gone now. It was owned by the Lagomarsino family in the late 1800s and purchased by Lockwood in 1916. The Peri family, which settled on a ranch in the Lockwood area in 1918, still operates the ranch.

"I haven't been up to the canyon in years," said Grace Lagomarsino, a Reno resident whose late husband, Mario, was a descendant of Lockwood's original family. The Lagomarsinos, according to Grace, came from an area near Genoa, Italy. Their hometown in the old country, she said, was named Lagomarsino. Grace remembers some of the history of the canyon, named after her husband's family. "That was one of the original routes to Virginia City," she said.

You can still reach Virginia City using the canyon's dirt road, about a sixteen-mile trip from Lockwood. Domenic Peri said he was told that in the days of the Comstock silver boom, the stagecoach took a day to get from Virginia City to what is now Lockwood, where the passengers, driver and horses spent the night at the Lagomarsino ranch. But what Peri remembers most from his own childhood were the smells, especially those from a tunnel built by the Lagomarsinos and later used by Lockwood.

"We used to go play in that tunnel," Peri said. "It's where they kept their salami and aged their cheese. The aroma of that salami — oh boy — and the cheese and the wine!"

Along with the smells, Peri remembers a sight that caught his attention as a boy: Carl Lockwood's new car. "In 1930, Lockwood bought a LaSalle roadster," Peri said. "It was red and charcoal, with real honest red leather seats. It had twenty-inch-spoke wire wheels. It had two spare tires in the front fender wells. It was magnificent!"

He probably couldn't drive it very far in Lagomarsino Canyon, which always has been best for horses, and now, four-wheel-drive vehicles. The trip is bumpy, but worth it.

"Isn't this canyon fascinating?" said Peri, one of nine children. "My dad used to have cattle in here. We used to come in on horseback. We'd pack a lunch. There was no one up there."

Domenic's younger brothers, Joe and

Bartender Colleen Conley works at the Lockwood Store and Bar and lives in Rainbow Bend.

Jim, run the Peri ranch in Lockwood. Things in the canyon have changed a little. "Now that big mountain is one gravel pit," Domenic Peri said. But you can leave the pit and dump behind for rugged terrain, history and one more of Domenic's stories — this one about hidden treasure in the canyon:

"There was nothing but gold and silver floating all over the place," he said. "There were a total of six banks in Virginia City. This robber robbed a bank of $300,000 and set off on horseback through the canyon to Lagomarsino. They captured him right at the ranch, but he didn't have the money. The story goes, according to my dad, that this robber either hid the money on the trail or had an accomplice that he handed the money over to. They never found the money."

Backers hope that an industrial park will put Storey in the big time

T he 21st century is under construction in Storey County. "It will be the largest industrial center in the U.S.," said Lance Gilman, a Reno developer who is creating the Tahoe/Reno Industrial Center near Interstate 80. "Storey County's millennium is about to change drastically."

For residents of nearby Lockwood and the rest of Storey County, the project is big — very big. "The development of the industrial park is the most significant thing, even going back a way," said County Commissioner Carl Trink. "I don't know of anything that could touch it." Perhaps the Comstock Lode — but that was a long time ago.

More recently, in September 1998, Gilman bought 102,000 acres on the north side of Interstate 80 at the Patrick Exit, about four miles east of Lockwood, and started planning the new development. His other projects include the Double Diamond residential and commercial complex in South Reno. On the land purchased from Gulf Oil, Gilman plans to devote 14,000 acres to the industrial park. The rest is hills and sagebrush.

Despite its Tahoe/Reno name, most of the park is in Storey County, with a section extending into Lyon County. "We want to keep it the way it is as much as we can," Kim Tun, Gilman's spokesperson, said of the rugged terrain. "We want to develop areas adjacent to I-80."

For Storey County, the industrial park could mean a huge boost in jobs, taxes and economic development. That is new for an area known mostly for legal prostitution at Mustang Ranch and Comstock history in Virginia City.

"Storey County has been very poor," Trink said. The public-private investment in the infrastructure amounts to twelve million dollars. The county put up $1.2 million, the state $2.5 million, and Gilman the rest. The area Gilman is developing sat empty for more than a decade, with little happening until he bought it.

"We envision creating a new millennium industrial park," said Storey County Planning and Building Administrator Dean Haymore. "This park is as big as the industrial areas in Reno and Stead put together. We've been working on this for twelve years. It's just starting to happen.

Dermody Properties of Reno bought a 210-acre piece of the park with plans for a

Rainbow Bend is a housing development beside the Truckee River, about ten miles east of Reno.

ten-building complex of warehouses and businesses. Construction of a 420,000-square-foot warehouse began in 1999 and Dermody started leasing space.

"It's larger than anything we have built in South Reno," said Dermody development director David Loring. "We believe the market exists for a very low-cost warehouse in that area." Along with Dermody, park occupants include Kaiser Aluminum and Hydroline, a hydraulic equipment manufacturer. Adjacent to the park is Kal Kan Foods, Incorporated.

"With the industrial park, we are looking at expanding our tax base," said Storey County Planning Commissioner Pat Shannon. "We're really trying to make this a big-time county."

Home brings a bit of the bayou to a sagebrush sea

Charlie Cheramie's lighthouse

C harlie Cheramie tells two tales about the old-time ship's wheel he used to make his kitchen table. "This is a genuine wheel that came off a steamboat on the Mississippi and the pilot was Mark Twain," Cheramie said with a grin.

Now comes the pause for effect, followed by the finish. "That's a better story than, 'I bought it at a thrift shop.'" He leaves you to figure it out. Did the wheel come from Mark Twain's steamboat or a second-hand store? It really doesn't matter. The wheel is unusual. Turning it into a tabletop makes it even more bizarre.

You could say pretty much the same thing for Cheramie's entire home. He and his wife Marie have created a nautical museum inside — except, that is, for the room that has been turned into a 1930s barber shop. On the outside — well, that needs to be explained one piece at a time.

Start with the lighthouse. That's what you see driving up the street. Twenty-two feet tall, it looks as if it should be sitting atop a big rock somewhere on the coast of Maine. It stands watch over Cheramie's lagoon which serves as sort of a front yard – an unusual front yard, just like the rest of the place. You

reach the other side of the lagoon by driving across a bridge. An island is in the middle.

"It's Jean Lafitte's pirate island," said Cheramie, who is Louisiana Cajun through and through. He pronounces it "Looziana." Born in Chauvin, Louisiana, he grew up on Bayou LaFourche.

"My dad was a fisherman and his father before him was a fisherman," said Cheramie, who spent his working life as a sales executive in California before retiring to northern Nevada in 1980.

Along with the pirate island, Cheramie's lagoon features a twelve-foot shrimp boat. "It's a copy of a shrimp boat from when I was a kid," Cheramie said. Everything in and around Cheramie's lagoon is almost life size. On one side is a Cajun fishing camp, on the other, a village with a church, hotel, saloon, general store and cafe — with a working kitchen.

The buildings are all made of stucco. They're not full size, but built to a scale where adults can move around inside, with a little bending over. The detail inside is amazing. The little church, complete with two pews and an altar, is copied from a seamen's chapel in Nova Scotia, to which Charlie Cheramie

A painted mask peers from inside an authentic deep-sea diving helmet in the Cheramie dining room. The diving outfit once was used for collecting sponges off the coast of Florida.

Charlie Cheramie stands on the deck of his Lockwood home outside the galley door of his almost-life-size shrimp boat model.

traces his ancestry.

The hotel has a lobby, complete with reception desk and room keys, and stairs you can climb to a second-story bedroom, with a bed. It reflects Cheramie's memories of the Monteleone Hotel in the French Quarter of New Orleans. The general store has a post office and fishing supplies for sale.

"The little store is from an uncle of mine I used to visit in Louisiana," Charlie Cheramie said. "The little saloon is a copy of the First and Last Chance Saloon in Jack London Square in Oakland. It's where Jack London wrote."

Building the village has taken some time, but Charlie and Marie enjoy the ongoing project. "I love to work with my hands," Charlie Cheramie said. "It's not finished. We have plans. The front of my home looks a little bit blank."

Inside the house — amid ship's wheels, hatch covers and fog horns discovered during a lifetime of searching flea markets and auction yards — Nick stands in one corner. He is a Greek sponge diver made by Marie Cheramie to fit inside the authentic canvas diving suit the couple picked up in Florida. The suit came with a brass helmet.

"I got a mask; I colored it a little bit," Marie said of the face inside the helmet. "I got a wig. I glued on its eyebrows and mustache."

Visitors still have one more thing to see — the barber shop with chair, clippers and all the rest — and Charlie Cheramie has one more story to tell: "I was in real estate in the San Francisco Bay area," he said. "I sold this man's house. He was a barber. He couldn't move until he sold the barber shop. "I had a buyer that wanted to move in now. That was a condition. "The barber shop equipment was for sale for $500. I was making $1,500 commission on the house, so I bought it from him. It's 1936 vintage."

It's perfect.

Lovelock

Tom Moura repairs his swather and Rosie Marcuerquiaga holds a variety of bolts in an alfalfa field on Moura's Lovelock ranch.

Heat, hay and history meet on main street

"If you can twist it three times and it breaks, then it's ready to bale," says Tom Moura, testing a handful of freshly-cut alfalfa from one of his fields.

When Mama Jean's Grill and Pastry Shop closed, Lovelock farmers mourned. The Main Street landmark had been their favorite gathering place for daily coffee, laughs and camaraderie. Before the doors closed on June 21, 1999, Mama Jean's was the place for scenes like this:

Pete Fundis can't find his chair. Sure, there's one in his usual spot, at the head of the first table, but it's not *the* chair. Fundis knows it. He looks around the restaurant suspiciously. Somebody's moved *the* chair, on purpose, just to get him going.

Fundis walks slowly from table to table, looking for his chair. Finally, Fundis finds it. He picks up the chair and brings it back to his place. His friends, local farmers gathered at the table for their morning coffee, roar with laughter. So does the waitress.

So did Jean Sherrer Hester, the town character who owned the place before it closed. Mama Jean's had lots of chairs, which all looked pretty much the same. But Fundis knew which one was his. "It had this rip down the side," said Fundis. The chair and the table were important parts of community life.

Lovelock is a farm town to its core, with acre after acre after acre of alfalfa growing in the heart of northern Nevada, just off Interstate 80 halfway between Reno-Sparks and Winnemucca.

Before Mama Jean's closed, Fundis and the farmers started arriving at 6:00 every morning to take their places at the table — always the same table — the one nearest the front door with eight chairs, including the one that belonged to Fundis.

By 6:45, most of the guys had arrived. By 8:00, they were all gone, headed for the rest of the day's work. At Mama Jean's, they talked about the weather — too cold. They talked about the price of hay — too low. Mostly, they drank coffee and teased one another.

"Everyone had their place at the table," Fundis said. "If you were a little late, you were out of luck." But Fundis isn't a farmer. He was the only one at the table not planting, growing or harvesting something. He's the retired owner of a trucking company.

"I'm the only foreigner," Fundis said with a grin. "I'm the only one that's not a DF." DF stands for "Damn Farmers" — which is what the group at the table called

Pete Fundis, right, shares a laugh and a morning cup of coffee with his farming friends, including Ricardo Arias, left.

John Aufdermaur sips a morning cup of coffee at Mama Jean's. The candle was an added touch when the power went out for about 20 minutes.

itself. The table wasn't just a table. It was the DF Table, until the group had to start looking for another table. A rumor was going around that somebody was going to buy Mama Jean's and turn it into a dinner house. A dinner house? That's not what the farmers wanted. They needed a place for morning coffee.

The closing of Mama Jean's was a sign of the times in Lovelock, where downtown business has been tough ever since 1983, when the freeway bypass was completed. Traffic on I-80 no longer has to stop in Lovelock.

"The freeway happened," said Hester, who gabbed for an hour after saying she didn't have time to talk. "That's been the downfall of little towns. You don't have to stop for gas."

Hester has seen a lot — and not just in Lovelock. Raised in Alabama, she drove to Alaska with her husband, a fisherman, in 1949 when Alaska wasn't a state but a frontier. When Hester's husband died a year later, she stayed in Alaska, doing what she calls "bush cooking" for construction crews, working in the most remote places of a remote land.

"You did the chain on the survey crew and you did the cooking," Hester said. "I'd be gone two or three months at a time. All your supplies were shipped in to you. You didn't just go to the market. When we did the last job, we were seventy-five miles from the nearest village." After twenty-five years, Hester finally left Alaska, looking for a place where the weather was a little nicer. She ended up in Lovelock in 1974.

"I saw this house," she said, "and I stopped right here. I bought it that day and slept on the floor that night. Lovelock was a booming little town. All the bars were open, all of them on Front Street."

Farmers take the long view. Most of them have been in the area most of their lives.

"I'd say Lovelock in about ten years will be back," said Larry Irvin, a DF, mentioning growth in other small northern Nevada communities. "Look how Fernley is going. You've got to get the corridor between Fernley and Reno built up, then the corridor between Fernley and Fallon, then they'll start out in smaller places. They'll have some big company that can't do what it wants to do around Reno, then it will come to a small town like this."

Two graduates find rewards of expression in the arts

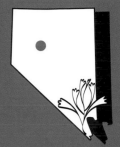

R uth Knight is a professional. Well, not really, at least in her own eyes. But she earned sixty dollars. That's what an art-lover paid for her sculpture of a boy on an elephant — Knight's first sale.

The piece by Knight, who graduated from Pershing County High School in 1999, was part of a show at the Governor's Mansion in Carson City. The young sculptor isn't planning a career in art. Now a freshman at Ricks College in Idaho, she plans to major in elementary education. "I've thought about illustrating children's books," she said.

John Jansen, also a Pershing County graduate and artist, specializes in "fantasy" paintings. "Wizards and castles," said Jansen, who had a variety of paintings and drawings in a recent Lovelock youth art show. "I like to do that kind of stuff."

Jansen *is* planning a career in art. "I want to get a double major, probably graphic art, then a science," he said before starting his first year at Brigham Young University in Utah. "After working as a graphic artist, I'd like to go back to school and get a doctorate in art, then teach. That way I can work as an artist."

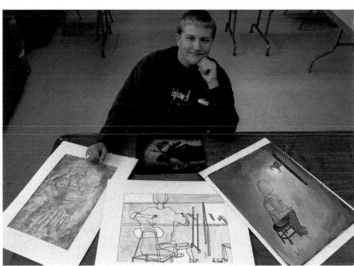

Top: Budding artist Ruth Knight displays some of her work at Pershing County High School.
Bottom: John Jansen shows his sketches at Pershing County High School.

Before Mama Jean's Grill and Pastry Shop closed its doors in 1999, Jean Sherrer Hester, left, and Belinda Smith used to joke with their customers.

Until that happens, people worry about the price of hay and the temperature outside. "What's the forecast for the weather?" Ricardo Arias, another DF asked. The high is supposed to be somewhere in the mid-seventies.

"It's eighty degrees out there somewhere," Gerald Munk said.

For Lovelock farmers, *eighty* is the magic number. It's warm enough for the alfalfa to grow fast and for bees to pollinate the plants, providing seed to sell and use for next year's crop.

"Eighty is better than seventy and ninety would be better," Irvin said. "When it's a hundred, we bitch that it's too hot. The price of hay is probably more important than heat." The price is down around Lovelock, mostly because of weak currency in Japan, where the farmers usually export a lot of alfalfa.

"Last year, the cheapest hay I sold was $105 a ton," said Bing Wesner, a DF regular. "This year, you get $40 for it. The Asian dollar went so bad, our export went to nothing. It's down to probably ten percent of normal."

On top of that, cotton prices dipped.

"Everybody in California, instead of planting cotton, planted hay," Wesner said. "That added to the hay supply. Demand went down and supply went up. Grain did the same thing. Two years ago, it was $160 a ton. Last year, we got $70." But Wesner keeps on planting. So do the rest of the farmers.

Pershing County has other businesses, such as mining. One company, Eagle-Picher, is a leading employer in the county. The county also has the state prison, which opened in 1995.

Farmers have been here for a while. The first farmers settled the area in the second half of the nineteenth century. Many of those pioneers came from Portugal and are remembered every year — usually during Memorial Day weekend — at the Portuguese Festa in Lovelock.

"The tradition was that back in the 1200s there was mass starvation in Portugal," said Tom Moura, a lifelong Lovelock farmer and descendant of one of the Portuguese pioneers. "The queen offered her crown and all her jewels if ships would come and rescue the country with food. They did come. So this was just a festival of thanksgiving."

Moura's ancestor, Manuel Moreira, came to Nevada in the late 1800s. His father, Manuel Moura, arrived in 1920. "I went to UNR for school," said Tom Moura. "That's as far from Lovelock as I've ever gone."

Moura isn't one of the DFs, but his situation is similar. "That's our dilemma this year," he said, pointing to bales of hay stacked near one of his fields. "Piles and piles of hay sitting here. It can't sit there forever. We've got this new crop coming. You don't want this to compete with the new crop. That's last season's crop. It doesn't do us any good, but I don't know what we can do."

Moura would like to see some kind of large farming business, such as a dairy, start in the area and buy local hay. "That's my side of the thing," he said. "We need an outlet for our products. We sell to California, we get a freight bill. We need something like a dairy, a local buyer."

Lovelock farmers get multiple crops from their alfalfa fields, cutting hay four times a year — if the weather's right. "We had a pretty good little frost this morning," Moura said. "It just kind of stunts the growth for a day — as long as we get some warm weather."

Alfalfa grows in abundance around Lovelock because the Rye Patch Reservoir was built in the 1930s, allowing farmers to control the flow of the Humboldt River and irrigate their fields. "Rye Patch was really our savior for this valley," Moura said.

Celina Galindo, a freshman at Pershing County High School, lives on the Star Creek Ranch where her father, Salvador, has been the manager for seventeen years. For Galindo, it's a ninety-minute bus ride to school in the morning and home in the afternoon.

"We study on the bus for tests," said Galindo, who also works in a Lovelock

Coffee and conversation — especially about crops and the weather — are part of the morning tradition for Lovelock farmers.

child-care center. "After school, I sleep or do my homework." On weekends, she has the ranch. "If my dad needs help, sometimes I go out and ride with him, gathering cows. It's kind of peaceful, but sometimes we get bored — like in the summer, if we don't do anything."

Sometimes, when the farmers meet over coffee, the talk turns from hay prices to beef commercials. The television ads urging viewers to eat more meat are running jokes among the DFs. The farmers, who also raise cattle, are assessed a small percentage of their beef sales to finance the ad campaign.

"You pay a dollar a head, then they put that ad on where they throw a steak on a barbecue and everybody's supposed to run to the market and buy meat," Irvin said with a chuckle. Then the talk turns to other questions, such as where to meet for coffee.

"Good restaurants have calendars on the wall," said Fundis. "I don't know why. The more calendars, the better the restaurant."

Lovelock's courthouse on Main Street is thought to be the only working round one in the nation.

Quirky round courthouse tells a tale of two counties

Justice is supposed to be blind. It comes with a few more quirks in the Pershing County Courthouse, built in 1921. The court has no jury box, but rather a semi-circle in the middle of the room where jurors sit facing the judge.

"You have to stay awake; the judge is looking right at you," said Jeanie Norcutt, deputy court clerk for the past twelve years, "but I've seen them sleeping in the front chairs and the back chairs."

The courthouse is round — one of the most unusual public buildings in the state and in the nation. "You don't see buildings like this anymore," said Pershing County Recorder Darlene Moura. Inside, seats for spectators form a large semi-circle between the jury enclosure and the interior wall. That not only puts the jurors in front of the judge, but in the middle of the audience.

Moura's office, along with those belonging to other county officials, used to be along the hallway circling the courtroom until they moved across the street in 1999. Now their offices are in a brand-new office complex, but some were reluctant to move out of the unusual courthouse, leaving it to the judges, lawyers and jurors.

"I have mixed emotions," said Sharron Montes, who works in the Recorder's Office. "It's a unique building." Montes misses the tourists who showed up at her door, wanting to see the courtroom.

Along with other county workers and Lovelock residents, Montes speculates about whether the Lovelock courthouse is the only round one in the country. Locals believe it could be the only one still in use. A courthouse built in Bucks County, Pennsylvania, in 1960 has round and rectangular sections.

"To my knowledge, Lovelock's is the only working round courthouse in the country," said resident Roger Mancebo. Lovelock got a round courthouse because Winnemucca received a square one.

Early in the twentieth century, Pershing County didn't exist. Lovelock and the ranches that dominated the surrounding area were part of giant Humboldt County, with Winnemucca as the county seat. In 1918, the county courthouse in Winnemucca burned down. At the same time, Lovelock citizens were complaining about paying taxes and seeing the money spent in Winnemucca. They wanted their own county. In 1919, the state legislature created Pershing County, named

The jury box is in the center of Lovelock's circular Pershing County Courthouse.

for General John "Black Jack" Pershing, commander of U.S. forces in World War I.

Next, Lovelock wanted a courthouse. Famous Reno architect Frederick J. DeLongchamps, who designed many of the state's most recognized buildings, was hired by Humboldt County to design a new courthouse in Winnemucca. He also was hired by Pershing County to build one in Lovelock.

"The plans were almost identical," Mancebo said of the Pershing and Humboldt courthouse designs. "When Lovelock got the plan back, they were very upset. They said they didn't want to have anything to do with the Humboldt County Courthouse. They challenged DeLongchamps to have something a little bit different and that's how we ended up with the round courthouse."

That's one version of the story. Another is that DeLongchamps simply decided, on his own, to design something distinctive for Lovelock, so he patterned the Pershing courthouse after a Roman temple, the Pantheon.

Either way, the courthouse at the top of Main Street in Lovelock catches your eye. The building is topped by a large dome, which can play tricks with acoustics inside.

"When it rains, it sounds like a downpour because of the echo," Norcutt said. Some say that's enough to keep the jury awake.

A rainy street in downtown Lovelock is seen from inside the Pershing County Courthouse,

An old wagon symbolizes Lovelock's farming roots.

Lovelock residents optimistic about the future

First impressions of Lovelock depend upon which way you turn your head at the town's only stoplight. Look west up Main Street and the picture looks pretty prosperous. The unique Pershing County Courthouse —a round building — sits atop the street. The post office, utility company and other businesses stretch in a neat block from the courthouse to the intersection.

"I picked this spot right here because it's a one-stop shop," said Jeri Fredericks, who opened Jeri's Unique Boutique near the courthouse in 1999. "It's kind of right in the general area. Every morning people park at ten o'clock. They go to the post office; they pay their power bills. Women from the courthouse come during lunch."

Look east down the rest of Main Street and the sight isn't so nice. The railroad tracks are at the foot of the street. The view finds a closed casino and a closed restaurant.

"I feel we've gone so far down, I don't see how we can recover," said longtime resident Glenda Seibert. "When I was a kid we had clothing stores, dime stores, a bowling alley, a movie theater. All those things are just melting away."

Lovelock has struggled ever since the freeway bypass opened in 1983, allowing motorists to drive between Reno-Sparks and Winnemucca without going through the small farm town. "I think that hurt us badly," Seibert said. "Before, people had to come through town. Now, when you're on the freeway and all you see are these raggedy buildings back here, you just go right on by."

The train doesn't stop anymore in Lovelock, a town founded by the railroad. Civic leaders hope to improve the lower end of Main Street by restoring the old depot and turning it into a Chamber of

A five-week-old puppy is one of the new arrivals on Tom Moura's ranch.

Rosie Marcuerquiaga says she has been cutting hay in the Lovelock area for the past fifty years. Here she's driving Tom Moura's swather.

Commerce office or visitor center.

When it comes to the future of Lovelock, some of the town's most optimistic people are kids. "New businesses open as old ones close," said Alecia Collins, a student at Pershing County High School.

Other students list the new attractions in town. "We've got a Taco Bell and a McDonald's," Cheri Belanger said. "We never had those before."

Lisa Christofferson comes up with one: "A Fashion 200 opened."

Lovelock's condition depends on your viewpoint.

"Personally, I'm very optimistic," said Librarian Jeanne Munk. "People think General Motors is going to come in here and put in a new plant. No, that's not going to happen. Growth is going to be slow."

Rosa Galindo, left, and Benje Robles cram for a final in the hallway of Pershing County High School in Lovelock. Both students are honor society seniors. They will graduate in 2000.

Minden

Grazing near Minden, these cows become part of the scenery.

Minden farms lose ground to city folk

One brown-faced bull stands out in a crowd of black-and-white dairy cows at Milky Way Farms in Minden.

Houses are replacing cows on what used to be farmland in Carson Valley, where the way of life is changing from rural to suburban.

"There's no agricultural future here," said Crystal Hellwinkel, sixteen, whose family operates one of only two dairy farms left in the valley. "All the people are moving in. We're getting crowded out."

Once, Carson Valley had many dairy farms. A short time ago, the number fell to a mere dozen, but Crystal's father, Chris, a third-generation dairy farmer in the valley, wants to stay.

"I've been in it all my life," said Chris Hellwinkel, who milks 150 cows twice a day. "I'll keep it going as long as I can hang on."

The family has discussed moving to Idaho, or to somewhere else that's not filling with subdivisions and residents who dislike sharing their new neighborhoods with old cows and dodging slow-moving farm machinery on the roads.

"When the tractor's on the road, people don't have enough patience to wait," said Crystal Hellwinkel, who wants to become a doctor, not a farmer. "You can tell they're all from the big city. People don't like the cows

— the smells and stuff."

Douglas County's human population has risen from 28,810 to 41,420 since 1991. Many of the newcomers live in subdivisions such as the Gardnerville Ranchos, which has about 10,000 people.

"We have a lot of retirees," said Bob Spellberg, manager of the Gardnerville Ranchos General Improvement District. "We have a lot of people who work up at (Lake Tahoe)." Many are in the Stateline casino business. They aren't farmers.

Dick Bonebrake is a Carson Valley resident who isn't a farmer, but he doesn't mind the cows or their smells. "I'm not a big open space advocate," Bonebrake said, "but I love the ranches. I love the smell of them. I think we do need some kind of a growth control. One thing I'm against is everybody throwing up fences around their yards. People talk about open space but they live in boxes."

Craig Witt sells them fertilizer. That's how Witt, forty-three, who used to milk cows, keeps his farm in business. "We have lousy soil," Witt said of the front and back yards in Carson Valley. "When people used to come to buy manure, instead of turning

IMPORTANT DATES
- 1906: Town founded on land owned by H.F. Dangberg Jr., as the last stop on the line for the Virginia & Truckee Railroad. The daily train leaves Reno at 8:30 a.m., arriving in Minden at 10:30 a.m.
- 1907: Minden flour mill opens next to the railroad tracks.
- 1908: Minden creamery opens.
- Oct. 20, 1909: The Carson Valley Farmer's Bank opens.
- 1912: The Carson Valley Improvement Club, a building listed on the National Register of Historic Places, opens for dances and other town activities.
- May 1912: The C.O.D. Motor Company opens. It remains in operation as one of the country's oldest family-owned car dealerships.
- 1916: Douglas County seat moved from Genoa to Minden.
- June 11, 1917: Grand opening of the Minden Inn.
- 1920: Businessmen form the Minden Commercial Club as a town governing board.
- 1961: Don Bently moves from Berkeley, California, and starts Bently Nevada, a worldwide engineering company.
- 1966: U.S. 395 made a four-line highway through town.
- 1969: Bently Nevada acquires the creamery and the flour mill for corporate offices.
- 1975: New Douglas High School opens in Minden.
- 1979: Douglas County gives Minden legal status under the state's unincorporated town law.
- Aug. 10, 1984: Carson Valley Inn and hotel casino opens.
- October 1993: Douglas County acquires Minden Inn for government offices.

them away, I'd say, 'Yeah, I'll load you.' We'd have people come with ten pickups." Then suddenly Witt, who filled the suburban trucks with fertilizer between milking cows, hit on a new business.

"I started realizing what they wanted," he said. "They wanted nice fine stuff to spread in their gardens. Business was starting to pick up. I said, 'Some day, the manure will be worth more than the milk.'" So, in 1998, Witt sold his herd of 350 milk cows. He still raises cows for a dairy in Yerington, but his new business makes compost to spread in the valley's suburban yards. He also runs farm tours for kids and has a gift shop for their parents.

"We looked at selling the farm, but we don't want to sell the farm," said Witt, who owns 160 acres and leases another 140. "We created these other businesses to be part of our farm to make it sustainable, to make it work." Witt charges $4 per child for his farm tours. Annual business increased from 1,200 kids to 6,500 in 1998. "I see us being a model for a farm, showing how farmers interface with urban change," he said.

The valley's most modern farmer is probably Bently Nevada, a worldwide engineering company based in Minden that is growing a variety of crops on 8,000 acres. Ironically, the headquarters for Bently's engineering operations is the brick creamery building in Minden constructed in 1916 for the valley's growing dairy business. It closed in 1961. Early in this century, the creamery exported butter overseas. Now, Bently does the same with precision instruments. Farming is a relatively recent company focus.

"Mostly, we improved our irrigation methodology so we use much less water than the typical rancher around here does," said

company boss Don Bently, a scientist who grew up an Iowa farm boy and now specializes in equipment for industry. "We use flood irrigation only as a last resort. We sprinkle the soil with overhead sprinklers. There's nothing really fancy or novel about what we're doing, just good common sense." Bently raises garlic, alfalfa, oats and wheat. He also produces animal feed and compost. "I don't really treat it as experimental," he said. "It's how to produce profitable crops. It's not a playboy ranch."

Still, there are some things modern farming can't replace. Witt, who has worked with Bently, talked about his days growing up in Carson Valley: "My grandfather had a 1965 Chevrolet truck and we'd go down for the afternoon milking. The cows walked down the road. Old Petunia, she was the one I could ride. You waited for her all the time. My grandfather, he always had oranges. We'd eat these oranges; we'd talk about life."

A rooster keeps a watchful eye on visitors to Milky Way Farms.

Thomas McKenzie, left, Ryan Graves and Doug Carr, in front, play catch with a football in Minden Park.

Minden artist looks at development

About the artist:

Paul F. Ford Jr. of Minden has been a teacher at Carson High School since the fall of 1978. He has designed and conducted a beginning through advanced art program that uses a wide range of two- and three-dimensional media. In 1986-87, he taught painting and art history at Queensferry High School in Edinburgh, Scotland, through the Fulbright Exchange Teacher Program. His work has appeared at numerous exhibitions across the region and he has been active in the community.

Artist's philosophy:

My current work represents an ongoing series that covers the last five years. My influences include Native American basketry, Tibetan sand painting and conceptual art. Each work is composed of found materials adhered to wooden frames.

The colors are naturally occurring soils from Nevada's central region and Great Basin. The plant fiber woven and thatched into the surfaces also has been gathered in the same region. My overriding concern in creating these images is to focus attention on the visual impact development has had upon Nevada's landscape. Historical architectural footprints and portals have been used to frame the inevitability of this process.

Artist's comments about this work:

This "Footprint" artwork of Western Nevada Community College's new Douglas County Campus in Minden, was created with native soils, milkweed and marsh reeds to form a Byzantine octagon; the clouds over Job's Peak are billow altocumulus. One element which follows rapid urbanization is the creation of institutions of higher learning. WNCC opened this new campus in 1998.

Minden artist Paul Ford used native soils, milkweed and marsh reeds to create this octagonal piece. Photo by Tim Dunn

MINDEN

- Population in 1998: 6,533 (26 percent under 18, 38 percent 18-44, 24 percent 45-64; 12 percent 65-plus; 50 percent male, 50 percent female).
- Population in 2003: (projected)7,425.
- Median income: $41,680.
- Total retail sales: $38.261 million.

- Claim to fame: It was a planned community, surveyed and laid out before the first residents arrived.

- How it got its name: Town founder H. F. Dangberg Jr., named it Minden after his family's home in Germany.

- Local legend: H. F. Dangberg Jr., who created the town in 1906 as a stop for the Virginia & Truckee Railroad, which he used to ship beef, grain and wool from his Dangberg Land & Livestock Co. in the Carson Valley.

Town keeps its sense of self

From the top of a silo, Craig Witt can survey all the land on his compost and dairy farm in Minden.

C rystal Hellwinkel is a Carson Valley kid. She lives on a farm, attends Douglas High School in Minden and doesn't see any difference between the valley's twin towns, Minden and Gardnerville.

"I don't ever remember knowing where Gardnerville stops and Minden starts," said Hellwinkel, sixteen.

Matt Wilcks, sixteen, is another Carson Valley kid. He goes to Douglas High and lives in Minden. He thinks he notices a difference.

"I see Gardnerville as bigger, more of a high-tech type place, more citylike, more buildings," Wilcks said. "Minden is more gas and groceries."

Kolt Clore, another teenager at Douglas High, calls the two communities simply "town."

Gardnerville and Minden bump into each other on U.S. 395 in Douglas County. Motorists have to watch closely for the sign separating the two. The whole thing, complete with its growing number of fast-food restaurants and strip malls, looks like one place. Maybe more important, it feels like one place to many longtime residents.

"They're basically all one town now," said Matt's father, Todd Wilcks, thirty-nine, who, like his son, went to Douglas High and, like his son, was an offensive lineman on the football team. "There isn't much difference." But harmony is a relatively recent development.

"There was no love lost," said Guy Rocha, the state archivist and an expert on Nevada history. "It was pretty hostile. It's changing as we move into the 21st century."

Don Hellwinkel, seventy-six, who operates the historic C.O.D. Motor Co. in Minden, made sure he was never alone in Gardnerville as a kid. "I wouldn't dare go to Gardnerville without one or two friends," he said. "I'd get beat up. We didn't like them and they didn't like us."

But J.P. Lekumberry, thirty-four, co-owner of the JT Basque Bar & Dining Room in Gardnerville, recalls a friendlier rivalry. "We'd go down to the park and play football against the Minden boys," said Lekumberry, a Gardnerville native. "Most people here haven't lived here long. They don't know there's a Gardnerville and a Minden."

Officially, Minden and Gardnerville have remained apart, both unincorporated with their own town boards. Unofficially, they continue to be somewhat distinct, despite the growth that has fused them geographically. In 1964, 1966 and again in 1979, the combined-town issue was raised by local officials, but nothing happened.

"I think even now you would have a hard time combining the towns," said longtime Minden resident Ray Smith, who has written several books about the area and its history. "Even though they don't know why."

Craig Witt talks to his wife, Karen, on a two-way radio after checking his crop of red worms at Milky Way Farms in Minden.

Tom Cook, chairman of the Gardnerville Town Board, said he knows why. "One was a cow town and one was a sheep town," he said. "All the Basques came to Gardnerville and all the cow people came to Minden."

Smith pointed out another historic difference, describing the local atmosphere during the 1920s: "There was no booze in Minden, except for certain specific places. For a drink, you went to Gardnerville. That was the sin town. That's where the bootlegging went on."

The wet-dry gap was bridged long ago. Today, the biggest difference between Minden and Gardnerville — the reason they were, are and probably always will be separate — no longer exists. That was the railroad. H.F. Dangberg, Jr. wanted one. He was the biggest man in the Carson Valley when the 19th century became the 20th. To get a railroad, he created Minden in 1906. Gardnerville already was there, one mile to the south.

"Here comes another little town," said Wynne Maule, a Minden native and local historian. "It was all laid out and surveyed. That makes it a planned town, right from the start." Residents of Gardnerville, established in 1879, didn't like it.

"It was competition for the railroad," said Rocha. "It left a long-standing competition between the two communities, with people feeling very strongly that you identify them with the community they live in."

Gardnerville's business leaders wanted the Virginia & Truckee Railroad, which connected Reno-Sparks and Carson City, to serve their town. Dangberg, whose Dangberg Land & Livestock Co., owned vast stretches of Carson Valley, wanted the V&T to serve him.

"Dangberg was a crusty old S.O.B," Smith said.

Gardnerville citizens offered the V&T right-of-way and a depot location, for a price. Dangberg gave the V&T the same things, across his land and in his town, for nothing.

"In essence, he told the V&T, 'You stop at what will become the town of Minden and I'll give you the right of way,'" Maule said. "He owned most of the right of way from Carson City."

So, when the railroad was extended from Carson City it stopped in Minden, never going the extra mile to Gardnerville.

"He became the principal person," Rocha said of Dangberg, who needed the railroad to ship his grain, beef and wool. "He had a greater amount of control because of the way he engineered the railroad, with the terminus in Minden instead of Gardnerville."

Minden was Dangberg's company town. It was named after his family's home village in Germany. Gardnerville was originally settled by Danish emigrants; Minden, by Germans. Dangberg wanted Minden to be a

Minden's historic flour mill anchors the town.

dry town, at least to begin with.

"When they put the town in, they put in very severe deed restrictions," Smith said. "It was primarily against liquor. Dangberg was very much against bars. They didn't have zoning (laws), so they deed-restricted."

Minden's streets were straight. They still are. There was a town square. It's still there. There were brick buildings to grind wheat into flour, to process milk, to make butter and store goods. They still exist, many of them converted to office space by the valley's new giant, the world-wide engineering company Bently Nevada, which also owns large tracts of valley land, including what used to be Dangberg ranch properties. About the only thing missing from the modern Gardnerville-Minden landscape is the V&T Railroad, which went out of business in 1950. A franchise restaurant sits at the approximate location of the depot along U.S. 395.

What has been added is people and homes, lots of them.

"There is such an influx of newcomers,

they look at it and say, 'It doesn't mean much to me,'" Rocha said of the Minden-Gardnerville history.

Overall, Douglas County now has 41,420 people, most of whom live in subdivisions such as Gardnerville Ranchos, a self-contained community sprouted in the nearby desert.

"I came up in 1975," said one resident, Bruce Nystrom, who arrived in Carson Valley from Los Angeles. "I was sick and tired of L.A. Now you can see urban sprawl everywhere."

The kids see something else, a loss of tradition. They say fewer people attend local events such as Douglas High's homecoming football game and the Christmas tree lighting ceremony in the Minden town square.

"People move here and they don't know anybody, so they just stay home," said Matt Wilcks. All the changes are enough to make the fourth-generation Minden native want to get out of town. "I'll probably end up moving somewhere else," he said. "I'd like to (stay), but I probably won't."

Resident recalls how a handshake sealed a deal

Don Hellwinkel knows there's a shiny high-tech office waiting for him in the C.O.D Motor Company's new showroom, but Hellwinkel, seventy-six, is in no hurry to move. When Hellwinkel does, an era will end. So the modern office sits vacant and Hellwinkel stays in the old brick building on Esmeralda Avenue. For now, it remains headquarters for one of the state's most historic businesses.

"We're pretty proud of our heritage," said Hellwinkel, who manages to be gruff and friendly at the same time. But Hellwinkel, who, with brother Dan, operates a car dealership and garage that opened in 1912, figures history won't help his son Robert much when it comes to maintaining a small family-owned operation in the 21st century.

"We're going to have a hell of a time surviving," said Don Hellwinkel, who remembers when deals were made with a handshake and a drink instead of a signature and a credit check. Hellwinkel's office is a monument to a lot of good old days. He sits behind a cluttered desk and across from an old-fashioned oil furnace that stands in the middle of the room with a pipe leading to the ceiling.

"That's a 'sparky stove,'" Hellwinkel said. "All the old ranch houses had them. It's been here all my life. That old smoke stack is a fire hazard."

The scene is something out of a 1940s black-and-white movie.

"Don is in the same old office his dad used," said Wynne Maule, a Minden native who has written a book about the town's history. "He's comfortable there. You go in

Don Hellwinkel stands in the doorway of the old brick building that houses his Minden garage.

The historic C.O.D. Motor Co. harkens back to another era of old-fashioned service.

there and it looks like it did 50 years ago. About the only change is, there's a computer sitting there."

Hellwinkel as a kid polished Clark Gable's car. Now he does have a computer and he also has a 1912 cash register, complete with a small slab of marble above the money tray. Once upon a time Hellwinkel's father, Fred "Brick" Hellwinkel, bounced silver dollars on the marble. A genuine dollar made a distinctive ringing sound when it hit the slab.

"It's the only way they could see if it was a real silver dollar or not," Don Hellwinkel said.

The original owner of C.O.D. was Clarence Oliver Dangberg, a member of one of Carson Valley's most prominent early 20th century families. (The C.O.D. stands for Clarence Oliver Dangberg, not "cash on delivery.") Dangberg used to keep two jugs of moonshine whiskey in a small bucket called the "pickle barrel."

"When you bought a car, you had a drink of shine and shook hands," Hellwinkel said. The old bucket is still in the garage area behind Hellwinkel's new office. One more reminder of the past.

Brick Hellwinkel was the C.O.D.'s mechanic. Later, when Dangberg didn't have enough money to pay his wages, he became a partner in the business and took over the company in 1936. Don Hellwinkel grew up in his father's office.

Hellwinkel's C.O.D., one of the country's oldest family-run Chevrolet dealerships, for years was the only lifeline for motorists stranded on the highway between Reno and Bishop, California.

"He'd go tow cars all night," Don Hellwinkel said of Brick. "Sometimes he'd take me out with him to keep him awake."

While he talks, Hellwinkel can sit in his office and look across Esmeralda Avenue at the Minden Inn, which now houses Douglas County offices. It used to be one of northern Nevada's grandest hotels. Clark Gable would stay there when he needed an escape

Michael Gilligan, a twenty-five-year-old chainsaw artist, created this twenty-foot statue from a dead cottonwood stump on the west side of Minden Park in November of 1998. It took him eight days to sculpt his creation, which he donated to the town. He has since moved to New Orleans.

from Hollywood. Hellwinkel, the kid always hanging around the garage, made seventy-five cents for washing and waxing the movie star's black LaSalle.

"It was the place to go in western Nevada," Hellwinkel said of the Minden Inn. "A lot of movie people came here." Many of them wanted to go fishing, and they'd take the local kid. "A big wheel with MGM — I can't remember his name — he knew I liked to fish," Hellwinkel said. "He would pay for the privilege of going fishing with me."

But now the movie stars are gone and the Minden Inn is home to government bureaucrats, not Hollywood celebrities.

"I have a lot of uncertainty, any (car) dealer will tell you that," said Don's son Robert, who works in the new showroom. "The retail side is changing. There are so many more resources available to consumers." Don and Robert are trying to figure out how to succeed in the face of modern auto malls and a future that includes car

sales by computer.

"General Motors and Chrysler want us in a new building," said Don Hellwinkel, who is back to work after suffering a heart attack in 1998. "We won't be (in the old office) more than two more years."

The Old Minden Inn now houses Douglas County government offices.

Paradise Valley

Early morning sun illuminates Paradise Valley's Stonehouse Country Inn.

Far from the rest of the world, this rural community preserves its past

Manager Nita Kennedy hands bread to sixth-grader Meganne Cone, an after-school helper at Paradise Valley Mercantile.

IMPORTANT DATES

- **1863: Prospectors enter valley searching for minerals in surrounding hills. Miner W.M. Gregg returns to start hay ranch.**
- **1864: Fredrick William Stock establishes ranch.**
- **1866: C.A. Nichols establishes town of Paradise Valley. Fort Winfield Scott built.**
- **1868: Flour mill built.**
- **Feb. 6, 1871: Post office established.**
- **1903: Auditorium Hotel built.**
- **1935: Auditorium Hotel destroyed by fire.**
- **1973: "The Haunted West" movie features Paradise Valley.**
- **1980: "Buckaroos in Paradise" exhibition about ranching in Paradise Valley opens at Smithsonian Institution's National Museum of American History in Washington, D.C.**
- **1983: "The American Cowboy" Library of Congress exhibit features Paradise Valley.**

C ody Blasengame and Meganne Cone show up at the Paradise Valley Mercantile on Tuesday to help Nita Kennedy put away the weekly delivery of milk and bread. Nine-year-old Cody and Meganne, eleven, don't work at the little store, but at 3:00 Tuesday afternoon the time has come to help Nita, their pal. A lot of kids come for one of the town's little rituals.

"I just showed up because she needs help," Meganne said. "There are cool kids around here." The reward for Tuesday's labor is soda and candy for everyone.

"All these kids are pretty good," said Kennedy, who runs the store and acts as Paradise Valley's unofficial baby-sitter. "With the high-school kids, some of the older people will ask them to rake leaves and stuff, and they'll do it. They don't want to get paid."

Paradise Valley is tucked away in a corner of northern Nevada where Kennedy, Cody, Meganne and the rest of the local residents manage to keep the outside world at arm's length as they go about their daily business.

Directions to reach the community are pretty straightforward: Drive north of Winnemucca on U.S. Highway 95 for thirty minutes, turn right on State Route 290, go up and over a couple of hills, stop in front of the post office — then go back about fifty years. The twentieth century is ending and the twenty-first is about to begin, but Paradise Valley remains stalled in the 1950s and wants to stay there.

"This is where *real* living is," said Frankie Peterson, head teacher at Paradise Valley School. If you want to see how the town works, be at Peterson's school shortly before classes start at 9:00 a.m. Two straight lines of students face the flagpole outside the main entrance. Two students raise the flag and the Pledge of Allegiance is recited. Then, after a moment of silence, everyone goes inside.

"This is my interpretation of Paradise Valley," said Peterson, who grew up in the community. "There is that pettiness all the time, but when something goes wrong, there is sticking together and taking care of each other. That's what I really like about it."

As far as Peterson is concerned, Paradise Valley is aptly named. She left home briefly to attend the University of Nevada, Reno, and graduated in 1968. She did some student teaching in Sparks, but before long she returned to Paradise Valley.

"I said, 'If this is what teaching is in the big city, I want no part of that,'" said Peterson, who attended Paradise Valley School as a kid and now lives next door. "This country girl wasn't ready for that."

Many of the children she knows in Paradise Valley come from the nearby ranches that have formed the area's economic and social base for more than a century.

Paradise Valley is a rural community. The town is the post office, store, bar, school, creek, bridge, park and block of old, mostly-abandoned buildings from an era when Paradise Valley was the center of a thriving agricultural and mining region. The entire community sits in a postcard-perfect nook at the foot of the Santa Rosa Mountains, where isolation protects a way of life.

"They look at what's going on around them, even if it's down the road in Winnemucca, and their view is that they want to keep it the way it is," said state historian Guy Rocha. "Paradise Valley seems like it's almost lost in time."

People ride horses down the main street. If you need a gallon of milk but can't get to the mercantile before it closes at 6:00 p.m., just call Kennedy. She'll leave your milk outside the door and you can pay her later. Next door to the mercantile is the bar that's supposed to be open, but sometimes there's a delay.

"They were opening slow because they didn't have the key," Kennedy said. "The gal who owns it forgot and took the key to town. She was going to Winnemucca."

The big event in Paradise Valley every year is the Father's Day Picnic in the park. Sometimes, more than a thousand people show up to eat barbecue. Most of them come from out of town.

"You know they aren't coming just for the food," said Emily Miller, who came to Paradise Valley from Oregon in 1941. "They're coming for something else. It's the family

One resident says that Paradise Valley "is where real living is."

feeling, I think. These are things you don't find in the big communities."

One of the more heated arguments in Paradise Valley took place when organizers of the picnic stopped cooking sides of beef overnight in a covered pit and switched to grilling tri-tip.

"That was a big battle," said Justice of the Peace Liz Chabot, who also drives the school bus. "It's a family mess. We're a family."

Paradise Valley might be a long way from modern problems and freeway exits, but the place is a popular destination for researchers and experts looking for a culture to study. The community and nearby ranches have been the subjects of reports by the Library of Congress

Ranching is a full-time job, but this artist paints to relax

Jean Thomas lives with husband Keith in a stone farmhouse built in the 1860s. They raise cattle on the 7HL Ranch. When she's not riding, roping or branding, Jean paints. Her subject is Paradise Valley.

"That's the thing, Paradise Valley is unique," said Jean, who grew up and studied art in San Francisco. As a child, she spent summers in Paradise Valley. Finally, she moved from San Francisco with her family to the rural community in 1964.

"It's a full-time job," she said of ranching, but she paints, mostly watercolors of local scenes, to relax. "I love that," she said. "It's time for myself." Paradise Valley is picturesque, with lots of old buildings. "I like the water tower. Everyone paints that; with those trees all around, it makes a nice picture."

Jean also teaches art to local kids. "I demonstrated watercolor," she said. "We did a little bit of background in basic art."

If you're lucky, you might be able to get a picture from the artist who paints Paradise Valley. "I give a lot of my stuff away," she said. "If somebody sees something they like while I'm painting it, I put my whole self into it."

Top: Artist Jean Thomas and her dog, Mini, are part of a scene she loves to paint, the Rinehart Ranch in Paradise Valley.
Bottom: Thomas's watercolor of the Rinehart Ranch hangs in one of the bedrooms at the Stonehouse Country Inn.

PARADISE VALLEY

- Population in 1999: 236 (33 percent under 18, 45 percent 18-44, 15 percent 45-64, 7 percent 65 and older; 47 percent female, 53 percent male).
- Population in 1990: 187.
- Population in 2003: (projected) 261.
- Median household income in 1998: $27,083.
- Claim to fame: Authentic buckaroo country; subject of studies and exhibits by Smithsonian Institution and Library of Congress.
- How it got its name: Community first called Paradise City in 1866, but name changed to Paradise Valley in 1870 census. Name refers to town and entire region.
- Local legend: Edna Purviance, girl who became Charlie Chaplin's leading lady, born in Paradise Valley in 1896. She starred with Chaplin in thirty-five movies during silent era. Chaplin met Purviance in San Francisco.

and the Smithsonian Institution. Anthropologists from leading universities have dropped by for a look.

"Somebody out of Berkeley was here," Miller said. "Two girls wrote their master's theses on Paradise Valley. One girl wrote it on the cemetery."

From outside looking in, Paradise Valley must appear unique. Places like this are difficult to find, if not impossible.

"It's almost a lab setting for science," Rocha said. "People, whether they want to live there or not, look at it as the ideal." From the inside looking out, most residents feel fortunate. That's evident at the school, where fifty-one children are enrolled in kindergarten through eighth grade. The school has three teachers, counting Peterson.

"We have eighth-graders playing with kindergartners," she said. "You never see that in the city. That's all part of it."

So is Peterson's classroom where the students behave, even when the teacher forgets something and has to walk the short distance home to find it. "I tell my kids that I'll be right back," she said. "The kids are used to it."

In Paradise Valley, they grow up without

movie theaters, burger joints and shopping malls. They don't even have a gas station. They can fish in the creek, shoot squirrels in the fields or wash the trucks at the volunteer fire department.

"The fire chief knows where to find the teenage boys when he needs his fire trucks washed and waxed," Kennedy said. "He comes in here and finds the whole bunch."

One of Kennedy's Tuesday helpers at the store, Cody, is a Paradise Valley newcomer. His father works at an outlying mine. "It's better than the other place where we used to live," said Cody, who came from Utah with his family.

Kids also can ride horses, play video games in the store or lasso a bale of hay that Kennedy keeps outside.

"If you noticed, there's a bale of hay with a plastic cow head on it," she said. "They all show up with ropes and they have roping contests. There's a rope up on the store ledge. I just leave it up there for anyone who's bored. They can rope."

On summer evenings, before it gets dark, you can find baseball games in the park. Everyone shows up, so the teams often have more than nine players per side.

"You can't put a limit on it; so when the little kids show up, we put them in the outfield so they don't get hit when the bigger kids get up to bat," Kennedy said. "The high-school kids, when they come to play, if they hit it out of the park, they're out. They have to try to keep it in the park."

Kennedy doesn't have children of her own, so the town's kids, in a sense, belong to her. Their school pictures are on the store's walls, as are their awards. If a child has perfect attendance in school, it's honored on her walls. If she is away running an errand, kids in the store will take care of customers.

"There's not a kid out here I don't trust," Kennedy said. "If I go to the post office, they take messages. They do everything. They're here day after day. Parents call and say, 'Is my kid there? Can you send him home?' "

In Paradise Valley, it has always been that way.

"We don't have the problems you see in cities," Miller said. "Most of the kids here respect the teachers and everybody else. They don't know any different. Their parents didn't know any different. It's passed down from generation to generation."

One announcement stuck to the store wall tells customers that six Paradise Valley children will be making their confirmation in the Catholic Church. The ceremony will be followed by a potluck brunch in the community center; everyone is welcome.

"There is the Catholic Church and the Community Church in town," Peterson said. "Everyone supports both churches. They are going to have confirmation at the Catholic Church. Everyone will support that. The Community Church will have a huge Thanksgiving dinner, a potluck. Everyone will support that. It doesn't make any difference."

Peterson fears that Paradise Valley and its way of life are going to be discovered and, eventually, changed. "That's exactly what's going to happen," she said, looking at a field across from the school. "There will be houses right there. People already are moving into the area. They like the country atmosphere. But when they come in droves, we'll lose all this."

Already, small debates have started. "People raise sheep in town," Peterson said. "We have meetings where people who have bought property complain because they don't like the smell. We say, 'Wait a minute. You knew what it was like before you bought the property. Don't try to change us.' "

Changing Paradise Valley will be tough to do, according to Chabot. "In order for a lot of people from Winnemucca to move here, there is going to have to be some sort of industry in Winnemucca," she said. "They don't have the employment base. They have to have a way to support living this far out. There's a few people buying places, but I don't see any big boom."

That probably means Kennedy will continue needing help at the store to put away the bread and milk — every Tuesday.

At the end of the road, Ninety-Six Ranch became a Smithsonian exhibit

A dude from an outfit back East once came to northern Nevada and decided to find the end of the road. He wound up at the front door of Les and Marie Stewart on the Ninety-Six Ranch. The stranger worked for the Smithsonian Institution in Washington, D.C., and hoped to look at life in the real West. He had come to the right place.

"He said he was looking for a place at the end of the road," Marie said. "When you come in here, you have to go back the same way you came to get out. We're the end of the road."

Founded in 1864, the Ninety-Six is the heart of Paradise Valley as well as one of the state's most authentic old-time cattle ranches. Les can show you a covered wagon his ancestor, Fredrick William Stock, used a century ago. Stock arrived in Paradise Valley and started the ranch after giving up his search for gold in California.

The wagon, missing one wheel, sits in a field near the Stewarts' ranch house. Les makes no special attempt to preserve the wagon. It's not on display behind glass. The wagon is part of the ranch, along with the traditional circular willow-branch corrals and hand-hewn stone barns.

"You keep putting new willows on top," Les said of the local building material used by settlers to make corrals. "Those bottom willows, no telling how old they are."

The stone barns were built by Italian immigrant masons in 1919. One barn was used by the buckaroos who worked the cattle; another was used by the ranch hands who mended fences, cut hay and did other chores.

"The buckaroos considered themselves a little better than the ranch men," Les said. "The buckaroos kept their saddle horses here. The ranch men kept their saddle horses up there. They had to build separate barns for them."

The Ninety-Six herd includes some longhorn cattle. They add to the traditional feel of the place. "You've got to handle them right, just like all animals," Les said. "We still have a few left."

The old ranch house, now vacant, was built in 1897. The Stewarts built a new home in the early 1960s. The first house on the ranch was made of sod, constructed by Stock. Les and Marie know the history of the Ninety-Six and they're proud of it. Stock came to the United States from Germany in 1853 and settled in Dayton, Ohio, where he made barrels. He didn't stay long.

"He came down the Mississippi River and came around Cape Horn on a sailing ship to San Francisco," Les said. "He prospected for gold around Red Bluff, California, but he didn't have any success at that. He worked at a livery stable for a while, then he bought himself a freight wagon and oxen."

Stock hauled supplies from Red Bluff on

A handmade willow corral on the Ninety-Six Ranch keeps a young longhorn steer close to home.

the Sacramento River to mines in south-western Idaho. One of his trips across northern Nevada took him through Paradise Valley. "He decided he'd come back the next year and start a ranch," said Les, who started running the Ninety-Six when he was nineteen. Now he's seventy-eight.

Naming the ranch "Ninety-Six" was simple: It's the ranch cattle brand. At the Ninety-Six, cattle branding — like many things — is done the traditional way. Livestock is rounded up on horseback, roped, wrestled to the ground, then branded with irons heated in a sagebrush fire.

"It's kind of a neighborly thing," Marie said. "Everybody helps out. There are people from town who want to come out and help. It's kind of a social affair, really."

In 1979, Smithsonian researchers filmed a cattle roundup on the Ninety-Six. A year later, that film became the centerpiece for a "Buckaroos in Paradise" exhibit at the National Museum of American History.

"Branding has a special place in the life of the valley," the Smithsonian's report said. "It is social, recreational and, as a form of shared work, takes its place with the barn-raisings, bean-stringings and molasses-boiling celebrated in the folklore of the East. Branding symbolizes the cowboy for outsiders: no other image is so immediately recognized as a scene of a rider roping a calf or a group of men applying the branding iron."

The Smithsonian folks asked Les why he insisted on branding the traditional way. "If you're going to run cows and have a cow ranch, you ought to run cows and have a cow ranch, and do it a-horseback and not a-foot," he replied.

Marie understands. "It's a way of life," she said. "It's not a way to make a living. You like the life, and you like what you're doing and where you live."

Ranchers and environmentalists slug it out in Paradise Valley

T alk to a Paradise Valley rancher and the sore subject will come up sooner or later. Usually, it's sooner.

"The problem with any ranching community now is getting along with the federal government," said Marie Stewart, who operates the historic Ninety-Six Ranch with husband Les. "It gets to a point where if you're going to make a living, you're going to have to do something else."

The Stewarts and other valley ranchers claim that increased livestock-grazing restrictions on public land — for which they mostly blame "radical environmentalists" — are hurting their livelihood and could, eventually, put them out of business altogether. The Stewarts don't want to do anything else. The Ninety-Six was founded by Les's ancestor, Fredrick William Stock, in 1864.

Since there's been a Paradise Valley, there's been a Ninety-Six Ranch. It was the subject of an exhibit at the Smithsonian Institution's National Museum of American History in Washington, D.C.

"It's radical environmentalists," Marie said. "They want to get rid of ranching, mining and recreational land use. They want to lock it up for people like themselves."

Deanna Alder rescues lost dogs — and they show their appreciation.

Aged buildings flavor Paradise Valley's scenery with historical significance.

Philip Ferraro's ranch is 115 years old. He can trace as much history as the Stewarts, including a great-grandfather who founded the place. He shares something else with the Stewarts — a point of view.

"They're getting more and more regulations," Ferraro said. "They don't want us out there." Staying "out there" isn't easy. "It takes a different kind of person to handle that forty-below-zero wind chill," Ferraro said of working outdoors in the winters of northern Humboldt County. "There's six inches of snow on the ground and you're out there feeding cattle all day."

Charley Amos is the ranch manager for the area's biggest landowner, Nevada First Corporation, which has 280,000 acres. The company also controls 3.5 million acres of public-land grazing rights.

"We have an excellent relationship with the federal government," Amos said. "The highest and best use of the land is to raise livestock. That's our business. You can also have hiking, fishing and hunting. There's plenty of room."

Winnemucca

The old Winnemucca bridge

"Cows are on the way out," but this town has other attractions

Mike Olano, president of the Winnemucca Basque Club, cooks for the lunchtime crowd at his Winnemucca Hotel and Basque Restaurant.

IMPORTANT DATES

- **1853:** Trading post established on Humboldt River.
- **1860:** French trader settles on banks of Humboldt River near present-day Winnemucca and calls location French Ford.
- **1863:** Building that is now Winnemucca Hotel constructed.
- **Feb. 1, 1866:** Post office established.
- **1868:** Central Pacific Railroad reached town; name changed to Winnemucca.
- **December 1875:** Fire Department organized.
- **1889:** Grammar school opened.
- **July 20, 1908:** Nixon Opera House opened.
- **1957:** Winnemucca becomes last city in state to get dial-telephone service.
- **1977:** Humboldt County Museum opens.
- **June 5, 1978:** Star Broiler Casino destroyed by fire.
- **May 1982:** Convention Center opens.
- **June 1982:** Bob Cashell opens new Star Casino.
- **June 1983:** Nixon Opera House placed on National Register of Historic Places.
- **Sept. 28, 1983:** State fire marshal closes upstairs auditorium of Nixon Opera House.
- **May 1984:** Heavy winter snow melt causes record crest of Humboldt River, closes historic downtown bridge and floods outlying areas.
- **1985:** Uproar in Winnemucca over CBS "60 Minutes" report on alleged police brutality in town.
- **July 1992:** Nixon Opera House destroyed by fire.
- **April 1996:** Money magazine ranks Winnemucca eighth on list of best small boomtowns.

Mike Olano keeps smiling and cooking, although lunch business is slow at his Winnemucca Hotel. Times are tough in town, with the price of gold down and mine workers losing their jobs.

Olano, owner and operator of the Basque restaurant and bar, has seen it all before. Besides, nothing is as rough as what he went through as a kid. As a thirteen-year-old, he was a soldier in the Spanish Civil War.

"I saw a lot of things," said the seventy-five-year-old Spanish Basque who fought on the losing Loyalist side. "There was no food, nothing." So a downturn in the local economy isn't going to scare Olano, who left his homeland for the United States in 1948.

"It's pretty quiet," he said. "Mining went down and laid off a lot of people. I saw it in 1983. It slowed down until the mining came back."

Once again, Olano is content to wait. His hotel, in the historic heart of Winnemucca, opened in 1863 during the American Civil War. The oldest building in the community, it would be the oldest structure in a lot of towns. Olano has run the Winnemucca Hotel since 1965.

"We've had ups and downs before," said Stanley McCoy, a local construction contractor eating at the Winnemucca. "The guys building houses are hurting."

On the other side of town, former miners are learning to be truck drivers. "People are abandoning homes," said Ed Garfield, a student in Dean Hartwig's School of Trucking. "They're just packing up and leaving." In the parking lot of the Humboldt County Fairgrounds, he is practicing backing up and other maneuvers.

Garfield was an underground welder when mining in northern Nevada was booming. Now he hopes to graduate into a truck-driving career from the class offered through Job Opportunities In Nevada, a non-profit adult training program.

"It's an unhappy situation," said Jackie Kearns, manager of JOIN's Winnemucca office. "In 1989, this office served 129 people." During nine months from July 1998 through March 1999, Kearns' office served 927 people. "That's a terrible commentary," she said, "terrible in the sense that the community's need for this type of service grows so radically."

Teri Williams, executive director of the

Tri-County Development Authority, estimated that 400 mining jobs were lost in the first six months of 1999. "We have experienced significant dislocation," Williams said.

Winnemucca is hurting, but it's not dead. Far from it: community leaders are making plans to bounce back with increased tourism and more downtown business.

"We have a pretty strong community," said Kim Petersen, director of the Winnemucca Convention & Visitors Authority. "I don't think it's going to become a ghost town." Winnemucca has name recognition. A lot of people in the West know what and where it is.

Folks have been coming to Winnemucca for years to participate in events ranging from rodeos to an annual softball tournament that goes non-stop for forty-eight hours, with teams playing at all times of the day and night until a champion is decided.

Along with the visitors, Winnemucca is filled with old-timers who have been ranching, railroading or mining for most of the century. They talk about grandfathers, grandmothers, fathers and mothers who arrived before that. They're not going anywhere.

"My grandpa came out here after the Civil War," said Pansilee Larson, born and raised in Winnemucca. "He was a conductor on the old Central Pacific Railroad. He got his discharge from the Union Army. He was wounded in the Battle of Chickamauga and left for dead. They dug a trench they were going to put the bodies in. But one young surgeon saw him move."

So Larson's grandfather, Walter G. Case, was saved. Curator of the Humboldt County Museum, Larson is an expert on Winnemucca history — and she's part of it. Larson was among the leaders of a group trying to save the old Nixon Opera House, built in 1907 and 1908. The community landmark was gutted by a mysterious fire that broke out July 23, 1992, and raged until

The Winnemucca Hotel was established in 1863, one year before Nevada became a state.

the next morning. That was one of the worst nights of her life.

"Devastating," Larson said of the Nixon's destruction which was ruled arson. But the community has rallied with plans for a new performing arts center that has become part of the effort to strengthen the economy with facilities — the biggest of which will be an indoor arena for rodeos and other events. Civic leaders hope to start construction on the arena during 2000 and the arts center in 2001 or 2002.

"We have a unique Western flavor; we are cowboy country," Williams said. "It fits very nicely with our

1910 Brush

Monsters and rainbows on the walls

The first wall Teddy Swecker painted was in daughter Nikki's bedroom. "I painted a little English scene," Swecker said. "It was two little girls and roses." Next came the wall in son Rick's bedroom.

"I did Star Wars," Swecker said. Then she moved from bedrooms to the homes of friends. "My neighbor said, 'Paint my wall,' so I did her bathroom. I think I did flowers. Then I came home and painted my bathroom – a rainbow. I did rainbows all over the neighborhood."

Today, her murals are on walls throughout Winnemucca. She even has some in Reno. Schools are her specialty.

"The junior high school in Winnemucca was having trouble with graffiti," Swecker said. "They asked me to do a mural. It worked." On the school walls she painted giant pencils and pens, with ink flowing. Then she was asked to do something about the bathrooms in the Humboldt County Library. She painted monsters.

Now Swecker has branched out. She has illustrated two books for children and she wrote and illustrated one of her own, *Ducks Ducks*. Watercolors are her favorite medium.

"That was for me; I loved watercolors," said Swecker, who graduated from the University of Nevada, Reno in 1972 with a degree in fine arts.

Best known in Winnemucca for her murals, Swecker is painting more than bathrooms now.

Winnemucca artist Teddy Swecker works on a mural in the library of Jessie Beck Elementary School in Reno.

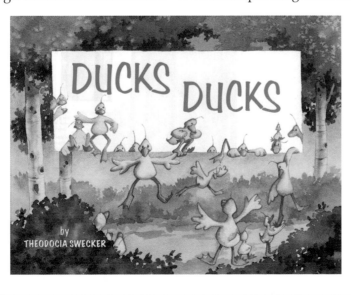

Suzanne Montero of Lowry High School in Winnemucca prepares to rope a calf in the Nevada High School Rodeo at Gandolfo Arena in Sparks.

community. It fits what we are."

Not everyone is so sure.

"I don't think it's a sound investment," said Lee Locke, who has operated a ranch and other businesses since coming to Winnemucca from Reno in 1947. "Cows are on the way out."

Williams figures Winnemucca's location on Interstate 80 and the cowboys who've been coming to town in summertime for years will fill it, if they can be convinced to return in winter.

"We have the capacity to host a 5,000-person event with their livestock," Williams said. "The types of people who come to these events don't fly. They're going to be driving. They'll have their horse trailers. Many of these participants are located in the Western states. We're right in the middle. We have what I feel is a nice geographic location."

Even if the arena is built and succeeds,

Winnemucca will continue to struggle with a basic economic problem — diversification — and how to replace the relatively high-paying mining jobs that are being lost with employment that offers similar wages.

"We have not been able to entice businesses with comparable wage scales," said Kearns, who serves on a committee trying to do just that. "We haven't had other industrial or manufacturing activity to absorb these people."

Kearns, whose family came to Winnemucca in 1946, has been in tougher spots. She spent twelve years as a teacher in Uganda in East Africa. "We had nine changes of government, all of them violent," said Kearns, who finally was expelled from the country by the dictatorship in power.

Kearns grew up on a Winnemucca ranch. "I came from a large family with

Katie Baker, front, and members of the Winnemucca Basque Dancers perform traditional steps at the annual Elko Basque Festival.

where it was a few years ago," Petersen said. "It's taken its toll. There's more competition. The pieces of the pie are getting smaller."

Today might not be the perfect time to build a new business in Winnemucca, but that's not stopping Chuck Austin, who bought Bikes and More on South Bridge Street in 1999. Austin, who went to Winnemucca High School, specializes in mountain bikes, skateboards and sunglasses.

"It's been off a little with the mining down," said Austin, who goes mountain biking in the vast open country around Winnemucca. "The sunglasses and the skateboard guys, they help pay the bills." To help his business, and just because he likes it, Austin is working with federal officials to designate a regional trail system for mountain biking. He sees the potential.

"When you're driving down I-80, you think it's flat," Austin said. "But if you look, there's the Humboldt Mountains. They're 10,000 feet high. Then you've got the Sonomas and Winnemucca Mountain. There's some neat stuff. There's streams and canyons. You can't see them from the highway, which is kind of good. If too many people see them, it would ruin it."

But they can ride the Bloody Shins Mountain Bike Trail outside Winnemucca that Austin put together with the Bureau of Land Management. The trail has seven, twelve- and twenty-two-mile loops. "That's the beauty of it," Austin said. "At my house, I'm a block away from dirt. I can be climbing a 7,000-foot mountain."

The great outdoors is part of what Winnemucca has to offer, along with cowboy culture and history, but residents figure the town will hang around just because it always has.

"It's a steady, slow pace," Locke said. "We just sort of move along."

numerous cousins," she said. "They all spent summers on the ranch. It was a great training ground to live and work as a team." She is the kind of person the director of the Winnemucca Convention & Visitors Authority probably is talking about when he refers to Winnemucca as a "strong" town.

"We've recently had an awakening," Petersen said of the community's economic battle. "The old-timers know mining is up and down. Some of the newer people are getting a little taste of the downturn." As often happens in Winnemucca, a boom came before the slump, when the town was riding as high as gold prices. "For a few years, it was going crazy," he said. "We couldn't keep up with the housing."

In the early part of this decade, new hotels were built and a Wal-Mart opened in Winnemucca. "Now it's settled back down to

Was Butch Cassidy here? A copy of a prison document hangs in the old building that once was a bank robbed by the Wild Bunch in 1900.

Butch Cassidy Days celebrate a debatable legend

Mary Ann Shannon sits at the scene of the crime. She is a secretary at the Winnemucca Tax and Accounting Service at South Bridge and Fourth streets.

"People come from other countries," Shannon said. "The wife won't come in, but the husband does. Then, when we get to talking, the wife comes in." When visitors show up, she becomes a tour guide, telling the most famous story in Winnemucca history. The problem? Nobody's absolutely sure of what's true and what's false.

On September 19, 1900, the building that houses the tax service was the First National Bank of Winnemucca. Three men entered the bank and robbed it of $32,640, giving birth to a legend. For years, the popular tale was that Butch Cassidy and the Sundance Kid — two of the Old West's most notorious outlaws — led the holdup with their Wild Bunch gang.

Winnemucca celebrates the event with Butch Cassidy Days each September. A small marker erected by the Boy Scouts in 1969 commemorates the robbery. Down the street is Butch Cassidy's Hole in the Wall Saloon and the Sundance Casino.

Everyone agrees the bank was robbed September 19, 1900. From there, however, the tale gets confused; it appears almost certain that Butch and Sundance weren't even in Winnemucca then. But that doesn't matter. People like the story, so it continues to be told.

"I'm all in favor of it," Lee Berk said of the Butch Cassidy Days celebration. Berk, a history buff who used to live in Winnemucca, started his Butch Cassidy research after leaving Winnemucca two decades ago. He's the guy who exposed the myth. He researched the robbery and, based on what appears to be solid evidence, concluded Cassidy and Sundance had no part in the holdup.

"There were some stories that people were upset with me for upsetting the Butch Cassidy apple cart," said Berk, a retired utility company executive who lives in Reno. "That's not true. There are so many possibilities and so many stories."

The one about Butch and Sundance became Winnemucca lore because a photograph of the Wild Bunch was sent from Fort Worth, Texas, to the First National Bank a few months after the robbery. An unsigned note thanked the bank for the cash. The photo of five men included Harry Longbaugh (the Sundance Kid) and Leroy Parker (Butch Cassidy).

The photograph became famous, as did Winnemucca, the supposed site of the last holdup pulled by Butch and Sundance before they fled to South America. A 1969 movie starring Robert Redford and Paul Newman as the outlaws probably added to Winnemucca's self-esteem.

After all, not every town had a bank robbed by Butch and Sundance. A painting of Butch, Sundance and the gang hangs in the Winnemucca Tax and Accounting Service, which still houses the bank vault. But Berk read documents, including letters from bank part-owner George S. Nixon, who was present on the day of the robbery. The leader of the three men who staged the holdup held a knife to Nixon's throat, marched him to the vault and ordered him to open it.

The robbers, who did not wear masks, never were caught, nor was the money recovered. In letters to the Pinkerton Detective Agency, Nixon denied that Cassidy was among the holdup men. Berk also found that Cassidy and members of his gang were known to have robbed a Union Pacific Railroad passenger train near Tipton, Wyoming, on August 29, 1900, twenty-one days before the Winnemucca holdup.

The bank robbers were known to have camped in a field at the CS Ranch north of Winnemucca ten days before the holdup. Cassidy could have committed both crimes only if he had made the 600-mile ride from Tipton to Winnemucca in eleven days.

"I figured that Cassidy couldn't have gotten there," Berk said. "He had to go on horseback." The new theory is that members of Cassidy's gang, without his help, robbed the bank.

"The presumption was that everyone in the photo was associated with the robbery," said state historian Guy Rocha. "They assumed that the gang in total robbed one place at one time. Butch and Sundance were in Wyoming at the time."

None of that appears to bother folks in Winnemucca. "It's fun," Shannon said of all the stories. "One guy came in and wanted his picture taken by the safe." Winnemucca natives tell about their ancestors' role in the events of September 19, 1900.

"My dad was nine years old," said Pansilee Larson. "Kids in those days would walk down by the river to skip rocks, as kids will do. That day, they walked by the livery stable and saw some strangers. I guess he had seen these guys out on the ranches, casing the town. They would talk to the boys about businesses in town. The robbers were the same cowboys who'd been talking to the kids."

Yvonne Hager tells a story about her father: "He was out at a ranch," Hager said. "One day, some people came by and asked, 'Would you feed these horses for us? We're cattle buyers and we'll be back in a few days.' My father said, 'Sure, I'll feed them for you.'"

"They came back in a few days. They saw the horses were well cared for, so they threw gold coins at him and they took off. Pretty soon a bunch of riders came and they said, 'It's the posse. They just robbed a bank in Winnemucca.' The Butch Cassidy gang, supposedly, that's who they were."

Larson's theory about the holdup is simple:

"If Butch wasn't here, he masterminded it. It was a well-planned robbery."

After the fire, the Nixon Opera House is still an invisible landmark

A twist of barbed wire is half-buried in the sand hills north of Winnemucca.

The night of July 23, 1992, might have been the worst in Winnemucca history. A fire, later determined to be arson, broke out at 10:00 in the historic Nixon Opera House, a community landmark for most of this century. By early morning, the blaze had gutted the building and scarred the town.

"The roof caved in about three a.m.," said City Councilwoman Joyce Sheen, a radio news reporter at the time. "It was an ugly night." The town had other smaller fires that night, all determined to be arson. No one was ever caught.

Built in 1907-8, the Opera House was lost that night. Seven years later, Winnemucca finally is recovering. Community leaders are planning a new performing arts center to be built — possibly in 2001 or 2002 — near the downtown location of the old Nixon.

Fighting over the Nixon raged for years before the fire broke out. Now it has stopped. Before its destruction, the Nixon was a building loved by many and hated by some. They argued about restoration of the Nixon, a portion of which was closed for safety reasons by city officials in 1984. Some said the money would be wasted.

"Some people thought it wasn't worth it; they wanted to start fresh," Sheen said. The fire ended the debate. Paul Vesco was mayor and a firefighter when the Nixon burned down. He remains mayor today.

"Some were mad and some were relieved to get rid of the dilemma the town was in," Vesco said of the emotions at the time of the fire. Getting over all the feelings has taken a long time.

"We worked hard to get the Nixon brought up to code, then somebody torched it; I'll never forget that," said Winnemucca native Pansilee Larson, a leader of the group who tried to restore the Opera House. She recalls dancing at the Nixon as a child.

Sheen wasn't born then. After joining the council in 1996, she became a leader of the long struggle to build a new facility. The first fight was over insurance on the old Nixon. Winnemucca went to court to get a settlement that ended up being about $2 million. After that, Mayor Vesco appointed a committee, with Sheen in charge, to figure out what to do next.

"The biggest thing I thought had to be overcome was the horrible division," Sheen said of the old Nixon bitterness. "I had nineteen people on the committee. I had representatives from business, casinos, the Chamber [of Commerce,] mines, schools, the Planning Department, the arts community. It was broad based."

The group decided on a center seating 600 to 825 people, to be built near the Convention Center and the park that occupies the site of the old Nixon. "You'll have an awesome City Center," Sheen said. It will take money. To go with the insurance cash, Humboldt County has pledged $900,000 and the city $785,000, provided other fund-raising efforts are successful.

"The community has to demonstrate support, or they could use the money for something else," said Sheen, who is pursuing government grants and private donations. "We need $2 million to $3 million more."

Thunder Mountain, on Interstate 80 at Imlay, is about thirty miles west of Winnemucca. The main building at Thunder Mountain is covered with sculptures such as the one above.

Yerington

On a hot summer afternoon, Jeff Spurlock flies high off a bridge into the Walker River in Yerington.

"We're decent small-town America"

Yerington's landmark water tower dominates the landscape.

Mike Lommori worries that his hometown is getting soft. After all, finding anyone willing to run, jog or even walk 10 miles carrying a 120-pound bag of grain on their back is becoming tougher and tougher. Lommori did it in 1964, defending Yerington's honor against a gang of Pennsylvania coal miners in the great sack race. He has become something of a town hero.

"I don't know what kind of guys we have now," Lommori said with a chuckle.

The sack race is an on-and-off tradition in this tidy farming community in the lush Mason Valley, where residents love to celebrate just about anything — including a stunt first performed in 1910 that became one of the state's most bizarre athletic events. Folks haven't seen a great sack race since 1996, and they're getting itchy.

"Maybe for the millennium," Lyon County Economic Development Director John Sanderson said, seeing an opportunity to revive the unique contest. "We just can't get contestants for it. We've tried. It's a brutal event."

Harry Rutherford Warren didn't think the event was a big deal when he completed Yerington's first sack race on February 15, 1910. Warren operated a ranch about ten miles outside of town. One day, five of Warren's workers bet the boss $600 he couldn't carry the 120-pound sack of wheat the ten miles from the ranch to town. Warren took the bet.

Rules for that first sack race were that the heavy bag of wheat couldn't touch the ground and Warren had to reach Yerington in four hours. Judges were appointed to watch his progress. The road to town was dirt and mud, so Warren's brother walked ahead to make sure of the footing. When Warren stopped to rest along the way, he held the sack on his knee to make sure it didn't touch the ground.

Warren reached Yerington in three-and-a-half hours, winning the $600. The story of the first sack race ends with the winner carrying a young boy on his back around a local bar for a victory lap. Various re-creations of Warren's trip have taken place, with contestants carrying 120-pound sacks of grain on their backs, sometimes running around the high-school track and sometimes through downtown streets.

"It's one of the most grueling sports

IMPORTANT DATES

- **1854:** N.H.A. "Hock" Mason drives cattle through what later would be named Mason Valley on his way to California. He returns five years later.
- **Aug. 6, 1871:** Mason Valley Post Office established.
- **Nov. 20, 1879:** Town is named Greenfield.
- **April 1, 1894:** Name of town changed to Yerington.
- **1907:** Yerington incorporated as city.
- **1909:** Lyon County seat moved from Dayton to Yerington.
- **Feb. 15, 1910:** Harry Rutherford Warren carries a 120-pound sack of grain from his ranch ten miles to Yerington, creating an event that becomes the Yerington sack race.
- **1911:** Electricity reaches Yerington on power line from Reno.
- **Jan. 6, 1912:** Thompson copper smelter begins operation.
- **1912:** Courthouse built.
- **1912:** Yerington Grammar School No. 9 opens.
- **1919:** Walker River Irrigation District formed.
- **1924:** Topaz Lake reservoir completed.
- **Aug. 17, 1924:** Story in San Francisco Examiner claims real Garden of Eden has been discovered in Mason Valley. Locals don't believe it.
- **1951:** Anaconda copper mine and plant open.
- **1964:** Yerington High School teacher and coach Mike Lommori wins sack race against team of coal miners from Edinboro, Pennsylvania.
- **1976:** Yerington celebrates U.S. Bicentennial for nine days, raising money for the formation of Lyon County Museum.
- **1978:** Anaconda closes copper operation.
- **1980:** Yerington Grammar School No. 9 closed.
- **1988:** Restoration begins on Yerington Grammar School No. 9.
- **1990:** Mason Valley Fish Hatchery completed.
- **Dec. 20, 1998:** Yerington Grammar School No. 9 reopens as Jeanne Dini Performing Arts Center.

events I've ever seen," Sanderson said. "When we get fired up to do it, we do it."

The last race was in 1996. After Warren, the most famous victory belongs to Lommori, a twenty-six-year-old teacher and coach when he carried the bag for ten miles, seventy laps around the Yerington High track, on July 4, 1964. Lommori ran the straight-aways and walked the curves, finishing in two hours, twenty-seven minutes, and fifty-nine seconds.

"We had to do it," said Lommori, who led six Yerington sack racers in defending the town's honor. "We'd been challenged by that group of miners."

The Edinboro, Pennsylvania, miners had read newspaper accounts of the race and decided to try it. Six men were sent to Yerington.

"We had to run it twice," said Lommori, a Yerington High wrestling coach whose teams during one incredible period won 107 straight dual meets and twelve state championships. "We had to qualify. We had twelve guys who wanted to do it. We had to cut that down to six." On race day, Lommori was ready. By then, the 120-pound bag was part of him. "After you trained with it so much, you hardly felt it," he said.

Lommori, a former fullback on football teams at the University of Nevada, Reno in the 1950s, is now retired from the school district. He's also out of sack racing. But he remains a big part of Yerington, where people remember favorite sons.

"We know who we are and we kind of like it," Sanderson said. "We're Yerington. We're decent small-town America."

One of the big things in Yerington is the business of waving. Everybody in town does it, whether they know you or not. About the only thing to do is wave back. Perhaps the wave is a local tradition, like the sack race, except it happens every day and you don't have to carry 120 pounds of wheat on your back.

"We'd drive down the street and people would wave at us," said Maureen Williss, who moved to Yerington from San Diego with husband, Dan, three years ago and didn't know what was up. "I'd say, 'Dan, do you know them?'" They didn't then. They do now.

"I came here kicking and screaming," said Dan Williss, who didn't like giving up his season tickets to San Diego Chargers football and San Diego Padres baseball games in exchange for quiet life in a small town, "but I'm happy now."

San Diego was too crowded for Dan and Maureen, and a scary place to raise kids. Maureen had friends who had moved to Yerington. The Williss family followed. Then Dan and Maureen were lucky enough to get jobs — he with the local plant of a national manufacturing company and she with county government — something not always easy to do in a small town.

"My Chargers' and Padres' season tickets, those are the only things I miss," said Dan, who went back to San Diego with Maureen in 1998 to watch the Padres lose to the New York Yankees in the World Series.

Yerington is isolated. Not enough to keep residents from driving to Reno-Sparks and Carson City, or even as far as San Diego, but just enough to keep the outside world at a long arm's length.

"We're just a little more off the beaten path," said David Fulstone II, a local farmer

Good morning! Neil Herrin propels his cart toward Main Street, passing neighbor David Fulstone on the way.
David Fulstone is a rancher and the "Garlic Guy" of Yerington. He is also the son of longtime Smith/Mason Valley physician Dr. Mary Fulstone. His license plate reads, "GARLIC."

Artist's stained glass leaves mark all over town

Ed Recanzone retired a number of years ago and needed something to do. He tried woodworking. It didn't work. He tried refinishing furniture. It didn't work. Then, he found something. Stained glass.

Recanzone's daughter, Joan Harned, operated a stained-glass shop in the San Francisco Bay area. She taught her dad.

"That's what got me started," said the eighty-nine year-old, who owned a clothing store in Yerington.

Today, Recanzone's glass is all over town. You can see it in everything from saloons to churches. The bell tower of the Holy Family Catholic Church is decorated with Recanzone's stained-glass windows. Two Recanzone pieces are mounted behind the bar of Dini's Lucky Club in Yerington. The doors of the Lyon County Museum are highlighted by Recanzone's stained glass. He has done doors all over town and windows in churches outside town. But now his work has slowed.

"I experienced a tremor in my fingers," he said. "I try a little bit. I get frustrated."

Ed Recanzone made this stained glass panel more than thirty years ago. It was his first. Since then he has created stained glass windows for churches in Yerington and Smith Valley. The window shown below is in the Yerington United Methodist Church.

YERINGTON

- Population in 1998: 2,890 (27 percent under 18, 28 percent 18-44, 24 percent 45-64, 21 percent 65 and older; 51 percent male, 49 percent female).
- Population in 2003: (projected) 5,433.
- Median income: $22,114.
- Total retail sales: $52.492 million.

- Claim to fame: Lyon County seat, center of Mason Valley, one of state's most productive agricultural areas.

- How it got its name: Named for Henry M. Yerington, general manager of the Virginia & Colorado Railroad, April 1, 1894 — although the railroad didn't go through town. Before that, the town was known as Pizen Switch for a small saloon in the area made from willow branches. Locals called the place the "Switch" and the liquor served there "Pizen." In 1879, the name was changed to Greenfield because of the surrounding green fields. Yerington was incorporated as a city in 1907.

- Local legend: Joe Dini Jr., who has served in the state Assembly since 1968. He's been speaker almost continuously since 1987. He's also the longtime owner and operator of Dini's Lucky Club, a Yerington landmark founded by Joe Dini Sr. in 1933.

Yerington's Jeanne Dini Performing Arts Center was formerly Grammar School No. 9.

and member of the Lyon County Commission. He and others try to explain how Yerington has missed the rapid growth taking place in Carson Valley and other formerly rural northern Nevada areas where houses are replacing cattle. You don't have to go through Yerington to get anywhere else. You don't arrive by accident. The town is on Alternate Route 95. Going to Yerington means going out of your way.

"We don't have any people who commute to work," said Sanderson, who showed up in town from Reno one day and stayed. "We are also the only town of any consequence in Nevada that's not on a major highway. We don't get the transient population. We don't get the problems that go with that. It's a nice valley."

Another tip-off about Yerington is the main street, with its all angle parking, not parallel. That was a conscious decision by town planners when they undertook a major construction project to upgrade the main street in 1992. Switching from angle to parallel parking, they figured, would make additional room for more traffic. Most important, the change would be a sign that Yerington was no longer small.

"It's a serious issue," Sanderson said.

Yerington also has no parking meters or traffic lights. Motorists don't have to be prompted to stop for pedestrians — they just do it.

"Nobody out here uses turn signals because we all know where each other is going," City Manager Roland Adams said with a chuckle.

About the only traffic anomaly is Neil Herrin, who zips along downtown sidewalks in a three-wheel motorized cart. The town looks after the sixty-seven-year-old, who figures he looks after the town.

"I run errands for them," said Herrin, who starts his morning rounds about 7:45 and finishes around 9:00. "I do a lot of things for the people around here. A lot of people do things for me." A town softball field is named for Herrin, who used to be the scorekeeper. A bad leg no longer allows him to climb the steps to the press box.

"He's a tough little devil," David Fulstone, father of David Fulstone II, said of Herrin. "Everybody knows Neil. You've got to watch him. He just turns when he wants to about half the time."

The Fulstones grow alfalfa on a 400-acre ranch about two miles outside of town. The son, the one who serves on the County Commission, is known as "Davey." The father, David, is seventy-five.

"If you mention me, you'll have to mention garlic," said David. "I'm kind of known as the 'Garlic Guy.' I always raised garlic to make my braids." Fulstone, who drives around with a rear license plate reading "GARLIC" on his pickup truck, used to make garlic braids for about 1,000 of his neighbors. He's cut the number to about 300 and buys the garlic from out of town.

Another hot item in Yerington is zucchini squash. A lot of people grow it in their gardens. If you're not careful — and even if you are — you'll find a bag in the front seat of your car. People just leave it.

"The only time we lock our cars on Main Street is in the summer," said Fulstone II. "That's to keep somebody from putting a bag of zucchini squash in your seat. Everybody grows a garden and they have too much."

With 50,000 acres of farm land being cultivated in Mason Valley, Yerington is thoroughly rural, but Sanderson warned against looking at Yerington as some kind of hick town caught in a Norman Rockwell painting.

"If all you see is sticks and rural, that they're so backward they don't have a stop light, you've missed the point," he said.

Look a couple of blocks off Main Street and you see a high-tech auditorium for music, plays and other performances that cost $1.8 million. The Jeanne Dini Performing Arts Center, named for the late wife of Yerington casino operator and longtime state Assemblyman Joe Dini Jr., opened in 1998 with performances of Shakespeare's plays.

"We like things urban people like," said Kathy Smith, who serves on the volunteer board that operates the 154-seat center. "But we choose to live in a rural area."

Events sell out in the center housed in what used to be historic Yerington Grammar School No. 9, a stately brick building the district was using for storage until the community saved it.

"This building looked horrible," said School Board member Debbie Arrighi. "It had been a building the town was proud of. There were rooms filled with old typewriters. This was a building the town could rally around."

A lot of local folks had gone to the school, built in 1911-12 and closed in 1980. Much of the money for restoration came from a state grant. But townspeople came up with some unique fund-raising stunts to get the rest. They sold bricks from the old school for $25 each. The building has a tower and an old-

Longtime Yerington resident Bob Schendel owns an historic downtown building, constructed in 1918, which houses his Crescent Garage.

fashioned school bell. For $5, you could ring it. A lot of people did.

"That was important to people who went to this school," said Jim Sanford, a board member who went to the school. "I yanked on (the bell rope) two or three times for my $5."

Another longtime Yerington resident, Bob Schendel, isn't sure if saving the old building was worth all the money.

"It just seemed to me to be an awful lot," said Schendel, who owns another of Yerington's historic buildings, the Crescent Garage, constructed in 1918. "At least they didn't tear it down." The seventy-five-year-old was raised in Yerington, then went away to work in big cities. He came back. "One of the reasons I moved back was I could walk to work," Schendel said. "I live about a half-block down the street. You can go fishing in fifteen minutes; you can go hunting in fifteen minutes. You can be away from people in fifteen minutes. You don't make as much money in a little town like this. But you make a living and you have more time to yourself."

A trip back in time offers fill-ups and clean windows

At Ed Hillygus's gas station, people stop for gas and end up staying an hour.

D uring his thirty-one years as a mathematics teacher at Yerington High School, Ed Hillygus warned lazy students to pay attention or they'd end up pumping gas for a living. Now, when the old teacher's former pupils drive by the corner of South Main and East Bridge streets, they see Hillygus pumping gas.

"I have a good time doing it," said Hillygus, who's keeping a family and town tradition alive by operating his tiny service station that has been sentenced to death in the 21st century. "There's a lot of harassing and joking, especially when former students come by."

The Hillygus gas station is a community landmark. Built by Ed's father, Lowell, shortly after the original building burned down in 1939, the station is made of wood and looks its age — a relic straight out of some Depression-era movie. Inside Ed's office is an adding machine that doesn't work and an electric heater that's unplugged. In the window, there's an advertisement for the local square dance club and a season schedule for the high school basketball team.

All of it is from another era and comes to an end in 2002. That's how long the federal government has given Hillygus to upgrade his gas storage tanks. He can't afford it, so he'll close and turn the little building over to the Lyon County Museum. The corner gas station will be history. Motorists can buy gas at other stations and get it cheaper at some of them, but they can't stop and visit with Ed at the other places. He won't pump their gas personally at the other places. Ed won't give their kids candy with each fill-up at the other places. And one more thing — Ed washes windows.

"I'd better scrape that off," Hillygus said as he cleaned a customer's windshield. "You'll get a ticket for having ice on the window." A child sat in the front seat. "Have you been good?" Hillygus asked. "OK, I'll get you a sucker." Washing windows and handing out treats are big deals at the Hillygus station. Lowell always took care of the windows and kids.

"My dad started that," Ed Hillygus said. "My dad was a big tease; the kids came by for the water fights. My dad had a boat and we'd go water skiing every Sunday. Kids would hang around and go with us." Ed paused for a moment and remembered: "All those things that seemed so ordinary at the time seem so

Top left: David Fulstone, whose mother was Mason Valley's only doctor for many years, chats with Maxine Ford, his neighbor, born in Yerington in 1909.
Top right: Debbie Arrighi worked with a community team to save the Yerington Grammar School No. 9 and transform it into the Jeanne Dini Performing Arts Center.
Bottom left: David Fulstone II is a county commissioner and rancher in Yerington.

significant now."

When Lowell died in 1978, Ed's mom, Clara, took over and ran the place herself for almost twenty years, taking care of the windows and kids. She died in 1995. Ed has been pumping gas ever since.

"I'm doing it as a family tradition," said Hillygus, fifty-seven, whose wife, Barbara, teaches English at Yerington Middle School. "I don't know. I guess it doesn't make a lot of sense."

It does to Herb Fawcett, one of the locals who buys gas from Ed. "You know why I come here?" asked Fawcett. "I have to fight him to keep him from washing the windows. He's just a heck of a nice guy." Fawcett stops for gas, then stays for an hour to visit with Ed. "I remember his dad," Fawcett said.

That's when the place was a Texaco station. Ed Hillygus lost the big oil company franchise in 1997. "They said we didn't (have)

the image Texaco wants," Hillygus said. People in town were so mad they cut up their Texaco credit cards. Now they pay cash for Ed's gas. A car goes by the station and the driver waves. Ed and Herb don't know who the motorist is, but they wave back.

"It's kind of like a huge family," Hillygus said, describing Yerington. Hillygus always has been a big part of it. He coached boys' basketball at the high school, along with boys' and girls' golf. His girls' teams won state championships in 1994, 1995 and 1996. Now those kids stop at Ed's for gas.

A large juniper tree stands in front of the station. Ed finds a picture — one of his favorites. The photograph shows Ed as a child; the juniper is a sapling.

Yerington needs jobs to keep youth

Adam Gibbs loves his life as a kid in Yerington, but he can't stay. Yerington has just about everything the eighteen-year-old enjoys: the town is small, rural and friendly, but is missing one thing that's important to Gibbs — an ocean.

"I can't stand the desert," said the Yerington High School graduate who wants to attend the Coast Guard Academy. "I like being on the water." Gibbs feels trapped in a landlocked, northern Nevada farm town. It was great growing up, but now it's time to leave. "It's a cool place," said the student vice president, "but I do want to get out of here."

The dilemma faced by Gibbs is common for Yerington teenagers: they like their hometown, but — unless you're a rancher, teacher or work for local government — opportunities to make a living are few.

"Yerington does need some change, maybe gradual," Mayor Doug Homestead said. "My parents had four kids and I'm the only one who lives here in Yerington now because there's no economic base to get jobs." Homestead and other community leaders want to attract some industry, similar to what has been moving into Fernley. That small northern Nevada com-

Yerington High School senior Stacy Tibbals clears a hurdle during track practice after school.

munity is in a better location for business, on Interstate 80 about thirty minutes east of Reno-Sparks. Yerington is out of the way, on Alternate Route 95 in Lyon County.

"We're kind of off the beaten path," Homestead said. "We've got to get something in here to keep our young people here. They're all moving away." They don't want to — they have to.

"Those courthouse jobs are pretty much taken," said Yerington native Stacy Tibbals, seventeen, when she considered the possibility of working in county government.

Yerington High School student Adam Gibbs, center, sprints near the end of his afternoon track workout.

"There's not much to do here once you're done with school."

At one time, Yerington's biggest business was the Anaconda Copper Company's mining pit that opened outside of town in 1951. Though it closed in 1978, Yerington has survived and maybe even thrived.

"Businesses and mining have come and gone," said Lyon County Commissioner David Fulstone II, a local rancher. "The real base of our valley is agriculture."

Tibbals, a senior at Yerington High, plans on going to college somewhere and probably won't come back. "Some stay, not many," Tibbals said. "Last year, a lot of kids went to Oregon." When she goes, she will miss some things, though:

"Everywhere, people say 'hi' to you. They hold doors for you."

The adults in Yerington want to preserve that way of life. They fear growth will ruin it. But they also know if Yerington doesn't grow, it might not survive.

"You don't have to go big time," City Councilman Darryl Carrigan said. "But it's really important that we bring something in here so we can keep some of our better kids here when they come back from college."

A new Nevada image has slowly eclipsed the old—so long embossed with dust, sage, and untamable distance. A massive influx of construction money, an expanded wave of social democracy, a breakdown in the old codes of morality, an unprecedented mobility, and a revolution in consumer technology have revitalized the state. ...The Nevada genre — with its distinctive art forms, its premier showmanship, its sparkling virtuosity, its secluded mines, ranches, and ghost towns — is an American original.

  Wilbur S. Shepperson, "A New Shrine in the Desert," East of Eden, West of Zion

Economic and Tourist Centers

The Reno skyline at dusk.

Carson City

The silver-domed Capitol building shines in the winter air.

Carson City was designed as state capital — and it'll stay that way

Family members cheer Carson High School graduate Marco Urbina Jr., as he receives his diploma.

No matter what people in power say, Maxine Nietz can't get over the fear that someday, somehow, Las Vegas will replace Carson City as Nevada's capital.

"It's just based on counting heads," the longtime Carson City resident said of the perceived threat from fast-growing Las Vegas. Carson City's population is 51,860. The Las Vegas-Clark County metropolitan area has almost 1.3 million people. "We look around in the Legislature," she said. "We look at where the state budget goes, where the population demands that it go."

Nietz and other Carson City folks long have been proud of their capital city status. They're particularly keen on being one of the country's smaller capitals, but its size also has made Carson City a bit insecure.

"It's a real Carson City paranoia," said Fred Nietz, Maxine's husband. "They are already building new structures (in Las Vegas) to house government agencies. The more they build, the more the paranoia of Carson City increases."

Although the state bureaucracy has a strong presence in Las Vegas, a statement from Governor Kenny Guinn's office said the capital isn't going anywhere. The

governor is from Las Vegas. Another new-comer, State Controller Kathy Augustine — also from Las Vegas — tried to reassure nervous Carson residents that their city wouldn't lose its claim to fame.

"I don't think that will ever happen," Augustine said.

Mayor Ray Masayko thinks downtown traffic is a more important issue. "A lot of us in Carson City say until we get traffic off the main street, the Capitol and historic district will never be able to be enjoyed by people on foot," he said.

Carson City's main street is U.S. 395, which funnels a heavy load of traffic through the middle of town. A $228 million bypass is planned to take U.S. 395 and its nonstop parade of vehicles around the east side of the city, but relief is at least a few years away. Construction on the first phase should start in 2000, with completion of the entire bypass in 2007 or 2008. Until then, plenty of traffic will go with the paranoia.

"I hope in twenty, thirty or forty years Las Vegas doesn't take us over and become the capital," said Candace Duncan, executive director of the Carson City Convention & Visitors Bureau. Duncan and others become

IMPORTANT DATES

- **1851:** Frank Hall, a gold miner who doesn't strike it rich, is one of the first white settlers in the area that would become Carson City. Hall and five companions establish a ranch and trading post. They shoot an eagle and stretch the skin over the door of their log cabin, calling it Eagle Station. The surrounding area comes to be known as Eagle Valley.

- **1858:** Abraham Curry from New York tries to buy a site for a general store in Genoa. The price is $1,000. Curry refuses and joins three partners to buy Hall's ranching claim for $1,000 - half in cash and half in horses. Curry plans a town and promotes it as the future state capital.

- **1861:** Nevada Territory is created and the first Territorial Legislature meets in the Warm Springs Hotel, owned by Curry, two miles out of town. Curry builds a streetcar to transport the legislators from town to his hotel and back. Also, President Lincoln appoints Orion Clemens as territorial secretary. Clemens, paid $1,800 a year, brings brother Samuel with him to Nevada as his "private secretary." Samuel Clemens changes his name to Mark Twain and becomes a famous writer.

- **June 17, 1863:** A volunteer fire brigade is formed when 20 men raise $2,000 to buy an engine, originally owned by the Warren Co. of Boston, from Marysville, Calif. Warren Engine Co. No. 1 still operates as a volunteer unit of the city's regular fire department.

irritated when they read about Carson City's supposed inconvenience for Las Vegas-based bigwigs, sometimes portrayed in accounts of the cost of flying Southern Nevada lawmakers to such capital events such as the governor's State of the State address.

"Issues like that always come up," Maxine Nietz said. "When you hear a series of small things like that over a period of time, it does get to you."

History is on the side of Carson City, which was designed as the capital before Nevada became a state. Abraham Curry, Carson City's first and probably best promoter, came to northern Nevada in 1858. He and three partners — John Musser, Frank Proctor and Benjamin Green — bought the original town site, planned Carson City and pushed it as the future state capital. Of the four founders, Curry is the one best remembered. He stayed in town for the rest of his life.

State historian Guy Rocha reminds listeners that when Carson's past was first recorded, it was Curry telling the story. "He had lasting power," Rocha said. "He cast the long shadow."

In 1861, the first Territorial Legislature met in the Warm Springs Hotel outside Carson City. Curry, who owned the Warm Springs Hotel, built a streetcar to transport lawmakers the two miles between his hotel and town. On October 31, 1864, Nevada became a state and Carson the capital. In 1870, the cornerstone was laid for the Capitol building, made from sandstone hauled from a local quarry — owned and operated by Curry.

"It's really sad we forget about old Abe Curry," Candace Duncan said. "The cemetery even spells his name wrong. We should thank him for making us the capital."

Masayko said fears of losing the capital are groundless because the state has spent millions constructing new government buildings in Carson City in recent years. "The

state of Nevada has made a statement here in Carson City that they have committed to keeping the state capital here," he said. "That comes from the legislative building expansion, all the state office buildings and the folks who are performing the state's business."

Masayko compared Carson City's status to that of Sacramento, California's capital. It doesn't matter, he said, that Sacramento is smaller than Los Angeles and San Francisco. "Sacramento is going to keep the state capital and so is Carson City. San Francisco and Los Angeles aren't going to take it away from (Sacramento). Las Vegas and Reno aren't going to take it away from us. Don't give that a second thought."

But Maxine Nietz does.

"The reason is that other city down south and their needs," she said. "When we look at those kinds of things and count the heads, that's where that fear comes from."

Room 308 in Carson City's St. Charles Hotel looks as if stagecoach driver Hank Monk just left it.

At heart, still a small town

Mark Amodei, a state senator from Carson City, checks the agenda in his law office.

Lots of kids want to grow up and be famous, but Jared Tatro figures he's got an edge. The Carson High School graduate already is planning his campaign to become a U.S. senator.

"I kind of have an advantage in Carson," said the seventeen-year-old whose father, Tom, was on the city's Board of Supervisors. "Tatro is a pretty well-known name here. I've met a lot of people. That helps with politics. With politics it does work out. I only have to meet so many people. I have to meet 40,000 people, not 400,000."

The teen, a lifelong resident of Carson City, already has taken what has become the traditional first political step in a community that used to pride itself on being the nation's smallest state capital. Tatro was Carson High's student body president, an office once occupied by Paul Laxalt, the city's most famous neighborhood kid who made good.

"The Carson City I knew and grew up in no longer exists," said Laxalt, a Washington attorney who was governor from 1967 to 1970 before serving two terms in the U.S. Senate. "Like most (kids), I didn't really like the place. You know how kids are — there's never enough to do. Looking back on it, they were absolutely wonderful days. It was a carefree small Nevada town."

Laxalt remembers a state capital with dirt streets and 1,450 residents — when he was the forward on Carson High's 1938 and 1939 state champion basketball teams. Since then the city has grown. In recent years, even since the 1990 census, the population has risen from 40,443 to 51,860. Carson City no longer is tiny. It hasn't been the country's smallest capital for a long time.

"The distinction has been gone for thirty-five years," said Guy Rocha, a Carson City resident and state historian who lists eleven capitals smaller than Carson City and expects more after the 2000 census. "It's pretty to remember, but the Carson City of today is a pleasant — no longer little — burg."

Despite the growth, some things haven't changed. A Carson City youth, such as Tatro, still can grow up to be relatively famous, do it relatively quickly and stay relatively close to the old neighborhood.

"If a kid like Tatro wants that, he can get himself into a position here; he can run for office," said Rocha, who said teenagers with the same desire in big cities must overcome more competition. "The 'local kid makes good' here is easier and it's high profile quickly. Here, you can emerge very rapidly."

That's part of living in a medium-sized capital that once was small and remains intimate.

- Oct. 31, 1864: Nevada becomes a state and Carson City the capital.
- 1866: A branch of the U.S. Mint is established on a site donated by Curry. The mint, like other government buildings in Carson City, is made from sandstone from Curry's quarry. Today, it's the Nevada State Museum.
- 1869: The Virginia & Truckee Railroad opens and becomes famous carrying ore from Virginia City's Comstock Lode.
- 1870: Cornerstone laid for the state Capitol, made from Curry sandstone.
- December 1890: Stewart Indian School founded as Carson Indian School.
- 1897: One of the most famous prizefights of the century takes place at the racetrack on St. Patrick's Day, as Bob Fitzsimmons knocks out "Gentleman Jim" Corbett in the 14th round for the world heavyweight championship.
- March 22, 1919: First airplane flight across the Sierra from Sacramento to Carson City.
- 1950: Virginia & Truckee Railroad ceases operation.
- 1969: Carson City and Ormsby County consolidate into city-county government.
- 1970: Legislature building completed.
- 1975: Carson High School boys basketball team wins Class AAA state championship, the last large-school state title for a Nevada team outside Las Vegas.
- 1978: City begins growth management. Ordinance limits growth to 3 percent annually.
- April 1980: U.S. government closes Stewart Indian School.
- 1992: New Supreme Court building opens.

"I know this may be overused, but it was a Huck Finn-Tom Sawyer town," said Dean Heller, a neighborhood kid who has grown up to be Nevada's secretary of state. "I never wore shoes. I didn't like Sunday. I had to wear shoes to go to church. It was summer and you didn't wear shoes. You didn't wear a shirt. You had a tan like you wouldn't believe. You had tough feet."

But that isn't enough to get elected. It's harder to make good in Carson City than it was when Laxalt grew up. Now, you've also got to win in Clark County, home to most of Nevada's population.

"I'd get my tail kicked in Clark County and make it up in the north," said Laxalt, who recalled racing bicycles with his friends down Carson Street to the Capitol. "It's nearly impossible to do that now."

Local kids continue to try. Heller, thirty-eight, served two terms in the Assembly representing a Carson City-area district, then twice won statewide election for secretary of state, most recently in 1998. He is mentioned as a possible Republican candidate for governor.

"Half the staff here I went to high school with," Heller said of the workers in his office. "My mom was a cheerleader at Carson High. I remember going back to the alumni (basketball) games and watching Laxalt play and my mom cheerleading."

If Heller gets to be governor, mother Janet wants just one thing. "The Governor's Mansion — I'd like to have Christmas in there," she said with a laugh. Janet Heller, who grew up in Carson City, already has been to the mansion. It was a place to play with her friends, Governor Charles Russell's children, during the 1950s. Maybe Carson City isn't so small and friendly as it used to be, but it's still a place where the governor rides his bicycle down the street.

"My wife is from Southern California," Heller said. "When she came up here, one of the first things she saw was former Governor

Secretary of State Dean Heller hunted frogs as a boy in Carson City and likes recreation-league hoops.

(Bob) Miller riding his bike. She said, 'I've never seen a governor. I've never seen a U.S. senator. Now I'm watching the governor go down the street.' She's used to it now."

In Carson City, Heller was Huck Finn. "Years ago, we would go down to the (state) prison and the old sewer; we'd jump in because there were frogs," Heller said. "There were frogs all over the place. We would literally get buckets full of frogs and bring them home." Heller enjoys this story. To him, the tale is Carson City at its best.

"We'd even jump the fence to the prison grounds. They had a barbed wire fence that was kind of the official line you didn't cross. We'd all jump over that fence because you'd see these frogs all over the place. We'd grab

An excerpt from Robert Laxalt's untitled memoir in progress

CARSON CITY

- Population in 1998: 51,860 (22 percent under 18, 39 percent 18-44, 24 percent 45-64; 15 percent 65-plus; 50 percent male, 50 percent female).
- Population in 2003: (projected) 56,800.
- Median income: $39,076.
- Total retail sales: $785.9 million.

- Claim to fame: State capital.

- How it got its name: Named for the Carson River, which was named by John C. Frémont for his friend and scout Christopher "Kit" Carson.

- Local legend: Paul Laxalt. The local boy who made good, Laxalt grew up in Carson City, was elected Ormsby County district attorney in 1950, lieutenant governor in 1962 and governor in 1966. He served two terms in the U.S. Senate. Laxalt is a Washington lawyer.

As far as Western towns went, Carson City was a polite town. From the time I was a young boy, I said hello to everyone I met on Main Street and they said hello to me. Nobody said I had to. It was just the accepted thing to do, from the governor on down to the town drunk who slumped out of the whorehouses just off Main Street.

The fact that Carson was a small town obviously had something to do with this. I could walk from one city limit to the other in half an hour. Main Street meant a grocery store, a butcher shop, a shoe store, a clothing store for men and one for women, a couple of cafés, a pool hall, a hardware store and five saloons.

Interspersed between them were ponderous buildings such as the courthouse, the U.S. Post Office, the state library, a one-time U.S. Mint and the depot where the Virginia & Truckee short-line railway stopped. In the middle of town rose the State Capitol of Nevada, with its spiraling dome and winding balcony in a setting of sprawling green lawns and dark elms.

To find someone's house it really wasn't necessary to know all the street signs because houses were identified by their occupants, not their locations. The west side of town was the high-toned part, spreading down to the Governor's mansion, its gracious homes and lawns under a canopy of cottonwood trees. The east side of Carson had smaller homes and beyond them were Indian shacks and Chinatown, until it was burned down by design.

Robert Laxalt

On Main Street, people who worked in government wore suits, neckties and hats. Their wives wore proper dresses and summer frocks and hats. The so-called working class wore blue overalls, the ranchers wore high boots and big hats. Indian men wore cast-off clothes and squaws who sat against the buildings on Main Street wore blankets to help the sun warm their old bones.

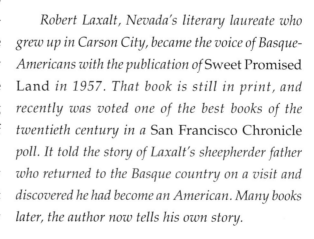

Robert Laxalt, Nevada's literary laureate who grew up in Carson City, became the voice of Basque-Americans with the publication of Sweet Promised Land *in 1957. That book is still in print, and recently was voted one of the best books of the twentieth century in a* San Francisco Chronicle *poll. It told the story of Laxalt's sheepherder father who returned to the Basque country on a visit and discovered he had become an American. Many books later, the author now tells his own story.*

these frogs and they'd be yelling at us from the (guard) tower to get back over the fence. We'd catch a few more frogs and jump back over."

Times have changed. Years have passed since Heller hunted frogs.

"The world you enjoyed is the world that's being rapidly phased out," said Guy Rocha. "What we're doing now is preserving the ambiance of Carson City."

Some of it can be seen every Tuesday at the Carson Station Hotel Casino, where a group of twenty-two elderly men, most former state administrators, sit down for lunch. They call themselves Charles Russell's Old Men's Club after the ex-governor who died in 1989. Russell's Club has been meeting and eating weekly for thirty-one years.

"That group represents another era," Rocha said. "Carson City is in transition. The newcomers don't know them. You can tell how long a person has been here by whether they know those people or not."

Another sure sign of an old-timer is somebody who remembers when the city had more cattle and sheep than cars.

"There were no paved streets; we ran our sheep through there," Laxalt said. "In high school, there were only two kids with cars. We hated their guts."

Along with old classmates, Carson City also has old familiar buildings. Heller works in the Capitol, where he used to deliver newspapers. Elsewhere along Carson Street, Heller and everyone else can walk to the former U.S. Mint (now the Nevada State Museum), the maroon-brick St. Charles Hotel built in 1862, the old post office that now serves as the office for the state's Tourism Department and other community landmarks.

"You look around town now and com-pare it to thirty years ago and things have changed — but a lot of things haven't changed," said attorney Mark Amodei, another neighborhood kid making good who won his 1998 race for state Senate. "The federal building is still there when you drive down the main street. The prison is still there when you drive down East Fifth Street. A lot of the sights that anchor you in the town are still the same."

So are some of the traditions. Amodei was student body president at Carson High and served as a congressional intern for Laxalt in Washington. Amodei also played on a state championship basketball team, Carson High's last, in 1975. His downtown law office resembles a city museum. He's got coins from the old mint. He's got a basketball from the championship team signed by all the players. He's got a stone from the walls of the old Virginia & Truckee Railroad depot.

"They did it all by hand," Amodei said, holding the stone for inspection. "There was a guy with a hammer and chisel mak-ing whatever you see here. See the chisel marks on that?" Yes, the marks are present. The stone is important to Amodei as part of Carson City's past.

"Carson has changed a lot in thirty years, but it's still Carson," he said. "It's a town of 50,000, but you still hear people complaining that everyone knows everyone else's business."

Room is a museum to a colorful character

A portrait of George Tufly, Nevada State Treasurer in 1865, hangs inside the St. Charles Hotel, which he once owned in downtown Carson City.

Room 308 at Carson City's St. Charles Hotel is reserved for Hank Monk. Nobody else may stay there. Inside are personal items, equipment and a small bed for Monk, a Sierra stagecoach driver from 1852 almost until his death on February 28, 1883. The restored St. Charles, across Carson Street from the Capitol, was headquarters for Monk — who loved wild rides and hard liquor.

"Local history remembers Hank Monk as the man who could drive when he couldn't walk," writes Nancy Miluck, a regional author who lives in Genoa. "Drink seemed to incapacitate his legs, but never impaired his driving ability; it is told through generations that he was often carried from the saloon to the coach to resume his run."

Monk, who drove the famous Bonanza Toll Road between Virginia City and Placerville, California, stayed at the St. Charles, which opened in 1862 and is advertised as Nevada's oldest hotel. The tiny Monk room is maintained by Karen Hamann, who bought the St. Charles in 1996. Hamann has turned most of the maroon-brick building into office suites. But Monk — who is buried in the Carson City Cemetery — is honored with Room 308, which is actually a museum.

Monk was known for drinking a toast from his whiskey bottle every time he reached the top of Kingsbury Grade between Carson Valley and Lake Tahoe. On one trip, the bottle came in handy.

"Testimony to his courage was given in the tale of Hank's being accosted by a robber on the Kingsbury Grade just as he was taking a sip from his ever-present bottle to mark the crest," Miluck wrote. "With his whip hand, he threw his bottle to knock the robber out and then tossed the brigand into the coach and delivered him to the sheriff at Friday's Station."

Another version of the tale was written by Phyllis Zauner in *Carson City — Capital of Nevada*. Zauner wrote that Monk, upon seeing a bandit along the road, "slowed the team to a walk, poured the last of his whiskey over his head, and slumped down in a simulated stupor. When the highwayman saw his condition, he contemptuously ignored the drunken driver and turned to robbing passengers. Monk stealthily grabbed a length of iron pipe and laid the robber out cold."

Sweat, steam evoke bygone age of iron

The 1910 McKeen Motor Car No. 22 is Chris DeWitt's latest work in progress at Carson City's Nevada State Railroad Museum. This is a self-propelled coach that carried passengers on the Virginia & Truckee Railroad until 1948, two years before the famous Comstock line ceased operation. DeWitt's job is to make the McKeen look and act the way the car did in its prime. He's the museum's supervisor of restoration.

"I like railroads, but I was never a train buff," said DeWitt, a metallurgical engineer in the San Francisco Bay area before coming to the museum in 1981. "It's a lot of fun."

DeWitt and his three full-time assistants are state employees with jobs most kids would envy: they play with trains.

"This has a certain amount of class," Lee Hobold, one of DeWitt's mechanics, said of the McKeen. "It's ugly in its own way."

The seventy-foot-long car that ran a half-million miles during thirty-eight years of trips between Reno and Minden-Gardnerville is bruised and battered. The gasoline engine and wheels are gone. The McKeen was used last as a plumber's office on South Carson Street before being donated to the museum. DeWitt figures two or three years are needed to restore the car. That's how it is with most of the work DeWitt and his crew do in the maintenance barn behind the railroad museum, where the historic engines and cars are studied, stripped and rebuilt. The barn is noisy and cluttered. Nothing happens in a hurry. Restoration takes time.

Work on the McKeen began in 1998 but research comes before repair. The process is similar for every engine or car that ends up in DeWitt's shop. Museum historians must decide how they want the relics to look. They check records and old photographs. They talk to people. At the museum, historians and mechanics don't always agree.

"We have to do a lot of research on the paint work," said Hobold, who collected toy trains as a youngster. "A lot of time, we'll talk to old-timers. Sometimes we question the research. We argue back and forth." After working in the restoration shop for a decade, Hobold has found the wood in the old train cars one of the most important details. "We try to use the same kind of wood — Douglas fir and oak," he said.

Hobold started in the restoration shop as a volunteer after moving to Carson City from Los Angeles. Much of his work is dirty and hard. Sweat is a big part of restoring historic steam engines. "Everything is heavy on a locomotive," he said. "Everything is greasy and everything has to be cleaned up."

Much of the museum commemorates the V&T Railroad, founded in 1868 to haul silver ore from the Comstock mines to the Carson River. Old cars and engines aren't difficult to find.

"When the V&T would get rid of equipment, there would be records of where it went," Curator John Ballweber said. "It's still out there. You can't really hide a train car."

The McKeen car was sold by the V&T to be used as a restaurant in Carson City. Then it became the plumber's office.

"Everyone knew it was there," Ballweber said.

Hobold and the other mechanics completed work in 1999 on the V&T's steam engine No. 27 which pulled the line's last train May 31, 1950. The old engine had been on display in Virginia City.

"That was a very complicated project," Ballweber said. "It's a steam locomotive with a lot of parts." If a part is missing, you can't buy it at a hardware store. You've got to make it in the restoration shop. That's what might happen with the McKeen if an original gas engine can't be found.

"We have the blueprints," Hobold said. "We could fabricate an engine for it, but that would be expensive." The McKeen car is rare: About 200 were build by the McKeen Motor Car Company in Omaha, Nebraska. They were made mostly of iron.

"This is a completely different project," Hobold said. "We're used to wooden cars and steam engines."

1910 McKeen Motor Car

Dayton

Downtown Dayton

Changing Dayton clings to its identity

Dayton artist Steve Saylor introduces Hemingway, one of his pet cats.

Steve Saylor is a renowned artist whose work is known across the country, but when Saylor first came to town in 1972, he was just a kid from back East with long hair and a ponytail. Nobody seemed to mind. In fact, the cowboys, miners and other old-timers in this historic community looked out for the stranger.

"I remember feeling honored, being asked to be one of the four guys in the volunteer fire department," Saylor said. "They even let me drive the truck."

That's how Dayton operates. Gold was discovered here in 1849 by prospectors from California. Ever since, people have been coming to Dayton looking for all sorts of things. Sometimes it's peace and quiet. Other times it's adventure. Most of them end up fitting in.

"I came here because of the characters, to paint their faces in their environment," said Saylor, who has been painting pictures of his neighbors for almost three decades. "People have looked out for me as I stumbled along."

Characters are accepted here. Guys with nicknames like "Swiss Bill" and "Cadillac" have been part of the landscape, just like the tiny downtown's historic buildings.

"I remember the old yodeler's name, 'Swiss Bill,' " said Julie DeWitt, who arrived in Dayton from Sacramento sixteen years ago in a blizzard. "He'd yodel on his way home from the bar at night. Everybody could hear him at two in the morning. It was wonderful to wake up and hear Swiss Bill."

DeWitt didn't come to Dayton to hear Swiss Bill yodel. That was a bonus. "This is the first really small town I've lived in," DeWitt said. "It took me just about a year to adjust to a rural, quiet, slower pace."

But that pace, whether DeWitt and others like it or not, is picking up. Subdivisions are sprouting, with more to come as Dayton evolves into a bedroom community filled with newcomers commuting to jobs in nearby Carson City, the state capital.

"In ten years, we'll be the size Carson City was twenty-five to thirty years ago," said Barbara Peck, an eighteen-year resident and chairperson of the Dayton Regional Advisory Council. "We're at 8,000 (in the area) now. Easily, we'll double that."

Peck doesn't want to see that happen. "This is never going to be the same community," she

IMPORTANT DATES

- **1849:** Gold discovered.
- **1851:** Settlement established.
- **Early 1850s:** Spafford Hall, the first permanent settler, builds a trading post and the site became known as Hall's Station.
- **1861:** Dayton becomes Lyon County seat in Nevada Territory.
- **1863:** Odeon Hall, constructed by the Odd Fellows Association of Dayton for $32,000, opens.
- **1869-1878:** The four-mile Sutro Tunnel is dug through the mountains from Dayton to Virginia City. The tunnel, financed by Adolph Sutro of San Francisco, was used to drain hot water from the Virginia City mines.
- **1870:** Union Hotel opens.
- **1911:** Courthouse burns and county seat moved to Yerington.
- **1960:** Marilyn Monroe and Clark Gable come to town to shoot scenes for the movie "The Misfits."
- **Aug. 17, 1974:** Revival of annual Santa Maria Day festival.
- **April 28, 1981:** Fire destroys Dayton Station, a popular downtown restaurant.
- **1990:** Three large manufacturing companies move into Dayton industrial park.
- **Jan. 27, 1990:** Rededication of the Bluestone Building, originally constructed in 1862, which is now the District Courthouse.
- **May 11, 1991:** Dayton Valley Country Club opens.
- **1992:** Population doubles from 1980, U.S. Highway 50 east from Carson City widened to four lanes through town.
- **1995:** Federal government begins cleanup of mercury contamination in the Carson River.

said. "I will probably move, ten years down the road."

Dayton has been growing for a decade. Peck predicts the population increase will accelerate if the sewer plant is expanded. "We are talking about a multi-million-dollar project," she said. "It's all because of the growth. Once that's resolved, I predict a huge explosion in population."

Dayton is not an incorporated city. Most of its services come from Lyon County, which is responsible for the sewer.

"The capacity is becoming a concern," said County Manager Stephen Snyder. "With the focus on growth there, we are currently working on that. We are nearing capacity."

Before long, Peck claimed, Dayton will become a city — incorporating and dealing with utilities and other growth-related issues. "We're going to have to incorporate," she said.

Dayton has a tradition of providing for itself. When townspeople wanted a library, donations were collected to cover a large share of the bill. One of the latest projects is a pool with an anticipated cost of $280,000. A task force is soliciting money and volunteer labor.

"They always come through," Jannette Hoffert, volunteer coordinator for Dayton's well-used community center, said of her neighbors. "We kind of proved that over the Christmas holidays when we were short money in the food bank for turkeys. We put it in the newspaper and we had money from heaven."

Another Christmas emergency arose when the town came up eighty-nine short of the 327 presents sought for needy kids. "We started making phone calls," Hoffert said. "We got donations. We came up with those eighty-nine presents in three hours. That's what we need to preserve."

As Peck and others worry about Dayton's future, the federal government is cleaning up a problem from the town's past — mercury contamination. Officials of the Environmental Protection Agency said cleanup of the toxic mercury left from Dayton's gold mining days is 80 percent complete.

"There is a lot of mercury all over the region," said Wayne Praskins, the EPA's Dayton project manager. "It's only a problem if concentrations are high enough and people are close enough. Most of it's been washed into the river system."

Mercury was used in 19th-century refining procedures to extract precious metals from ore that was processed in mills along the Carson River.

"The goal is to prevent contact with highly contaminated soil," Praskins said. "We're replacing it with clean fill."

That will remove contamination, but leave Dayton with the struggle of keeping its small-town identity in the face of rapid change.

An old firetruck, one of many for sale, sits in a Dayton vacant lot.

Edna MacDiarmid and
the Union Hotel

T he past lies shallow,
a thin line of foam, driftwood set down
on a lake's edge, on the high water
mark along the river.

Records need not lie deep,
first or last white settlement
not yet in dispute or put to ground,
ornamented with superlatives.

Edna reclaims her story from photos,
diaries, yellowed books, flyleaves of Bibles
or memories stored in high ceiling rooms,
one mind going into and out of shadow.

Into the sunshine of Marilyn Monroe,
filming *The Misfits*,
taking time to visit, bringing Edna a plate
of tacos and gentle conversation.

Clark Gable remarked to Edna, the postmaster,
Dayton's post office might not have been
the largest, but it was certainly the most
colorful he had ever mailed a letter in.

The cracked walls remain covered
water damaged wallpaper patterned in diamonds
of green and maroon, fading watermarks.
Her hotel was famous, she laughs
for its two-story outhouse no longer
beside a free-standing, quarried-rock wall
which served as the Pony Express station
and stop for the Overland Stage.

Dayton is not the same, she says, no
foot traffic passes the Union Hotel doors,
no children play in the streets,
adults aren't as sociable any more.

Some have the tendency
to move here and shut the gate,
single-generation Nevadans, still developing
their sense of place
for whom the past must be reclaimed
in telling and listening, moments like this
when time slows to a walk, nods, stops
to pay its respects to Edna MacDiarmid.

*Bill Cowee,
poem's author*

Edna MacDiarmid

DAYTON

- Population in 1998:
3,690
(27 percent under 18,
38 percent 18-44,
24 percent 45-64;
11 percent 65-plus;
52 percent male,
48 percent
female).

- Population in 2003:
(projected) 4,461.

- Median income:
$31,155.

- Total retail sales:
$9.254 million.

- Claim to fame: Site
of gold discovery
in Nevada, 1849.

- How it got its
name: Surveyor
John Day drew
town boundaries in
1861; residents of
the settlement
agreed to name
their community,
known first as Gold
Canyon, after him.

- Local legend:
Gold miner James
"Old Virginny"
Finney is said to be
the man after
which Virginia City
is named. His
grave is in the
Dayton Cemetery.
The story also goes
that Finney was
bucked off a mule.

1849 seems like yesterday

The steer burger at the Wild Horse Saloon on Main Street is a half-pound of ground beef that costs $5.25 and takes a long time to eat. Before you get started, Joe France — co-owner of the bar-restaurant housed in one of Dayton's oldest buildings — wants to point out a few things.

"We've been working on this for two years," said France, who restored historic covered bridges in Oregon before finding his latest project: the Wild Horse, which first opened in 1887. "We wanted pictures, all of Dayton. All of this stuff on our walls has been given to us by people who live here."

That's important to France because those are the folks working to restore the history of a town claiming to be the birthplace of Nevada after decades of being ignored as an important spot on the state map.

"Dayton was kicked aside," said Laura Tennant, a local newspaper editor who organized a 1999 celebration of the 1849 discovery of gold not far from the Wild Horse. "Our history was kicked aside."

Now it's being brought back a little at a time by Tennant, France, Ray Walmsley and others like them. Some, including Walmsley, whose great-grandfather moved to Dayton in 1859, have been in town a long time. Others, including France, who started work on the Wild Horse in 1996, are newcomers.

"We've had a lot of people move into the newer part of the community," said Steven Saylor, who has developed a national reputation as a Western artist after coming to Dayton from New York in 1972. "The community is changing those people more than they are changing the community. I've never had such a feeling of community. We hope we can keep that."

Dayton, where the early digging for gold led straight to the mining of the Comstock Lode, was overshadowed by Virginia City, Nevada's famous boomtown and historic landmark. Dayton also lost to Genoa, which takes credit for being the state's first settlement. But Dayton is growing, mostly with residents of subdivisions outside the old downtown area who commute to work in Carson City on U.S. 50 or make the longer drive to Reno-Sparks.

Tennant hopes growth somehow will provide money for restoration.

"It's basically untouched," she said of the old downtown. "It's slowly decaying and disintegrating."

France is completing work at the Wild Horse, where old photos and paintings of Dayton and its people will be displayed in the restaurant. Across Main Street, the Bluestone Building — constructed in 1862 as a mining warehouse — stands as Dayton's best rehabilitation job. Fixed up and rededicated in 1990, it houses the District Court and other offices.

"They're talking about putting (downtown) back the way it was," Saylor said. "We want to put back the old board sidewalks. We want to put the gaslights back. We want to move the power lines. Nobody really cared. Now, we do care."

Saylor lives up the street from the Wild Horse in a home built in 1856 that Walmsley's ancestors owned. When Saylor first moved in, he had no running water or electricity. He hauled drinking water in five-gallon jugs from a faucet a couple blocks away. Saylor had six jugs; one lasted a single day. Electricity came in 1974, but Saylor carried water until 1976 when he connected to the sewer system.

"That changed things," said Saylor, whose art hangs in the Capitol in Carson City. "I didn't realize what a chore it was until I didn't have to do it anymore."

The fifty-year-old, who is part of the color of Dayton, lives in the home with wife, Johnye. They're surrounded by twenty-two cats, seventeen peacocks, seventy-five chickens, two horses, three dogs, three turkeys and one quail.

"We're trying to find her a boyfriend," Johnye said of the quail.

Gold was discovered practically in their back yard. People in town give directions to the 1849 discovery site as if they're explaining how to reach a drug store.

"When you go into Dayton, turn right at the light and stay on Main Street," said Bob Cox, president of Dayton's historical society. "The next place is Steve Saylor's house. Gold was discovered right behind where he lives."

Down Main Street from the Saylors and across from the Wild Horse, Edna MacDiarmid, ninety-three, lives in the Union Hotel. MacDiarmid, who came to Dayton from Saskatchewan, Canada, in the 1940s, is part of Dayton's color, as is the two-story Union, built in 1870. MacDiarmid, who served as Dayton's postmaster, bought the hotel and lives there alone, except for Carol Taylor, whose bedroom was the old post office. Taylor takes care of MacDiarmid, who is surrounded mostly by memories.

"Every Saturday night we had dances," said MacDiarmid, who allowed the town's youngsters inside her hotel for the festivities.

"I had teenage dances and I'd lock the door. I'd tell the kids, 'If

The sun sets on the old homestead at Winters Ranch in Dayton.

This pastoral scene is on Winters Ranch in late afternoon.

The Union is important because the hotel and its chief resident have so many connections to the rest of the town. When Tennant married in 1968, her wedding reception took place at the Union. When Saylor, new in Dayton and poor, couldn't pay his post office box rent, MacDiarmid came up with the money.

"She's a neat old gal," Cox said.

Before moving into the Union, MacDiarmid lived in another downtown hotel, the Fox. That's where she met Tennant, a teenager who wanted to spend the last year of high school in Dayton after her mother moved to Carson City.

"I was pretty independent," Tennant said. "I went door to door to see who I could live with." MacDiarmid took her in.

"There's a lot of camaraderie, people helping each other out," Saylor said of Dayton.

That's what April Logue, a graduate of Dayton High School, likes about the town. "It's neat knowing people," said Logue, who moved from Los Angeles to Dayton with her parents in 1986. "A lot of people you talk to in Carson, they don't have the same kind of experience we're having. I think we have an advantage."

But Logue and her classmates leave Dayton for Carson City and Reno-Sparks to do everything from clothes shopping to movie watching. "It's kind of a dependent community," Roman Timoshkin, eighteen, said of Dayton.

"We live out here, but we have to go to Carson for everything else," said Logue, whose parents are among the U.S. 50 commuters with jobs in Carson City. The kids are hoping growth will produce other stores and businesses to go with the large supermarket under construction near the subdivisions.

These students are growing up in a different Dayton than the town occupied by Tennant, Saylor and MacDiarmid.

you go out you're not coming back.' It was too close to the saloon. I was an old crab."

The Union Hotel is a possible target for restoration. MacDiarmid lives on the ground floor; the nine upstairs bedrooms are closed.

"It would take a ton of money to bring it up to code," Cox said. "All the (bedrooms) are filled with the original metal beds. You can't go up there."

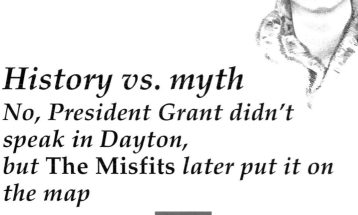

History vs. myth
No, President Grant didn't speak in Dayton, but The Misfits *later put it on the map*

Marilyn Monroe loved tacos. Every afternoon, the glamorous movie star would bring a batch to share with friend Edna MacDiarmid at the Union Hotel on Main Street.

"Marilyn used to come over with her tacos," said the ninety-three-year-old Union owner and one of only two residents in the 128-year-old hotel. "She was very gracious and very nice."

MacDiarmid, who came to Dayton from Canada in the 1940s, has seen many visitors pass through town. Monroe showed up in 1960 with Clark Gable, Montgomery Clift, Thelma Ritter, Eli Wallach and director John Huston to film scenes for *The Misfits*. The picture — also shot in Reno — was the last completed by Monroe, who died two years later.

Cooks on the movie set made the tacos.

"*The Misfits* put us on the map," said Bob Cox, another longtime Dayton resident. The film's makers were seeking an Old West town as the backdrop for a rodeo and wild-horse roundup.

"It was about 1,000 people (watching) when they shot some of the scenes," MacDiarmid said. Other than MacDiarmid's

memories, about all that's left to remind locals of the movie is the Old Corner Bar on Main Street, where some scenes were shot and a dry lake bed outside of town named Misfit Flats.

In 1982, another movie legend — Clint Eastwood — came looking for the Old West when he was starring in *Honkytonk Man*, a film about a 1930s-era country singer. Cox got a part in the picture as an extra. But he never appeared on film.

"We got left on the cutting-room floor," he said. Cox made $30 for his trouble and a dog he owned also was used in the movie. The producers paid $40 for the dog.

"I had a bloodhound they wanted," Cox said. "Why pay him $10 more than me?"

Along with Monroe and Eastwood, Dayton takes credit for another famous guest — Ulysses S. Grant, Civil War hero and eighteenth President of the United States. A bronze plaque on the front wall of the Odeon Hall & Saloon, another of Dayton's nineteenth-century buildings, proclaims that Grant stood on the balcony and addressed a "responsive group of townspeople" in October 1878.

No, he didn't, said state archivist Guy

Rocha, an expert on Nevada history. Grant, president from 1869 to 1877, had left the White House when he visited the Comstock.

"Grant did not speak in Dayton," Rocha said. "He did not speak from the balcony of the Odeon Hall." Rocha cites a local newspaper account of the Comstock tour that said Grant "passed through" Dayton, but "did not stop or pause" in town.

"It didn't really happen, I guess," said Ray Walmsley, seventy-three, whose grandmother was born in Dayton before Nevada became a state. "History is chance."

Rocha said historical myths such as the Grant story are common in Nevada and across the country. "What happens with people later is they want an association with an ex-president," Rocha said. "They have a bad case of the 'George Washington slept here' syndrome. Nevada is full of that. Every place is full of that. They want great events to happen in their town."

Ninety-three-year-old Edna MacDiarmid, who was Dayton's postmaster for many years, lives in the Old Union Hotel.

Who was first in Nevada?

New Dayton evidence questions Genoa's longtime claim

hen Dayton resident Ray Walmsley is asked if his historic town gave the state its start, the response is quick.

"There were people here before anyone was in Genoa," said Walmsley, whose great-grandfather was an arrival in 1859. But when Genoa resident Nancy Miluck is asked if her historic town is Nevada's birthplace, the response is equally emphatic.

"It is! It is! It is!" Miluck repeated, shaking her head for emphasis as she sat in the living room of a 150-year-old house on First Street. As Nevada ends one century and prepares for the next, the argument about who got here first heats up.

Genoa, situated in a picturesque spot at the foot of the Sierra, always has taken credit for being the state's first white settlement. Although gold was discovered in Dayton in 1849, both communities trace their permanent roots to 1851. That's when miners occupied Dayton, with farmers and merchants settling in Genoa.

A sign at the edge of town proclaims "Genoa — Nevada's First Settlement 1851." A flier advertising Dayton's celebration of the 150th anniversary of the discovery of gold proclaims it "The Oldest Town in Nevada." Nobody outside Dayton paid much attention to that claim until 1998, when state archivist Guy Rocha, an expert on Nevada history, sided with the upstart.

"There were always people (in Dayton) mining," he said. "When historians began to write, the voices heard were the voices of Genoa, not of Dayton."

Today, the voices in Genoa accuse Rocha of a publicity stunt.

"That's being hustled, I think, by the state historian," Michael Miluck, Nancy's husband, said of the dispute. "They're stirring it up to get good stories out if it. I don't think they really believe it."

Voices in Dayton are proclaiming Rocha a hero. "We were jumping with joy," said Lee Vecchiarelli, who works in one of Dayton's oldest buildings — the one on Main Street, constructed in 1887, that houses the Wild Horse Saloon.

Dayton won the race to be first by a matter of weeks, Rocha said. After the initial gold discovery, California miners returned permanently to the site near the Carson River in May 1851. Rocha cited diaries in which the first Dayton settlers write about a group from Salt Lake City led by forty-two-year-old merchant John Reese, traveling along the Carson River, headed for what would become Genoa.

"I have assumed all along, as most Nevadans have, that Genoa was the first settlement," said James Hulse, retired University of Nevada, Reno history professor. "But if there is new evidence, we ought to take a look at it. It's not unique for history to be turned around after finding new evidence."

Reese is credited with erecting the first permanent structure in 1851 at the Genoa site — which initially was called Mormon Station — arriving in June and building a trading post. The Dayton miners lived in tents, something Genoa's defenders are happy to point out.

"Does a settlement exist when you have a hole in the ground or a tent?" Michael Miluck asked. "As far as setting up the general store, the post office, things like that, Genoa was the one that did it."

Elko

Rope tricks by Felix Luna and the Charros Arenas Mexicanas are part of the Basque parade as it passes the Elko County Courthouse.

Elko changes with the times but it's still real cowboy country

A casino and polar bear survey an older part of Elko's main street.

Cowboys looking for jobs can check the upstairs bulletin board of the J.M. Capriola Co., at Fifth and Commercial streets: "Wanted," reads the notice. "Three/four cowboys. March through October. Slackers need not apply. Experience/ references required. Contact Glen Alameda, Saratoga, Wyo."

That's a long way to go to herd cows, but if you're a cowboy in the closing days of the twentieth century, you take work where you can get it. Elko and the wide-open spaces surrounding it might be cowboy country, but the landscape is changing. Work for guys who've spent a lifetime riding and roping are scarce.

'It's getting hard to get a job," said twenty-seven-year-old Frank Dominguez, who's been a working cowboy since he was fourteen. "There's not so many big outfits. You call around. You call the cow boss at these big ranches. You get to know them. They get to know you. It's not like it used to be."

But enough of the Old West remains to keep Dominguez and men like him coming back for more. The work is hard, the hours are long and the pay is terrible. Other than

that, being a cowboy — or "cowboying," as the *real* cowboys call it — is a great life.

Dominguez has tried getting off his horse and living in town. "I've tried it for a couple of months,"he said, "but I've always got to get back."

Elko celebrates the cowboy, whether he's the real one, such as Dominguez, or the mythical ones who exist in memory and legend. That's one of the things that makes the town distinct.

"Elko is the capital of cowboy culture, certainly in the Far West," said Guy Rocha, state archivist and Nevada history expert. That culture is everywhere, from Dominguez to the area's famous saddle makers, J.M. Capriola and Eddie Brooks; from Sarah Sweetwater, the local artist who started recording buckaroo lore in the 1970s, to the Elko High School kids who practice their roping during their lunch hour and the Western Folklife Center with its annual Cowboy Poetry Gathering that attracts visitors from around the world.

"This old high desert, it's home to me now," said Brooks, a sixty-six-year-old Texan who once made a saddle for President Lyndon Johnson. "When I first came here,

In Lamoille, about twenty-five miles from Elko, the sun sets behind the entrance to Ruby Dome Ranch at the base of the Ruby Mountains.

you could get on a horse at Elko and ride plumb to Idaho without hitting a fence. Now, it's fenced more. The mines came. They took a lot of the country."

Elko has grown because of gold mining. Since 1980, the population has more than doubled, rising from about 8,000 to more than 22,000. Mining slowed with the drop in the price of gold in 1999. But the big companies, Barrick and Newmont, continued to dig and people kept coming to town.

"Elko is a city," Rocha said, "not a town."

Mandi Alleman, who has lived in Elko since she was six months old, has seen the growth up close. "My dad's an optometrist," the Elko teenager said. "If he got eight eye exams a day, it was a good day. Now, he's working his butt off. He has twenty exams a day. The business is just really growing. There's construction all over. They're building these new subdivisions all over town."

Kyle Blackburn used to go hunting a short distance from town. Now he can't: the old hunting ground has become Spring Creek, a community with lots of homes and a high school of its own.

"There are so many houses out there, you can't get away from civilization," he said.

"Even if you go over to Ruby Valley or Star Valley, the place to go hunting is an hour away. There's a lot of houses."

Steve Burrows is one of the newcomers, arriving in town four years ago when his father changed jobs. "It's made the town a lot more open," the teen said of the rapid growth. "Outsiders coming in find it a lot more welcoming. I know I did. It's a lot more open than other towns I've been in."

Giovanni "Pooch" Puccinelli is a native who left after high school graduation in 1981 and returned in 1995. The growth occurred while he was gone. "It shocked me," Puccinelli said. "It was an 'old boy' town. When I left here, there was only one subdivision on the north side of the freeway. I'll bet there weren't 4,000 people out at Spring Creek."

But some things haven't changed. schoolteacher Pat Sheehan still paints herself green on Saint Patrick's Day, which is also her birthday. The kids at Northside Elementary love it. In 1999, her last year at the school before retiring, Sheehan was honored at a surprise Saint Patrick's Day-birthday assembly. Mayor Mike Franzoia showed up and Sheehan's fellow teachers wore green tinfoil wigs.

The sculptor who recorded cowboy poetry

If Sarah Sweetwater asks you to come over to help unload a few things and bring them into the house, be careful: you'll probably need a forklift. Chairwoman of the art department at Great Basin College in Elko, Sweetwater is a sculptor who likes carving marble. That's heavy stuff.

Elko artist and teacher Sarah Sweetwater places one of her sculptures in the solarium of her home.

"I always make my pieces larger than life," said Sweetwater, who once had eight tons of marble shipped from Italy by way of Oakland, California. Friends help her with the lifting. If you show up for work, expect Sweetwater to feed you.

"I like to do things over food," she said. "A good Texas woman likes to do things over food." Sweetwater is a good Texas woman. She legally changed her last name from Whisenant to Sweetwater, the name of her west Texas hometown. "I love the way it sounds," said Sweetwater, who loves cutting marble. "My voice is in stone."

Sweetwater's other true love is Elko's cowboy culture. She started recording cowboy poetry in the 1970s as part of a state-funded arts project.

"What I found was, they were still going to the bunkhouses after dinner and reading poems to each other," she said of the first cowboys she recorded. "That was their entertainment." Sweetwater took her tape recorder all over northeastern Nevada. Elko bars were among her best spots for finding poems and bizarre experiences.

"One night I was doing some recording and this old guy came home with me," Sweetwater said with a laugh. "He slept on my couch. He announced the next day that he was retiring at my house. I had a boyfriend who didn't think that was a good idea."

On Idaho Street in downtown Elko, Pauline Beitia watches the annual Basque Festival parade from her pickup truck.

"That is the character of Elko, to do bizarre and fun things like that," said Sweetwater, Sheehan's longtime friend.

The community remains isolated on Interstate 80, about halfway between Reno-Sparks and Salt Lake City. In some ways, Elko is as much influenced by Utah as Nevada. Local television sets receive broadcasts from stations in Salt Lake City and Boise, Idaho.

"We're smack dab in the middle of everything," Blackburn said. "Boise, Salt Lake, Reno." But they're close to nothing. "We measure time in hours on a bus." Yes, the bus thing. In any conversation with Elko kids, it has to come up, sooner or later.

They go everywhere on buses — to football games, basketball games, track meets, speech contests and band concerts. The rides are always long. To Reno and back is four hours each way, and that's an average trip.

"We just plan on it," said Alleman, who played soccer at Elko High School. "That's something we have to do that a lot of other schools just don't understand. The Reno schools, they complain so much about traveling to Elko, but it's one time out of their whole season. Some come once every

two years."

Elko kids know every bump, turn and twist in I-80. The lead story in one issue of the Elko High School student newspaper was a long report on the ownership change at a popular freeway truck stop about halfway between Elko and Reno. The kids talk about long trips with pride. It sets them apart, like a badge for being from Elko.

"It's a terribly self-sufficient town and always has been, stubbornly so," said Jan Petersen, program director of the Northeastern Nevada Museum. "It's literally in the middle of nowhere."

But, she'll tell you, Elko has its own orchestra and theater company, and its own ski lift. "There has been a ski lift in Elko since the mid-1940s," said Petersen, whose ancestors came to the area more than a century ago. "It was a rope tow that ran off a 1938 Dodge truck. Then they got this lift from someplace that had gone bankrupt in Idaho. They got a good deal on it."

In Elko, you've got to do things for yourself because you're too far from just about everything. The isolation has helped Elko maintain its distinct cultural traditions.

Saddle makers are on one street, Basque restaurants and hotels on another.

Miguel Leonis is the co-owner of the Star Hotel, which opened in December 1910 and remains a traditional Basque place today. "I came when I was twenty," said Leonis, who immigrated from Spanish Basque country to the United States in 1966. "I came to gather as much money as I could in two years and go back. It never happened."

After working as a sheepherder in central California and a butcher in Los Angeles, Leonis came to Elko and the Star a decade ago. He and many of his customers speak the ancient Basque language. Tourists and locals fill the traditional family-style dining room

The Star maintains the Basque custom of long-term boarders who stay in the upstairs hotel rooms and eat three meals a day in the dining room. In the evenings, the old-timers sit at a round table near the bar tended by Leonis and play *mus* (pronounced "moose"), a Basque card game.

"It's got a wonderful tradition," Petersen said of the Star. "When I was the telephone operator, their business phone was a pay phone."

Every year, the National Basque Festival is held in Elko on the Fourth of July weekend. That festival and the Cowboy Poetry Gathering in January are the community's biggest celebrations.

The largest breakfast might be at Toki Ona, a Basque restaurant across the street from Petersen's museum office. "It's chicken fried steak and gravy," Petersen said with a smile. "It's one of those heavy breakfasts that lasts until 3 o'clock in the afternoon. You can see this gravy gluing your arteries together, but it's wonderful."

So is Petersen's tale about Pete Itcaina and the Silver Dollar Bar in downtown Elko. "It's a Basque story," she said. "It had to be before Prohibition. There was this guy, Pete Itcaina, he got thrown out of the Silver Dollar

Basque dancers Nicole White, ten, and Antonia Lee, nine, came to Elko from Salt Lake City to compete at the Annual Basque Festival.

by the bartender. He went to the guy that owned the place and paid cash for the bar. This was about ten thirty or midnight. He went back and fired the bartender."

The Silver Dollar is still around, along with a lot of Elko history. The trail the pioneers took to California ran through the middle of what is now downtown. Since the days of moving west, millions of people have passed through Elko. Now they come on Interstate 80.

"We have an interesting mix of cultures," said Petersen, whose great-great-grandfather, Elijah Yeates, followed the railroad into town in 1868.

Dominguez hopes the cowboy way of life continues. "I want to do it as long as I can," he said. Around Elko, the ranching tradition remains strong. Roundups are done on horseback, and branding with fire and hot irons. That's the way it has always been.

"There's still a lot of outfits that do it the traditional way. If it's big country, that's the best way to do it," said Brooks, the saddle maker. "It's the last of the big country."

Frank Dominguez has been a working cowboy in the Elko area since he was a teenager.

With a view of snow-covered Ruby Mountains, a sculptured horse marks the shop of saddlemaker J.M. Capriola in downtown Elko.

Are they cowboys or buckaroos?

On the cattle ranches in northeastern Nevada, cowboys aren't cowboys, they're buckaroos. And yes, the two are different.

"Buckaroos pertain mostly to Nevada, southern Idaho, southeast Oregon and California," said twenty-seven-year-old Frank Dominguez, who has spent almost all of his working life on horseback. "The tradition was kind of started by the Spanish. It's just a different style of working cows. You spend more time with your horses, making them good cow horses."

Dominguez and others like him might call themselves "cowboys" and the work they do "cowboying," but those are generic terms. In the strict vocabulary of the West, buckaroos are those you see riding the range around Elko. Buckaroo comes from the Spanish word *vaquero*.

"There is a fundamental distinction between ranch-hand styles," said Paul Starrs, a geography professor at the University of Nevada, Reno who studies the West. "Cowboys are the supposed lesser beings from Texas. The buckaroo is the elegant master, derived from California roots." A former ranch hand who has written a book about the American West, Starrs said Elko is "clearly,

unequivocally," the nation's buckaroo capital.

Cowboys ride different saddles, he said. Buckaroos use more rawhide equipment. "Chunks of Idaho, Washington, California and Nevada are clearly, distinctively buckaroo country," Starrs said. "Colorado, Montana and Texas are clearly cowboy country."

Being a buckaroo who cares abut how he looks on horseback is expensive. Most of a buckaroo's pay goes into his gear.

"It wouldn't be hard for most guys to be packing $10,000 worth of stuff," said Dominguez, who started punching cows for a living when he was fourteen. "You have your silver bridles. For a good saddle, you'll pay $2,500 or $3,000." The average pay for riding the range around Elko is $1,000 to $2,000 a month. Buckaroos do it because they like it, not because they're getting rich.

"I'd say in Elko County and northern Nevada, it's about as true to it as anywhere," Dominguez said of ranching tradition. "Here, everything is done on horseback." Ranches in northeastern Nevada are isolated. If machines break down, ranchers have a long trip to get them fixed. Men

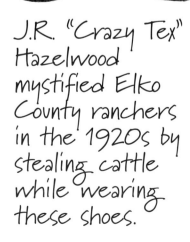

J.R. "Crazy Tex" Hazelwood mystified Elko County ranchers in the 1920s by stealing cattle while wearing these shoes.

Saddle-maker Eddie Brooks can look up from his work and see the Ruby Mountains from his studio in Spring Creek. Below: A tin can holds some of the leather-stamping tools Brooks uses to create his saddles

and horses are more reliable. But other, more personal reasons exist for ranching the old way.

"It's a pride thing," Dominguez said. "We want to practice our roping. Everybody wants to rope."

Ranching in northeastern Nevada is a balance between tradition and economics. In some cases, machines replace buckaroos. "We've cut back as we've gotten more mechanized," said Meg Glaser, whose family has been ranching near Elko since 1864. "Some of the big places have a crew that's strictly cowboying."

Glaser helps keep the tradition alive. She's the artistic director of Elko's Western Folklife Center, meeting place for the annual Cowboy Poetry Gathering. "They want to look good, they want to ride good, they want their horses to look good," Glaser said of the buckaroo way of life.

On the range, Dominguez and the other Elko buckaroos spend the summer tending herds, sleeping in tents next to the cattle. They'll come to town every couple of days to take showers. "You've got to stay pretty clean or you couldn't stand to be around each other," Dominguez said.

Eddie Brooks is another part of the

buckaroo culture. He makes saddles. "The ranch cowboys up here, they really appreciate it," Brooks said of his work. "They need real good stuff. When demand is for good saddles, it makes you bear down and do better."

The sixty-six year old Texan is a world-renowned craftsman who has made saddles that cost more than $35,000 for collectors, including President Lyndon Johnson. His average price for a working saddle, hand made with custom designs in the leather, is $4,000 to $5,000.

"There's a lot of difference in saddles when you're making them for these working cowboys that sit in them all day," said Brooks.

His wife, Linda, also knows her husband's customers. "It's a life, it's not a job," she said of the Elko buckaroos. "It's something you have to love. It's not something you just do."

The University of Nevada birthplace wants to expand its Great Basin College

A plastic chair in the creek provides a cool resting place at Thomas Creek Campground in Lamoille Canyon.

Elko is supposed to be about basics: railroading and ranching. The two Rs go a long way in defining the community, as does mining, but for the future, civic leaders see the city as a center of art and education.

"One of my visions is that this becomes a cultural center," said Sarah Sweetwater, chairman of the art department at Great Basin College in Elko. "We have the right scenery and the right isolation."

Surrounded by mountains and desert, the city offers plenty of landscapes to paint. The community already is host to one of the West's biggest cultural events, the Cowboy Poetry Gathering. But Sweetwater and others want more than that. The big dream is to make Great Basin College a four-year instead of two-year school in the state's public higher-education system.

Great Basin remains primarily a community college offering two-year programs, but "community" has been removed from the school's name. Great Basin now offers a four-year degree in teaching. Business administration is about to become another four-year program. More four-year programs could be added, but Great Basin — at least for the near future — will remain a "community" school.

"It will always be a community college with four-year programs," said Dorothy Gallagher, an Elko resident and member of the state's governing body for higher education. "It will always have a community-college mission."

But Mayor Mike Franzoia appears to want more. "The college is vital," he said. "I have four kids. I may or may not be able to send them to universities in Las Vegas or Reno. We want to have a choice. It's difficult for us to travel and pay those costs."

Elko's isolation sometimes does make it difficult to leave home for school. "Our students are place bound," Gallagher said. "They have families and jobs."

Great Basin has become a rallying point for the area. It opened without state funding in 1967 as Elko Community College. The townspeople raised $40,000 to start the school.

"They didn't know you couldn't run a college on $40,000, so they did it anyway," Gallagher said. "It's a big thing in the community. I don't know of any place in the state where an institution has more support.

Young Elko residents Josh Mudlin, eleven, and his sister, Lindsey, nine, pan for garnets in Lamoille Creek.

People feel it's their college."

Elko has a campus tradition. The University of Nevada was founded in Elko in 1874 before moving to Reno in 1885. "The university was in Elko until influential people in Reno said Elko was past its prime," said Jan Petersen, program coordinator of the Northeastern Nevada Museum. Elko still has a College Avenue which runs past the high school.

Sweetwater, who remembers teaching art in a locker room in the early years of Elko Community College, expects the arts community to expand, regardless of whether Great Basin does, because of rapid population growth.

"I love it," Sweetwater said of Elko's surge in population during the last fifteen years. "It means I have a wider range of students."

Along with the museum and the college, Elko has an orchestra and a theater company. "The mining has brought in these well-traveled people," she said of the industry responsible for much of Elko's growth. "We're richer because of them. They have brought to me this whole other dimension for which I'm really grateful."

The Community Presbyterian Church sits behind a neat picket fence in Lamoille.

Fernley

At the Fernley Fly-In Air Show, five-year-old Adam Sarosi of Silver Springs flies his own toy P-38 with his dad, Sky Sarosi.

Industry, golf courses and new houses are replacing alfalfa fields

Beth Mortensen takes a break from feeding her miniature horses on her Fernley ranch.

IMPORTANT DATES

- 1902: Congress passes National Reclamation Act.
- May 1904: Irrigated land opens near what is now Fernley.
- June 1904: Canal Township established.
- January 1905: First reference to "Fernley" in Southern Pacific Railroad timetable.
- June 1905: Truckee Canal opens.
- April 21, 1908: Post office named for town, "Fernley."
- 1910: Fernley Improvement Club formed.
- 1914: Fernley railroad depot completed.
- Feb. 5, 1921: Fernley High School established.
- 1935: Lyon County recognizes Fernley as unincorporated town.
- Aug. 15, 1950: Fire destroys Tourist Hotel and other downtown buildings.
- 1963: Construction on cement plant begins.
- 1978: Developer Jim Johnson proposes planned community of 40,000 near Fernley.
- April 1982: Truck Inn opens.
- 1985: Railroad depot closes.
- 1994: Wade Development Co. buys Nevada Pacific Industrial Park.
- January 1999: Amazon.com builds warehouse in industrial park.

Beth Mortensen and husband Neil took Sunday drives around Fernley just to check on the town. Who was cutting hay? Who was building a new barn? Who was coming and who was going? That weekly community survey started in the 1950s and continued for more than forty years. Beth and Neil watched Fernley develop slowly — a new house here, a store there — until one day, suddenly, they couldn't believe what they were seeing.

"It was the golf course area," Beth said. "That used to be a dairy ranch." Not anymore. Instead of cows, the town has the eighteen-hole Desert Lakes Golf Course surrounded by an 800-home subdivision under construction. Fernley, northern Nevada's millennium boomtown, is growing by the minute.

"It's got about 10,000 people now, if you count the whole area. We expect it to quadruple over the next twenty to thirty years," said Patty Wade, president of Wade Development Company, Inc., whose 5,000-acre Nevada Pacific Industrial Park is fueling the explosion. "We're changing the whole landscape of the town. It will be very much like Sparks."

Beth and Neil, longtime Fernley ranchers, took their last Sunday drive together in March 1999. "He was really in bad shape," said Beth, whose husband died two months later. "He told me, 'This may be the last time I get to see this,' so we took him around the whole thing, out to the golf course, out to the industrial park and the new buildings going up there. He did not get to see it again."

But Beth did. She took another Sunday drive about a month after Neil died. "I can't believe it," she said. "There are two more big buildings out in the industrial area. The houses have shot up since Neil was out. It's scary."

Beth Mortensen hangs on to the family ranch where she raises miniature horses, but all around her there are housing tracts where fields of alfalfa had been for almost a century. On Farm District Road, the center of Fernley's rural economy and lifestyle, developers are buying ranches — one after another.

"I don't like it, but you're not going to stop it; it's already happened," said Charlie Ceresola, one of the few remaining ranchers on the road. "The golf course was the dairy when I was a kid."

Ceresola says he will sell his land — for

the right price. "I said, 'When you get all those houses built, we'll have to go some- where,'" Ceresola said, describing one of his conversations with a developer looking for land. "I said, 'Run me out of here with $100 bills.' He seemed like a nice guy."

Diana, Charlie's wife, knows the devel- oper she wants to see. "Only if he's got a checkbook with something in it," she said with a laugh. Diana is part of Fernley's boom since she opened a deli, Udderly Crafty, and a gym, C1 Get Fit, named for her family's cattle brand, C1. Both businesses are in Fernley's heart. At one time, the site was occupied by community tennis courts; then it was the longtime location of the Country Store, a favorite local hangout.

"We used to have street dances in the summer," said Fernley teenager Michelle Peterson. "Where the gym is now, that used to be the Country Store. That used to be where the dances were. Where the parking lot is, they'd set up a band and everyone would just come out the whole night and just dance."

Like just about everything else in Fernley, it has changed — except for a few reminders of the past. The meat case in Diana's deli is from the Country Store.

Her gym opened in 1998 and now has 350 members. "I'm hoping Fernley grows even more," Diana said. "On the cattle side, you hate to see it. But for business, I hope it grows even more." She's fond of the family ranch on Farm District Road, but figures it's a losing battle.

"I tell my husband every day, 'Sell it! Sell it!'" she said. "Keep enough there for us and our horses and put the rest up for sale. We don't have enough water there to grow anything but alfalfa, and we don't have enough to grow that."

Marlin Hanneman doesn't blame the ranchers for selling. He remembers the way the town looked in the 1940s — with 350

Development vs. elbow room is the tale of this farmtown turned industrial suburb.

residents. "They couldn't make enough ranching in a hundred years for what they're being paid for the land," said Hanneman, who came to Fernley from Minnesota as a kid with his family in 1945. Now he owns a gas station and garage where his employees still wash the windows and check the oil with each fill-up.

Hanneman also owns a ranch fifty miles north of town. He says he used to watch the trains stop in Fernley to unload farm equip- ment and pick up livestock. "They'd leave off combines and tractors and everything else;

Artist's motto: Paint what you know

Painter Loni Kowalski's favorite subjects are right around her: she likes the ranchers, Indians and historic buildings found in Fernley, on the nearby Pyramid Lake Paiute Reservation and in neighboring Wadsworth. Her mother, Kris Hanneman, photographs many of the same things.

"I work from a lot of her stuff," said Kowalski, a Fernley native who has been painting for ten years. A series of prints has been made from three of her paintings: Fernley's historic railroad depot, the church in Wadsworth and a Paiute eagle dancer at Pyramid Lake.

Six of her paintings hang in Mary & Moe's Wigwam Restaurant Casino & Indian Museum, which features a large collection of western art. She has painted many portraits of the Ceresolas, a ranching family whose ancestors came to the area more than a century ago.

"I've done pictures of Stan and his dad, Bill," Kowalski said. "They're great subjects." When she's not painting, she sells houses in Fernley's booming real-estate market. "Everything is changing so dramatically," she said of the town's rapid growth. But she still finds enough of the Old West to paint.

Top: Little foxes painted by Loni Kowalski watch diners in the Wigwam Restaurant.
Bottom: Fernley artist Kowalski displays some of her other paintings at the restaurant.

FERNLEY

- Population in 1999: 7,696 (30 percent under 18, 39 percent 18-44, 21 percent 45-64, 10 percent 65 and older; 49 percent female, 51 percent male).
- Population in 1990: 5,164.
- Population in 2003: (projected) 9,028.
- Median household income in 1990: $30,677.
- Median household income in 1998: $32,929.
- Total retail sales in 1998: $39.709 million.
- Total retail sales in 2003: (projected) $51.536 million.

- Claim to fame: Northern Nevada's millennium boomtown, with a 5,000-acre industrial park, new subdivisions and growing population.

- How it got its name: "No one knows (who Fernley was)," said Guy Rocha, state archivist and a Nevada history expert. Rocha said the area first was called the Canal District in 1902 when Congress passed the National Reclamation Act which would bring Newlands Project water to irrigate local land. Several years later, Southern Pacific Railroad relocated its tracks through western Nevada and the town became a railroad siding. Rocha said the first time "Fernley" appeared was in a 1905 railroad timetable. "The railroad did the naming," he said. "They made a number of sidings. Managers decided how they got their names."

- Local legends: Joe and Patty Wade, husband and wife who own Wade Development Co. and operate Nevada Pacific Industrial Park, now fueling Fernley's growth by attracting business to the town.

those days are long gone," he said. "Where all the homes are now, there were little farms — on both sides of the highway."

Fernley's biggest crop is sprouting in the Nevada Pacific Industrial Park, bought by Patty Wade's company in 1994. Companies in the huge complex include Amazon.com, the Internet bookseller, and Trex, an outfit that makes building materials out of trash.

Wade's formula for Fernley is simple: Bring the industry, which creates jobs, which bring people, who bring stores and other services. In her view and that of others, Fernley then becomes a better place to live.

"With that comes the nice homes, the opportunities for all sorts of things," said Wade, a biochemist who wanted to become a doctor before she got into industrial development. "You bring in commercial. You base that on homes. When you get that critical mass of homes, that determines what retail comes in."

Fernley is a boomtown because Patty and husband Joe, who came from Southern California to Reno to build subdivisions, found flat industrial land next to Interstate 80 and the railroad.

"It's an absolute industrial haven," Patty said. "We could see it. This is a great crossroads, transportation-wise, and the land was relatively cheap. We realized we were running out of industrial land in Reno and Sparks."

The industrial park brought Greg Homol to Fernley from Arizona. He is a machine operator for Quebecor, one of the world's largest printing companies, which located its western operation in the park.

"It's a good place to live," said Homol, who bought a house in the golf-course development. "It's not as congested as Reno. As much as this place is growing, they need more services." And growth is bringing the services, one by one.

"After eighth grade, we got

Cattle are becoming scarce here — the golf course was once a dairy.

McDonald's," Michelle Peterson said. "We never had a fast-food place before." She used to spend summers working at the community pool, which now is surrounded by new homes. Other favorite spots have been turned into subdivisions. "Those are places where we used to play in the fields," Peterson said. "Where they're building apartments, there used to be a big ditch. We'd ride our bikes there."

Like Peterson, Cody Premo is a teenager who grew up in a different Fernley. "When we were high school freshmen, I knew everybody. Now I don't know anybody," he said. "The new businesses, they bring people in. A lot of people are moving in for jobs."

One of the newest tenants in the industrial park is Trex, a Virginia-based company that manufactures artificial wood out of old plastic garbage bags and sawdust. The resulting lumber is used primarily to build back-yard decks.

"We've got a product that's selling like hot cakes," said David Jordan, manager of the Trex plant under construction in Fernley. "We decided we needed a second plant site." The choice came down to Richland, Washington, or Fernley. "These folks did a better job of selling this place than the state agencies," Jordan said of Patty and Joe Wade. Once it's up and running, the Trex plant will employ 200 to 250 workers.

Brian Carter already is working, coming from the Trex home base in Winchester, Virginia. A native Virginian, he never had seen the desert until he arrived in Nevada. "It's an adventure," he said.

Although she has seen it going on for several years, Beth Mortensen still watches the arrival of newcomers and the ongoing construction with amazement.

"If somebody comes along and offers me a good chunk of money, I'd sell that," she said of the north side of her ranch. "The south end, I would like to keep that. That would be a pretty decent front yard."

Above: A view of the Desert Lakes Golf Course sells houses in Fernley. James Rose helps build them in a new development for Verner Homes. Below: In the industrial park, David Jordan manages the Trex plant, a Virginia-based company that makes artificial wood from recycled plastic bags and sawdust.

Mary and Moe's Wigwam Restaurant-Casino-Museum is a Fernley landmark

As a kid, Moe Royels usually carried a handful of rocks and arrowheads in his pocket. "They'd end up in the washer," said Beth Mortensen, Royels' sister. "My mother used to yell at him." But that didn't stop Royels, whose school-principal father enjoyed hunting for American Indian artifacts in northern Nevada.

"We have one of the best collections," Moe said of the arrowheads, artifacts and art that cover the walls of Mary & Moe's Wigwam Restaurant Casino & Indian Museum, a landmark in downtown Fernley.

You can eat at the Wigwam. The rib-eye steak sandwich costs $9.25. You can look at the collection, including a cavalry saber that's more than a hundred years old. Or you can eat and look.

"A lot of people come by just to see the stuff," said Moe, who has operated the Wigwam with his wife, Mary, since 1984. "We have rock clubs that come in, and school kids."

The collection is displayed on walls in the restaurant's bar and four dining rooms. It doesn't leave too many bare spots. Moe hasn't counted the arrowheads, arranged carefully in framed groups, but they prob-

ably number in the thousands. Along with the arrowheads there are stone tools and other implements. Most of the Indian artifacts come from within a 150-mile radius of Fernley.

Willow baskets and buckskin clothes are protected in glass cases. "Smoke and grease will eat that buckskin right up," Moe said. Many of those items came from the nearby Pyramid Lake Paiute Indian Reservation. Some were loaned; others were gifts. A plaque from the tribe is inscribed, "To Moe and Mary Royels in recognition of their efforts to preserve the Paiute culture."

Wilson Wewa, director of the Pyramid Lake Paiute Cultural Center, said tribal members have mixed feelings about the Wigwam collection. "There are probably some who don't like Moe having so much," Wewa said. "But he bought a lot of what he has from members of the tribe and a lot of elders gave Moe and Mary gifts."

Federal laws enacted in the 1970s and '80s prohibit collecting artifacts on tribal land. "I look on private property," said Moe Royels, who co-owns a ranch near the reservation.

Aside from the tribal artifacts, Moe and Mary have a large collection of Western art, most with Indian themes, much of it the work of local painters. A sixteen-foot mural created for the Wigwam by Reno artist William Moore depicts a panoramic view of Pyramid Lake and dry Winnemucca Lake. Every year, Mary and Moe put on an art show at the Wigwam featuring Moore's work.

"I like good art and so does Moe," Mary said. "That's where we started spending our money." They've had the entire collection appraised, from arrowheads to paintings, but they decline to disclose its value.

Ronald Seward probably doesn't care. A regular Wigwam customer, Seward comes

Mary and Moe Royels own the Wigwam Restaurant Casino & Indian Museum, a downtown Fernley landmark.

to eat and maybe talk a little. The paintings and arrowheads are simply background.

"A lot of people come in on Wednesday to drink coffee and talk. We don't know why it became Wednesday," said Seward, who discovered the Wigwam after moving to Fernley from Illinois. "I've only been here three years, but it seems like I've been here forever."

People have been dropping in at Mary and Moe's since she opened a hamburger and ice cream stand called the Dainty Cone in 1961. The stand had no art collection.

Mary and Moe married in 1964. Two decades later, they changed the name of the burger place to the Wigwam. The restaurant has undergone three expansions to accommodate customers and art; the most recent in 1995.

When Mary came to Fernley from Reno in 1960, Moe was already in town. He was a player on the football, basketball and track teams at Fernley High School. The teams won state championships during the 1956-57 school year.

"When Moe graduated, there were eight people in his class," Mary said. The two of them, Mary and Moe, have been fixtures in Fernley for a long time — just like the Wigwam, the steak sandwich and the arrowheads.

To incorporate or not? That is the question

Debra Brazell wants Fernley to grow up and become a city in the twenty-first century: "We believe the town is ready for incorporation. We're bringing this industry here. We believe to control the growth, we need to incorporate."

As chairwoman of the Fernley Incorporation Committee, her group is collecting signatures for a petition that would put incorporation to a community vote. That's something Fernley boosters tried and failed to accomplish in 1996 when incorporation backers obtained about half the petition signatures required for a vote. Now the farmtown-turned-industrial suburb, thirty miles east of Reno-Sparks on Interstate 80, continues the pattern of rapid growth that began in earnest in the mid-1990s.

The bigger Fernley gets, the stronger the drive for incorporation becomes. Many in Fernley want to govern themselves and stop depending upon Lyon County for decisions and services. After all, if northern Nevada has a millennium boomtown, Fernley is the one, powered by the business pouring into its 5,000-acre industrial park.

"For incorporation, we're long overdue," real-estate broker Rodger Denn said.

A quail brightens a fence post in Fernley.

"With the industrial park out there, the money it will generate will be fantastic for the town. We really have a lot of good things for this town."

Linda Gregory, a member of the incorporation committee, believes in controlled growth. "We can't close our eyes and say we want it the way it was twenty years ago," she said. "I want it to look like there is a plan. I want parks in the right places. I want businesses to locate outside the town proper."

Dorothy Furst isn't convinced. "Every few years, someone comes up with this idea that we have to incorporate," she said. "My mind's not made up."

John Wagner, owner of Fernley Electric, has seen the growth firsthand as he races to keep up with expanding business. "I've got five trucks on the road," said Wagner, whose father, Chuck, started the business in 1969. "What am I going to do about growth? It's my livelihood."

The same goes for Peggy Foley, who is selling new houses for Foley Realty on East Main Street. "I get home from work at night at ten-thirty," said Foley. "I get up at five-thirty."

Moe and Mary Royels own a landmark in Fernley's small downtown – Mary & Moe's Wigwam Restaurant Casino & Indian Museum. For them, growth means more business as well as a lot of changes to the town.

"We're happy for it to grow, but we don't want it to grow to the extent of Reno," Mary Royels said.

Her husband isn't sure growth can be contained, no matter how much everyone wants to try. "Once it starts," he said, "it's hard to stop."

Vietnam veteran Randy Craig clears dead flowers from graves at Veterans Memorial Cemetery in Fernley.

Genoa

Bev Smith, officially in charge of fun in Genoa, pauses with her dog Haida in front of an old barn she and her husband renovated on their property.

Feisty Genoa keeps the tax man at bay

Downtown Genoa and the Old Genoa Bar

Bernie Carter couldn't believe what happened when he first attended a meeting of the five-member Genoa Town Advisory Board.

"They voted not to collect taxes," Carter said with a chuckle. "I raised my hand and told them it was un-American. I didn't think you could do that."

In Genoa, you can. The tiny town at the foot of the Sierra, which claims to be Nevada's oldest white settlement, prides itself on being fiercely independent. Genoa's citizens, about 230 strong, spit in the eye of the federal government and view most actions of local officials with deep suspicion. Douglas County is allowed to count Genoa's money, but bureaucrats better not tell the town how to spend it.

"We've got a community that exhibits a spirit of individualism, that fights the federal government," said Carter, a board member. "It's not afraid of local government, including the county government."

But Genoa does worry about keeping its freedom in the 21st century as suburban growth in Carson Valley encroaches on the historic community. That's why residents see the county plan to run a sewer line through town as the latest threat to their way of life.

"It could open up all areas to building," Genoa resident Linda Sanfilippo said. "It could cause the type of growth that may not be exactly desirable here."

Genoa has no sewer system and County Manager Dan Holler has assured citizens they won't have to hook up if they don't want to. The line is supposed to connect the golf courses and residential developments on the north and south sides to the county sewer plant. The line, according to the plan, simply is passing through town.

"We want to stay away from mandatory systems," Holler said. "People could hook up as they desire." The line, he said, will be in place sometime in the next two years at a cost of about $2 million. Not everyone in Genoa is opposed.

"It's important that we understand there is a necessity for growth," said Barry Benzel, who lives in nearby Minden and owns a business in Genoa. "The sewer line represents some of that progress. It doesn't mean we have to build on every five square feet. But it does mean we have to build more because more people will be coming to town. There's an underlying distrust of the sewer line coming through. That has to be dispelled."

Today, it's the sewer line. Yesterday, it was the post office, a real war: Genoa vs. Uncle Sam. The battle lasted about twelve years. The result was a victory for the town, which got a scaled-down post office on Main Street, just south of Candy Dance Lane.

"It's kind of feisty," former Town Manager Ann Marie Evans said.

Kind of feisty? That's one way to put it. Let resident Bob Centanni tell the tale.

"When we found out what the post office was trying to do, there were a lot of individuals who rallied around and supported our position," Centanni said. "What the post office was trying to do was invade this small community with a very large facility, something way beyond our means."

Invading Genoa, as Uncle Sam found out, is tough.

"There were a lot of people we fought with," Centanni said.

They had meetings. They had arguments. Sites were proposed and rejected before an agreement was reached.

"Because of the support of all the people that rallied around, we are going to have a post office being built today that's going to be functional and much smaller in size," Centanni said.

Genoa pays for its independence. The biggest source of the town's power over its own affairs comes from one of northern Nevada's most popular special events — the annual Candy Dance. The event buys Genoa its freedom. Thousands from Nevada and out of state attend what has become a huge crafts fair on the last weekend of September. Last year, the event drew 320 vendors. Money from the event, about $90,000 annually, makes up the bulk of Genoa's budget and pays for street repairs, building maintenance and other municipal needs. The festival started in 1919 as a way to pay for street lights.

"The Candy Dance the last five years has really grown," Evans said. "The growth has allowed Genoa to sustain many of its projects."

In 1996 and 1997, Genoa didn't collect property taxes because the town had enough Candy Dance cash to fund the budget. The money goes into the town's bank account that's supervised by the county, but the dollars and cents belong to Genoa. That's important — but the Candy Dance is about more than money.

"It tells the world, 'We're Genoa,'" Evans said. "It has made us unique. It's very important to show who we are. It's us."

The tombstone misspells his name, but this is the grave of John "Snowshoe" Thompson in the Genoa Cemetery.

Don't let facts get in the way of conclusions

A bit of folk art decorates Bev Smith's barn door.

Two days after you move here you're a native.
    Longtime Genoa resident

I magine moving a house from Virginia City to Genoa in 1898 because it was cheaper than building new. Imagine a town that, up until a few years ago, had a town checkbook. Imagination mothers both challenge and contention. Some days it is hard to separate the two even if you want to.

Feelings of frustration are not new here —
a Mormon judge curses Genoa, the father
whose son was murdered in a quarrel
over a bridle refuses to bury him in the town
cemetery, legendary mailman Snowshoe Thompson
fights the government for his pay,
Dayton throws down the gauntlet claiming
title to the first permanent settlement in Nevada.

In all this, deer walk Genoa freely,
browse the lawns and windfall apples,
two men catch enough catfish to feed everyone,
generosity overflows following a forest fire.
In 1919, the town holds a dance, sells candy
to raise funds for street lights.
Eighty years later they still make candy
for the thousands who celebrate with them.
People stretch, pull apart, come together like taffy.
Now they debate volunteerism versus city employees,
new and old residents with different sets of answers.
There are times in the growth of many towns
when it is easier to be neighborly
than to be neighbors.

Bill Cowee is a member of the Ash Canyon Poets.

GENOA

- Population in 1998: 230 (27 percent under 18, 39 percent 18-44, 23 percent 45-64; 11 percent 65-plus; 57 percent male, 43 percent female).
- Population in 2003: (projected) 259 .
- Median income: $36,875.
- Total retail sales: $4.011 million.

- Claim to fame: "Nevada's first settlement," founded 1851.

- How it got its name: Settlement founded by traders from Salt Lake City and first was called Mormon Station. It was renamed Genoa (after the city in Italy) in 1855 by Territorial Judge Orson Hyde. But the Nevada town's name is pronounced "ju-NO-ah," not "JEN-o-ah."

- Local legend: John A. "Snowshoe" Thompson. Born in Norway, Thompson carried the mail on skis over the Sierra between Placerville, California, and Genoa in winter from 1856 to 1876. The "Mailman of the Sierra," who died in 1876, is buried in the Genoa Cemetery. The name "Thomson" on the tombstone is misspelled. His handwritten letters in the Genoa Courthouse Museum are signed "Thompson."

An old water pump sits near a cluster of apple trees in front of a home on Genoa's Main Street

Bears and candy mix with history

The outside world is closing in rapidly on the historic community of Genoa, which sits snugly in a postcard setting at the foot of the Sierra. Upscale development, complete with gated subdivisions and manicured golf courses, squeezes a town where longtime residents claim ancestors who arrived in covered wagons. But the local bear didn't notice. He lumbered through Bev Smith's back yard to reach the town park and a free meal. In Genoa, the bear is a welcome sight.

"The town park has a lot of apples," said Smith, who picked Genoa as the perfect place to live after searching throughout the West. "He's an interesting bear. He has this path in mind. He was probably taught as a cub. He comes through the fence to get fruit. He's really beautiful."

Before reaching Smith's back yard, the bear visited Ron Funk's neighborhood.

"He ate some apples," said Funk, an artist who moved to Genoa from Southern California in 1981. "He was eating out of a bucket."

The bear's journey included a stop at the home of Billie Jean Rightmire, whose great-great-grandfather came here in 1858.

"I grabbed my camera," said Rightmire, the town historian. "He was watching us. He ran off and went behind us."

The bear eats apples in the town park. Deer roam the streets. Funk paints landscapes. Rightmire points out Adam Uber's Hanging Tree on Genoa Lane. Smith is in charge of the community fun club. Every year, the Candy Dance is staged to raise money for town upkeep. That's Genoa, which claims to be Nevada's first white settlement — founded in 1851. Genoa also has soaring real-estate prices, plans for a new sewer line and fear of growth in a place that's attractive to newcomers because of its size.

"I don't think people who live here now have any idea, in the next five years the whole nature of the area is going to change," said real estate agent David Kuzawa, whose office is next to Genoa's handful of remaining 19th-century brick buildings. "This will be another Santa Barbara."

The area is just too pretty for developers to pass up.

"The Carson Valley is the garden spot of Nevada," Kuzawa said. "In this valley we have more water than the rest of the state combined. That's an exaggeration, but it's not far off. Because of that, we have trees and

A doe and her fawn feed on ripe apples in downtown Genoa.

pastureland. It's green."

That helped attract Genoa's original Mormon settlers from Salt Lake City. Today, it attracts home buyers.

Frank Durham, who sells property at the 415-acre Genoa Lakes golf course-residential development on Jacks Valley Road, said home prices have reached $300,000 and $400,000 as wealthy newcomers from California move in and around town.

"It was hay and cows until now," Durham said. "What I see in this valley is a huge sociological change. These people are wealthy, successful and cultured. You bring Marin County here and it's a culture shock."

But will the town still have room for the bear?

"We're going to get lost in the shuffle," Rightmire said.

The popularity of the Genoa area amazes Shirley Giovacchini, descendant of a pioneer family who works with Kuzawa.

"This is really the strangest phenomenon because when I was growing up here, the Genoa area was looked upon as the wrong side of the tracks," said Giovacchini, a town native. "It was not a good place to be. The people down in Gardnerville and Minden thought the scum of the earth was Genoa.

"I don't know when the change happened. I would say not until the 1970s; then, the foothills here became a prestigious place to be."

Jay Rhodes, who came to Genoa from Las Vegas in 1986, doesn't mix with the town's old-timers. He owns the Inn Cognito restaurant and bar, part of which is housed in what used to be a 100-year-old barn on Genoa Lane.

Rhodes, whose long gray hair and beard make him look like an 1800s mountain man, wouldn't mind some development.

"There is a faction of business people in this little town that would like to see a little bit of growth; it's an ongoing battle," said Rhodes, who is prevented from offering regular live music at his bar. "I like living here because it's quiet and close to the mountains. As far as interacting with the townspeople, I pretty much keep to myself. I find it easier that way."

Sue Haugnes, who bought the Wild Rose Inn bed and breakfast in 1998, is a newcomer

from San Francisco who enjoys Genoa's history. She's got part of it in her back yard, site of Elzy H. Knott's grave. He was shot to death March 8, 1859, over a dispute about a bridle. Next to Knott is the grave of Mary Williams, a child of his widow's next marriage.

"I look at it as a privilege to be taking care of a bit of history," said Haugnes, who tends the graves. "People have said to me nothing's going to happen to Genoa. I hope that's true."

Rightmire, sixty-five, who lives in the house she grew up in, and others among Genoa's 230 residents are doing their best to maintain the community's identity.

The town limits, Rightmire carefully pointed out, don't include Genoa Lakes and the nearby Sierra Nevada Golf Ranch.

"The town itself hasn't changed," she said.

The Old Genoa Bar, where Rightmire learned to dance as a youngster, occupies a building opened in 1863 and advertises itself as "the oldest continually operated thirst parlor in the state of Nevada."

A short walk from the bar is the Genoa Courthouse — Nevada's first — built in 1865. She went to class there after the courthouse

became the schoolhouse. Today, the place is a museum where Rightmire works as a volunteer guide.

"Adam Uber, they came in here and took him out of his cell," Rightmire said of the November 25, 1897, lynching in which about twenty angry townspeople removed Uber from the courthouse and hung him from a Genoa Lane cottonwood tree.

"It was a very dark, windy, cold night. There was nobody even aware this was happening. They actually shot him a lot. They used him for target practice before they hung him."

Uber was locked up for shooting local wagon driver Hans Anderson in a Carson Valley bar brawl.

The story goes that all the lynch mob leaders met with bad ends. One lost his leg in an accident near the spot of the hanging, another went insane, one took poison and still another committed suicide with a shotgun.

The hanging tree remains, with a plaque commemorating the event.

Rightmire doesn't want Genoa to lose the tree or any other local landmarks. She doesn't want Genoa to

lose its lore.

"I'm very protective of the town," Rightmire said.

So is Smith, a relative newcomer, who organizes Genoa's fun and games.

"Once a month we have a fun night in the Town Hall and we play games," said Smith, who helped organize the Genoa Events Committee three years ago.

"Last year, we learned how to play Mexican train dominoes. It's a kick. Now, we are working on swing-dance lessons."

When Smith first came to town, she made candy for the Candy Dance, which started in 1919 as a community fund-raiser to buy street lights. Today, the annual weekend crafts fair attracts thousands of northern Nevadans and provides Genoa with most of its budget.

Perhaps more important to townspeople, the funds allow Genoa to maintain some independence from Douglas County government.

"We raise our own money," Rightmire said. "When we want something done, we pay for it. I don't know how long we're going to be able to carry that off. We kind of work with the county, but it comes out of the Genoa budget. We like being independent."

Standing beneath the hanging tree, the bowed, almost twisted branch appeared to be the one used to "do the evil deed."

Does long-dead judge's curse linger?

When a car breaks down, a dog gets sick or someone's water pipes freeze in the historic town of Genoa, residents know why:

"Orson Hyde's Curse."

People in Genoa, the rest of Carson Valley and Washoe Valley have been living under it since January 27, 1862. That's when Hyde, a disgruntled judge in Genoa when Nevada was a territory, declared in a letter:

"You shall be visited of the Lord of Hosts and thunder and with earthquakes and with floods, with pestilence and with famine until your names are not known amongst men, for you have rejected the authority of God, trampled upon his laws and his ordinances, and given yourselves up to serve the god of this world; to rioting in debauchery, in abominations, drunkenness and corruption."

No one can mistake the Nevadans he had in mind. The high-ranking Mormon church official, who gave Genoa its name, was specific. The curse, Hyde wrote, "shall be to the people of Carson and Washoe Valleys."

Billie Jean Rightmire, a native of Genoa and town historian, has researched Hyde and his letter.

"He put a curse on Washoe and Carson Valleys," Rightmire said. "When something happens, we blame it on the curse." Perhaps the curse means something.

On March 16, 1882, Genoa was buried under a Sierra avalanche that destroyed buildings and killed nine people. On June 28, 1910, downtown Genoa was destroyed by a fire that left the courthouse, among other structures, in ruins. Hyde was angry when he cursed the early Nevadans, who were part of Utah Territory. He'd spent seven years in Genoa, then returned with other Mormons to Salt Lake City at the request of Brigham Young.

"Not quite seven years ago," he wrote, "I was sent to your district as probate judge of Carson County, with powers and instructions from the executive of this territory to organize your district into a county under the laws of Utah. But opposition on your part to the measure was unceasingly made in almost every form, both trivial and important, open and secret."

Apparently, locals didn't want the Utah man organizing them. But what Hyde really appeared to be angry about were tenants who wouldn't pay the proper rent on property the judge co-owned in the area, including a sawmill in Washoe Valley. Hyde estimated the sawmill, rented to a person named in the letter as Jacob Rose, was originally worth $10,000, but Rose didn't pay his rent in cash.

"On this rent he advanced one span of small, indifferent mules, an old worn-out harness, two yokes of oxen, and an old wagon," Hyde wrote. "This is all that we have ever received for the use of our property in that valley." Hyde wanted money. "That mill and those land claims were worth $10,000 when we left them. The use of that property, or its increased value since, is $10,000 more, making our present demand $20,000."

Hyde warned against trying to escape the curse by moving to California. "If perchance, however, there should be an honest man amongst you, I would advise him to leave," Hyde declared. "But let him not go to California for safety, for he will not find it there." Rose, for whom Mount Rose is named, remained and later owned a large ranch in Carson City.

Hyde's curse included a question for

Chris Cummins, Matt Martin and Taylor Lather of Genoa walk up Mill Street downtown after snowboarding in the mountains above town.

residents:

"We now tell the people of Carson and Washoe Valleys some things that will befall them, and the reason why they will befall them. But will you believe us?"

Lake Tahoe

Brian Spiersch of Reno paddles his ocean kayak around the giant granite boulders in Lake Tahoe at Sand Harbor.

From Great Gatsby to garage bands, the lake has seen it all

The MS Dixie II shows visitors the sights around the "Lake in the sky."

The standard summer uniform at Lake Tahoe is T-shirt, shorts and sandals. Bill Bliss remembers a different dress code, at least in the dining room of his Glenbrook Inn.

"Whether they liked it or not, I insisted on ties and coats for dinner," said Bliss, who descends from a family that created much of the lake's history. "I knew most of the guests. I grew up with them. They knew me. If they had serious complaints, I'd tell them, 'Don't bug me. You're lucky I let you in.' "

Bliss closed the Glenbrook Inn after the summer of 1975, ending an era at Tahoe. That was a time when the lake served as a quiet summer retreat for the rich and possibly famous of the San Francisco Bay area and the rest of California.

"From Memorial Day to Labor Day, they'd have their cottages, their cabins, their houses; it was like *The Great Gatsby,*" state historian Guy Rocha said, comparing the old Tahoe to F. Scott Fitzgerald's novel about 1920s high society on Long Island in New York.

"For San Francisco, Tahoe was their Long Island. It still takes place today, but it's not that elite. That was the 1930s to the '60s. The Stateline casinos went up and you started getting more people."

The folks Bliss knew not only dressed for dinner, they dressed to fish. Old Bliss family photos show men with fishing poles wearing coats and ties. Up and down the lake, they had picnics, they swam, they played tennis.

"It was like running a big weekend house party, to a large degree," said Bliss, whose great-grandfather, Duane L. Bliss, was a Nevada pioneer. Bliss State Park on the California side of the lake is named for Duane Bliss. His great-grandson, who lives in Carson City during the winter and spends summers at Glenbrook, considers the legacy of his famous ancestor.

"A very good case could be made that nobody did more damage to the Tahoe Basin than my family," said Bill Bliss, recalling the 50,000 acres of trees cut down by his great-grandfather. "There was just a tremendous demand for timber."

Duane Bliss, who came west from Massachusetts in

Bill Bliss

1849 as a seventeen-year-old, ended up in charge of the Carson and Tahoe Lumber and Fluming Co. at Glenbrook, which supplied Virginia City's Comstock mines with enormous quantities of wood. It made Bliss rich and Glenbrook famous.

Few signs are left of what happened. Glenbrook — a teeming lumber camp of the 1870s on the Nevada side of the lake with sawmills, tugboats and hundreds of men — is now a secluded community of multimillion-dollar homes and dramatic Tahoe views. One easily can miss it from the highway because the spot has only a single state historical marker to show its importance.

"It all came back in time," Bill Bliss said of the trees covering modern Glenbrook — trees that replaced the ones his great-grandfather cut. "And it came back without any help from committees, or ecological this and that."

Bill Bliss represents a different Tahoe, the one that existed before all the fighting started about saving the lake, development, government regulation, property rights, tourism and pollution; before the casinos and big ski resorts.

"We're so divided around this lake," said Edward Dilley, a Zephyr Cove businessman who operates a production company. "We're crazy with politics up here and the government agencies that put their fingers in all this."

To start with, two states — Nevada and California — share the lake. So do five counties and a bunch of special districts for water and other utilities. There's also the controversial Tahoe Regional Planning Agency, which tries to referee disputes and preserve the lake. Tahoe, the subject of national attention when President Clinton paid a visit in July 1997, is a battleground.

"We have very special needs up here," said Dilley, who, like many of his neighbors, came to Tahoe from one of California's overcrowded corners and stayed. "These

needs aren't being addressed by outside people. It's been the desire to chip Tahoe out politically and send it around the sun by itself."

Despite all that, Tahoe maintains a unique character, with its history preserved in some interesting nooks and crannies. One of these is a workshop on the North Shore where Craig Beck, a building contractor and real estate salesman, makes long-board skis. His skis are ten to fifteen feet long, with leather straps for bindings. They're what the miners used to go down hills in the 1800s. There's been a lot of skiing for a long time at Tahoe.

"They did it in the mining camps," said Beck, a forty-year Tahoe resident who organized the National Long Board Association. "I'm fascinated with the history of the sport. I wanted to make a film and I realized I'd have to make some skis to do it. Long-board skiing only existed here. The only time it happened was in the mining camps from about 1860 to 1911."

Beck has carved thirty-five pairs of old-fashioned skis used by racers in his annual long-board championships. Some of Tahoe's most famous modern skiers, including former U.S. Olympian Tamara McKinney, have dressed in historic costumes to compete in the race. They go very fast.

"The girls are in hoop skirts and they look like witches riding brooms," Beck said. "These things go faster than beans, twice as fast as beans."

Things used to be a lot slower. Once upon a time, Lake Tahoe was a world apart, one that flourished in the summer and closed in winter.

"Nothing was year-round," Bill Bliss said of the Tahoe he knew growing up at Glenbrook, the hotel his family had turned into a resort. "It was very understated. We had a golf course. We had tennis courts. We had rodeos. We'd put on three or four

This Paiute Shoshone buckskin doll, c. 1900, was found near Tahoe City.

Tahoe artist "was born with the smell of paint under my nose"

inda de Curtis estimates she's painted 8,000 pictures of Lake Tahoe and she'll paint a few more.

"I have three going," said the Italian-born Tahoe resident who works at her home studio in Zephyr Cove. "I just love the lake. Every day, I thank God I live in such a beautiful place." De Curtis says she paints the lake for another reason: it sells.

"Bread and butter" artworks for Zephyr Cove artist Linda de Curtis are paintings of Emerald Bay, her top-selling Lake Tahoe subject.

"It was the most successful subject," she said. "People appreciated it and bought it. When people buy it, it's like being on the stage and getting applause."

De Curtis paints the lake as it looks at all times of the year, but her favorite is Tahoe in the fall. "We not only have the blue sky and the purple mountains, we have the bright yellow of the aspens among the dark green of the pine trees. When you make a painting, you've got all the colors in it."

The artist, who has traveled around the world, learned to paint as a child in Naples, her hometown.

"My father used to be a professor at the Academy of Art in Naples," de Curtis said. "My three brothers are artists. I was born with the smell of paint under my nose."

She wanted to be a doctor, but couldn't get into college.

"I flunked Latin," she said with a laugh. "So I went to art school. I didn't need Latin for that. As an artist, you can go anyplace in the world and make a living."

Including Lake Tahoe.

LAKE TAHOE

- Population in 1999: 18,949 (20 percent under 18; 42 percent 18-44; 29 percent 45-64; 10 percent 65-plus; 52 percent male, 48 percent female).
- Population in 1990: 13,516.
- Population in 2003: (projected) 22,295.
- Retail sales in 1999: $172.72 million.
- Retail sales in 2003: (projected) $257.98 million.
- Claim to fame: The crown jewel of the Sierra Nevada, Lake Tahoe is one of the world's most famous bodies of water. It has been a longtime recreation and vacation spot, especially for northern Nevada and northern California residents.
- How it got its name: Washoe Indians camped around the lake and called it "da ow a ga," which means "edge of the lake." According to Washoe tribal history, white people mispronounced "da ow" as "Tahoe," giving the lake its name.
- Local legend: George Whittell, a multimillionaire from the San Francisco Bay area, owned much of Lake Tahoe's Nevada shore from the late 1930s until shortly before his death in 1969. His holdings included land that is now Incline Village. He built a French chateau-style mansion on a shoreline point south of Incline where his wild parties became part of Tahoe history.

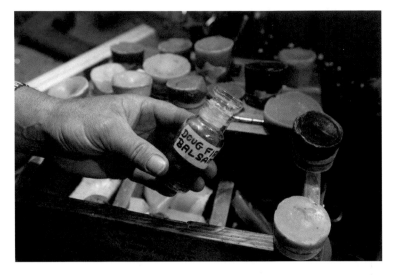

shows a year. My father was a frustrated roper."

As a youngster, Bliss worked as a caddy at the golf course, a garbage collector and a busboy in the restaurant. When his father, Will, died in 1960, Bill was faced with bigger tasks.

"We still owned 3,500 acres up here," Bliss said. "I had to sell property to raise money for the inheritance tax. I couldn't pay the bills. It's as simple as that."

Bliss sold most of the property to the U.S. Forest Service, and it remains untouched. He sold 700 acres to a developer; that's the modern Glenbrook with 230 homes. One of the homes belongs to Bliss. The inn has been turned into dwellings. The place — especially in winter when storms come and the waves are high — looks like the coast of Maine, not the shore of Tahoe. The golf course remains, but it's not a tourist stop. It has a gate with a guard.

"It was a different era," Bliss said of the old days, when the men dressed for dinner at the Glenbrook Inn. "It was something you took for granted. You look back on it, you find it was a tremendous era. It certainly makes me feel like an old geezer."

A short drive from Glenbrook, still along the Nevada shore, Houston Guy lives in Tahoe's modern era. He's a student at Incline High School. His father, Rich — that's right, Rich Guy — is the sales manager for ILOG, one of the growing number of high-tech companies producing software in small Incline Village offices that are turning the area into a sort of silicon forest.

"Two of the company founders are ski

Top: Craig Beck holds a bottle from his collection of natural waxes that he gathers from local fir and pine trees and uses on his hand-made long-board skis.
Bottom: Beck is dwarfed by the long-board skis he made at his Tahoe North Shore home.

buffs," Rich Guy said. "They grew up in the Oakland area. They always wanted to live in the mountains so they relocated here. When it comes to software, you can ship from anywhere. We do all our work over the Internet."

So does Antonia Neubauer, whose Myths and Mountains company in Incline Village uses computers to arrange exotic adventures — studying wildlife in Tibet, trekking in Nepal, or exploring the Amazon.

"You e-mail the itinerary, they e-mail the money into an account," said Neubauer, who came to Tahoe from Philadelphia. "You can work anyplace in the world."

If you can afford a house. Rich Guy said he might be looking for one in Reno. Incline real estate is expensive. But Houston Guy wants to stay at the lake.

"It's easy and simple," Houston Guy said of his Tahoe life. He's a musician, playing in the school band and the youth orches-

tra in Reno. On the side, he's the leader of a five-member garage band called Stereotype. When the band played a benefit, raising $5,000 for a local cancer patient, the story made the front page of Incline's local newspaper.

"You can get some acknowledgment," said Amanda Forman, a student at Incline High who was student body president. "When you see yourself in the newspaper it's really encouraging. It's a big deal." Forman figures she knows how Incline kids are viewed: rich, spoiled, skiing and driving fancy cars.

"I talk to people; they tell us what they think of us," Forman said. "Little rich kids up here. It's a huge stereotype. There are people up here who do fit that description. I have one friend like that, but there are a lot who don't fit that description. I drive a Volkswagen."

Deals, drinks, and one wild ride gave birth to Incline

This is one of those only-in-Nevada stories about the midnight ride that led to the founding of one of Lake Tahoe's best-known and wealthiest communities, Incline Village.

The characters include a commander, an admiral, a young Reno attorney and a captain — the Tahoe legend, the incredibly rich and slightly eccentric Captain George Whittell. The events include meetings in Reno hotel rooms and a bizarre trip up the Mount Rose Highway to Whittell's lakeside mansion.

The whole thing started in Seattle with the attorney, Bob McDonald. Now, at seventy-nine, McDonald is head of one of the state's most prestigious law firms — McDonald, Carano, Wilson, McCune, Bergin, Frankovich & Hicks in Reno. In 1958 he was looking for business when it all happened. Here's his story:

"A law school friend of mine who was practicing in Seattle called me and told me he was representing a retired commander in the Navy. The commander had a group of people who had an option to purchase some property from Captain George Whittell at Tahoe."

The law school friend wanted McDonald's help.

"I said I would do my best."

Then McDonald met a guy named Arthur Wood, a businessman from Oklahoma who had returned to the West Coast after buying a bunch of radio stations in Hawaii.

"He came through Reno and stopped at the Riverside Hotel and was looking for an investment in the West. He called me over to the Riverside. I went upstairs and talked to him about Whittell's property at Tahoe."

Wood was interested. McDonald told

A quiet Lake Tahoe is framed through one of the picture windows of Thunderbird Lodge, George Whittell's Mansion on the east shore.

Wood about the commander in Seattle who'd paid Whittell $50,000 for the sixty-day purchase option. Soon after that, McDonald and an associate were on an airplane to Seattle, representing Wood in an attempt to buy the option from the commander.

"We went to Seattle and met him. He took us to the Navy officer's club in Seattle and bought us dinner." They ate. Time to talk about the option. "He said 'I'm sorry, I never discuss business after dinner.' He got up and left."

McDonald called Wood. "He said, 'Get the hell on back here.' We came back to Reno." Wood upped his offer to $100,000 for the option and McDonald made another trip to Seattle to talk to the commander.

"We couldn't meet with him. He was a very strange person. Wood said come back to Reno." So McDonald did, not knowing he was being followed by the commander.

"I get a call from the Holiday Hotel in

A Steller's Jay keeps watch from a tree branch at Sand Harbor.

Reno. It's the commander. He said, 'Come over with the papers.' At the time, the price had gone up to $150,000. I went over there and he was in bed. He was a very large man. His stomach was sticking out and he was saying his rosary. It was draped over his stomach. He signed the papers. I thanked him."

Now Wood had the purchase option. The next step was informing Whittell that he was buying the land. This is where McDonald's story gets wild.

"I got hold of Whittell's lawyer in San Francisco. He comes up here. He was a reasonably good-drinking Irish sort of a fellow. We had until midnight to serve the papers so we head up to Lake Tahoe."

The route was the Mount Rose Highway, with stops along the way.

"At every bar, he had a couple of scotches. Every time we stopped, he'd call Whittell. He'd get Molly, the nurse, on the phone. She would tell him Captain Whittell was ill and not talking to anybody."

That didn't stop McDonald.

"We drove over there. It was a summer night, probably June, but colder than hell. Before you go down to the mansion, there was a phone booth sort of thing and a little house. An admiral was in there. He was a retired admiral who was hired by Whittell to guard the trees, to keep people from cutting trees on his property."

Whittell's lawyer, possibly fearing his client's wrath, refused to go all the way to the mansion with McDonald, who waited at the admiral's house. The admiral's first name was Jack.

"I went in and sat down with the admiral and his wife and got to know them quite well. She said, 'Jack, why don't you fix Bob a drink?' I had a martini. He had two or three. She said, 'Why don't you take Bob down there in the Jeep?'" So McDonald and the admiral headed for Whittell's mansion.

"The admiral drove me down there and

he went back. It was the darkest night. There was no moon. It was cold. I went around to the door. I saw a Chinese fellow sitting in there, so I knocked on the window. He jumped about nine feet. That's the last I saw of the Chinese guy. I went around to the other side of the house. Nothing happened.

"I looked up and there's Jack. It scared me to death. He had come back." Jack tried to get Molly the nurse to open the door. "He said, 'Molly, this is Jack; can you come out for a second?' She said, 'No, but I'll come to the door.'" That was enough. "I had the papers in my hand. She opened the door two or three inches. I shoved them through there. I got in the Jeep, Jack got in and away we went."

The 5,200 acres eventually were sold to Wood for five million dollars, according to McDonald. Wood developed Incline Village and offered McDonald $25,000 or a lakefront lot as payment for his services. McDonald took the money.

"We could have been billionaires. I took my $25,000. I didn't have any dough." McDonald got something else: a lifetime membership at the Incline Village golf course.

"I played once."

The Ponderosa Ranch portrays mining and logging, part of Lake Tahoe's past.

A door to the boathouse at the Whittell Mansion opens onto the clear waters of Lake Tahoe's eastern shore.

Whittell links Tahoe's past and future

George Whittell was extremely rich and just a little strange. The flamboyant playboy didn't want uninvited guests poking around his estate on Lake Tahoe's Nevada shore.

Fair enough. But a no-trespassing sign and a barking dog weren't enough for Whittell. Instead, he used a siren to scare the curious away from his mansion perched on a rocky promontory south of Incline Village. The siren still works. A button activates the siren near a window facing the cove where boats might approach the French-style chateau, known as the Thunderbird Lodge.

"He'd wait until they got really close, then he'd turn it on," said Phil Caterino, who runs the Tahoe office of the American Land Conservancy.

Someday, visitors may get a closer look at the imposing stone buildings. A complex deal that would allow some public access to the famous property is close to completion. The Del Webb Corporation, now owner of the Whittell property, is giving the estate to the federal government in exchange for public land it wants to develop in the Las Vegas area.

A miniature lighthouse sits near the boathouse of the Whittell Mansion.

At the end of a 500-foot tunnel from the main house to the boathouse on the George Whittell property, caretaker Bob England can see the lake.

Capt. George Whittell, sketched from a photograph in the Gatekeeper's Museum, Tahoe City.

That would take care of the grounds. The rest of the deal, which involves the University of Nevada, Reno, would cover the buildings, including the lodge, guest houses and the network of tunnels connecting the complex. Del Webb wants to join UNR administrators, who expect to use the mansion as a conference and research center, to form the Thunderbird Lodge Preservation Society.

"The society needs to get organized and get funded so the facilities can be open to the public," Del Webb spokesman Scott Higginson said.

There's a lot to see on the property. Whittell, whose family made a fortune in San Francisco during the Gold Rush era, built the Thunderbird Lodge from 1936 to 1939. He bought the property with the family money he removed from the stock market shortly before the 1929 financial crash. At one time before he died in 1969, Whittell owned almost all of Tahoe's Nevada side — 20,000 acres.

"This place is unique," said Caterino, whose organization helped set up the land-exchange deal. "The entire history of Tahoe is right here." The 140-acre property features prehistoric sites and locations where Washoe Indians camped long before Whittell showed up.

Along with his money, Whittell had a reputation for wild parties and wilder women. The parties he had at the lodge. The women, according to Caterino, he'd sneak through the tunnels into the guest houses so his wife wouldn't see them. Whittell didn't hide his parties. They were famous around the lake.

"There was a big spotlight," Caterino said. "He'd turn it on when he was having big parties. When he turned the light on, you knew the door was open and the booze was flowing."

Along with the fun and games, Caterino credits Whittell with keeping much of Tahoe's Nevada side undeveloped. Except for Incline Village and a few other spots, bulldozers didn't reach Whittell's land.

"Nevada gets beat up about Lake Tahoe development," Caterino said. "Compared to the California side, this is relatively pristine."

Reno

Reno has constructed arches to celebrate the city since 1899. This one, in 1928, first carried the slogan that became famous.

A place of neon, noise — and plain folks

In the kitchen at Casale's, Inez Stempeck chops garlic for homemade ravioli.

When Sammy Davis Jr. came to town, the party didn't stop until sunrise. The famous entertainer would finish his act at Harrah's Reno, then start another one a few blocks away for a different audience — the rank-and-file casino workers who'd been pouring drinks, serving dinners and cleaning tables for the paying customers a few hours earlier.

"He would rent the old Majestic Theater and show first-run movies," said John Maniscalco, who presided over a glitz-and-glitter era on Virginia Street as head maitre d' of the Headliner Room at Harrah's. "He'd invite the service people from all over Reno. There'd be a couple hundred waiters and bartenders. He didn't care who came. He'd arrange to have a film brought in that was not playing in town and serve cocktails at the theater. He'd be there until four or five in the morning."

Now Davis is gone. So is the Majestic. So are the dinner shows at Harrah's, with their star performers, thirty-piece orchestras, flaming desserts and silver champagne buckets. Maniscalco retired in 1999. His 400-seat showroom, which opened June 20, 1966, with Eddie Fisher singing, is named for Davis.

"When you'd see a thirty-piece orchestra on stage, the curtain would go up and it would be a magnificent setting up there," said Maniscalco, who was on the job as a captain in the showroom that first night. "There were lots of violins, lots of strings; sometimes there were harps and those kettle drums. It was exciting. It would give you goose bumps."

Not anymore. "You can't do that now," said Maniscalco, who used to be called "boss" by another of the showroom's regular performers — comic Bill Cosby. "It's cost prohibitive. You'd need about 1,500 seats to make it worthwhile. It's an era that's gone by."

Reno was a gambling town, and still is, but now it's a different time. Bill Harrah is gone. So is Pappy Smith. Harolds Club, which made Reno famous, is closed. So are other casinos. The city, once a gaming pioneer, struggles to keep its share of the tourist market. Committees meet. Strategies are proposed. Plans are made.

"It's going to be difficult because of the spread of gaming, whether it's in California, Oregon, Washington, or on the Internet," said Reno native Don Carano, owner of the Eldorado Hotel Casino, who grew up here during the other era. "It depends upon how aggressive we are and how much vision this city has."

When it comes to gambling, casinos, blackjack tables and neon, Reno always has had a split personality. Although it made casinos popular, Reno never has embraced gaming with the same fervor as Las Vegas, a 20th century boomtown built by casinos. Unlike Las Vegas, Reno clings to roots a lot older than casino gambling, which was legalized in Nevada in 1931.

"It was a more diverse economy, with a history," University of Nevada, Reno history professor Bill Rowley said of Reno. "This is the origin of the two Renos. When gambling was legalized by the Legislature, a lot of the establishments were low key. They didn't want to offend the general population. It took out-of-state people like the Harolds Club people to come in and open the doors on Virginia Street."

Before legal gaming, Reno was a center of what Rowley calls the "progressive" movement to create a society of farmers in northern Nevada. "To make the desert bloom," said Rowley, who is writing a book on the city's history. "This would be the future of Nevada, a back-to-the-land movement." But Rowley said the farm philosophy was opposed by what he calls Reno's "saloon crowd," whose views prevailed with the election in 1923 of Mayor E.E. Roberts, who promised a "barrel of whiskey" on every street corner.

The conflict between "respectable" and "casino" Reno has persisted. "Gambling was not accepted socially," said Roy Powers, long-time publicity director for Harolds Club. "Reno had a real strong society in those days. They looked down upon anyone involved in the gaming industry."

Today, we still have two Renos. The modern skyline is mostly the result of the 1978 casino boom, led by the opening of the MGM Grand, which became Bally's and today is the 2,001-room Reno Hilton. But the other Reno, the one without the neon and noise, exists in places such as Cerveri's Drug Store on the corner of Lake and East First streets downtown. Ernest Cerveri, eighty-two, who opened the place in 1948, has no plans to retire.

"It's a funny thing," he said. "People come by in the morning and say, 'Ernie, you're still working.' They come by again at 4:00 or 4:30. They say, 'How in the hell can you do this? We're tired already.' They're just young punks. If the Lord keeps me in good health, I'll keep working."

Here's how old-fashioned Cerveri's is: it's got a soda fountain with nine stools. Milk shakes cost $1.70 and malts go for $1.80.

Keep looking and you can find more of the

Colored lights on casinos define the downtown Reno skyline at night.

Ernest Cerveri

other Reno in the kitchen of Inez Stempeck, owner and operator of Casale's Halfway Club. Her place smells great, especially when she's making ravioli. The pasta is fresh every day. The sauce simmers for eight hours.

"Have you ever tasted her cooking?" asked Marie Thompson, who has known Stempeck for fifty years and drives all the way from Carson City for her old friend's ravioli. Thompson stands in Stempeck's kitchen at Casale's, an East Fourth Street institution that started life as a roadside fruit stand in 1937. Stempeck was a kid then. Her parents, John and Elvira Casale, ran the business and were part of the area's large Italian community.

"It was halfway between Reno and Sparks," said Stempeck, who does what she calls all the "major" cooking in the restaurant-bar that looks like an old wooden house and sits amid East Fourth Street's weekly motels and trailer courts. "We sold all kinds of fruit and grapes to make wine."

The ravioli began cooking in 1940. "We started selling ravioli to go," said Stempeck, "That's all we had for years. Then we went to meatballs-to-go." The restaurant opened in 1942 and the eating hasn't stopped. Inez Stempeck has been in charge of Casale's since 1969, after the death of her husband, C.S. "Steamboat" Stempeck.

Thompson still gets her food to go. The day's load includes a jar of minestrone soup, meatballs and, of course, ravioli. While waiting for the fill-up, customers have fun hanging around the kitchen and talking to Inez, who is a little piece of Reno history.

"My dad was from Genoa and my mom was from Florence," she said of her parents' hometowns in Italy. "My dad came over in 1913. My mom came in 1920. My mom was a 'picture' bride. My dad's sister sent her picture over. She was here two days and he married her."

Before you leave, Inez tells you why she has a big rock painted green in front of her little restaurant. "One year I rented the place out for Saint Patrick's Day," she said. "So I'm in here fixing corned beef and cabbage. I go outside to look and they're painting everything green. I said, 'Hey, I'm renting out the place and I'm fixing dinner, but I didn't tell you to paint the place.'" She left the rock green.

Stempeck's family story is a fairly common one in Reno. The town has been attracting overseas emigrants for more than a century. The Caranos were among them. Don Carano, a successful local attorney who opened the Eldorado in 1973, then joined gaming giant Circus Circus to launch the Silver Legacy Resort Casino in 1995, has said his Italian ancestors showed up in northern Nevada at the turn of the century because the area's railroad yards had jobs. Today, the yards are gone. Newcomers find employment in casinos.

That's how it was for Fun Fu, who escaped from mainland China to Hong Kong as a teenager in 1962 and came to Reno in 1971. She worked at John Ascuaga's Nugget in Sparks, then the MGM, and for the past twenty years in the Eldorado's keno department.

"I almost got killed," Fu said of her dash with a childhood friend across the Chinese border to freedom. "They were shooting machine guns. We ran." Fu's husband, Tim, also an escapee from China, was a longtime Reno

- 1926: Reno Arch dedicated, honoring completion of nation's first Transcontinental Highway, which ran through heart of Reno.
- 1929: Reno slogan, "The Biggest Little City in the World," adopted.
- March 19, 1931: Gov. Fred Balzar signs bill legalizing gambling.
- Feb. 23, 1935: Harolds Club opens.
- Oct. 30, 1937: William F. Harrah opens bingo parlor on Center Street.
- Dec. 17, 1947: Mapes Hotel opens, state's first high-rise hotel.
- 1955: Flood results in $3.8 million in damage.
- April 3, 1962: Fire destroys Golden Hotel.
- Oct. 10, 1969: Harrah opens downtown hotel.
- 1973: Eldorado Hotel Casino opens, first north of railroad tracks.
- June 30, 1978: William F. Harrah dies.
- 1978: MGM Grand opens along with other new casinos downtown in Reno's casino building boom.
- Dec. 17, 1982: Mapes Hotel closes.
- Feb. 3, 1995: National Bowling Stadium opens.
- March 31, 1995: Harolds Club closes.
- July 28, 1995: Silver Legacy Resort Casino opens.
- Jan. 1, 1997: New Year's flood.

casino cook. Their sons are in college. Wayne, the oldest, is a graduate engineering student at Stanford University. Younger brother Frank studies art at the University of Nevada, Reno.

"We saved our money penny by penny," Fun Fu said. "We never bought fancy clothes. We saved for their education. This is what I planned."

Rosa Molina had similar hopes when she fled a civil war in El Salvador and came to Reno in 1982. Molina was a teacher in her Central American home country.

"I could see my students being killed," said Molina, who spoke little English and went to work in Reno as a hotel-casino maid. In 1999, her two children, Cecilia Khan and Rhina Guidos, graduated from UNR with master's degrees. And Rosa Molina is a leader in the area's growing Hispanic community in her job as director of Latinos for Political Education.

"I had my daughters go to school no matter what it took," Molina said. "I didn't want them to work in casinos like I did."

Like many of his Reno neighbors, Maniscalco came from someplace else — New Jersey. "I came here to go to UNR," said Maniscalco, a college student when he went to work at Harrah's. "Before I graduated, I had a wife, a family and a mortgage." He stayed at Harrah's. "It was a good job, a great job," said Maniscalco, who became the showroom's head maitre d' in 1970. "It had all the pizzazz of a fine showroom."

Stars still come to Reno. Natalie Cole, Johnny Mathis, Olivia Newton-John and the Righteous Brothers are among those who appear in the Silver Legacy's Grande Exposition Hall. These aren't dinner shows; they're concerts.

The old-time Reno casino folks acknowledge the business has changed, but they believe something important is missing. "I don't think they know how to have fun anymore," said Powers, who had plenty of laughs at Harolds Club. "They take them-

Geese enjoy the morning sun by the Truckee River.

selves too seriously." That's something Powers never did. He once convinced Reno that Harolds was entering a world-champion camel rider from the French Foreign Legion in the annual Virginia City Camel Race.

"I had a guy picked out to play this role," Powers said with a laugh. "I got this great uniform. He was a rugged-looking guy. We had this reception committee. The press met him and I took him to the Rotary Club and put him on a TV show. I did all the talking. He'd just nod and smile."

The world-champion camel racer turned out to be a Harolds Club employee. "He was the stage manager in the seventh floor showroom," Powers said with another laugh. "No one detected it. The newspaper did stories on him." Just about everyone, it seemed, was having a good time.

"It was New Year's Eve every night in Reno," said Harry Spencer, spokesman for the old Mapes Hotel. "You didn't want to miss anything. It was a party town, better than New Orleans."

Artist creates humor in mixed media

C heryl Tenk is one of Reno's divas. "That's a group of us," Tenk said. "We're friends and fellow artists."

One of the winners in a contest to create work for the 1999 Biggest Little Art Show in Nevada III, Tenk works with a variety of methods and materials.

"I like to combine paper, clay, wire and paint," the fifty-year-old artist said of her multi-media style. She used clay, paper and paint to create "High Roller" on the front of a playing card for the art show that's traveling around the state. Her card was the queen of spades.

"I thought if the queen came to town, she'd be a high roller," said the Lovelock native who lived in Elko and graduated from Reno High School. "I took clay and reproduced her face. I made the bottom part of the card look like a blackjack table, then I had to sand down the back of the clay to make it thin enough to meet the criteria. We couldn't go beyond an eighth-of-an-inch thick."

Tenk has been showing and selling her work for five years.

Cheryl Tenk

Examples of Cheryl Tenk's art

RENO

- Population in 1999: 211,756 (22 percent under 18, 45 percent 18-44, 23 percent 45-64, 10 percent 65 and older; 51 percent male, 49 percent female).
- Population in 1990: 171,521.
- Population in 2004: (projected) 241,542.
- Total retail sales in 1998: $3 billion.
- Total retail sales in 2004: (projected) $4.127 billion.
- Median household income: $41,070.
- Claim to fame: Place where legal gambling was made popular. Early casinos, such as Harolds Club and Harrah's, drew tourists to Virginia Street. The town was also a divorce capital.
- How it got its name: Myron C. Lake, rancher from California established Lake's Crossing toll-bridge on Truckee River in 1862. Lake charged $1 per head for livestock and 10 cents each for pedestrians to use bridge. With coming of railroad in 1868, town was named for General Jesse Lee Reno, Union officer killed in Civil War.
- Local legend: William F. Harrah, founder of Harrah's Reno and Harrah's Tahoe hotel-casinos came to Reno from Southern California and opened bingo parlor on Center Street Oct. 30, 1937. He bought his first full-fledged casino, Mint Club, June 20, 1946. He opened hotel in December 1969. He brought big-name entertainment, world-renowned automobile collection and other innovations to northern Nevada . He died June 30, 1978.

Horses teach the meaning of friendship

Horse-trainer Joe Donohue gets a warm greeting from Riker, a four-year-old gelding.

Joe Donohue hasn't lost his accent. Despite years of living in the rural quiet of Reno's north valleys, Donohue's voice is straight out of downtown New York's noise and hustle. But he can talk to horses, especially a stallion named Myriah.

"This guy has taught me everything," said the fifty-three-year-old, who credits the horse with changing him from an Eastern city boy to a Western country man. "The reason I call him Myriah is he moves like the wind, so graceful and quiet. He taught me how to ride, really ride. He taught me what trust was. He taught me what friendship was."

Donohue hasn't seen the popular 1998 movie, *The Horse Whisperer,* starring Robert Redford as a renowned horse trainer. He doesn't plan to watch the film and he doesn't have to, because he plays the Redford role in real life.

"He thinks like they do," said Sabrina Zackery, Donohue's partner in the training business. "He's in their heads. It's the most amazing thing to see. A lot of trainers manhandle horses. He doesn't do that. He's very communicative — body, mind and soul."

Donohue, who trains horses with Zackery on a ten-acre ranch in Red Rock, steps into the corral where Myriah and another horse, Chase, stand next to one fence. At the sound of Donohue's voice, accent and all, Myriah and Chase take off at a gallop. Donohue calls out again. The horses change direction. Donohue calls again. Myriah and Chase slow to a trot, then a walk. Donohue and the horses seem to be a single, perfectly meshed unit.

"People have a horse, they want him broken in thirty days," said Donohue, who takes ninety days and longer to get horses to respond instantly to voice commands. "They think horses are like cars. This guy and I have been together for twenty-one years. You talk about rapport!"

Donohue always is calling Myriah "this guy." They've been friends since he captured the horse in 1978, after folks in Red Rock dared the kid from New York to do what nobody else could.

"They said if I could catch him, I could have him," said Donohue. "They knew me. It was more of a joke. Here's this guy from New York City."

The Vietnam veteran who left the Navy

Horse trainer Joe Donohue, who works with hard-to-handle or abused horses, rides Myriah, his companion of twenty-one years, at the ranch north of Red Rock.

in 1968 was on his way from Southern California to Canada to become a farmer when he stopped in Reno and stayed. He did some of the usual things a northern Nevada newcomer usually does, including work for a casino-supply company. At first, he figured he just was passing through on his way to the Canadian prairie. When he learned to shoe horses, he reasoned he'd probably need that in Canada. Instead, it turned into a business in northern Nevada, and that resulted in a home in Red Rock.

"People say, 'Horse shoeing? That's a lost art,' " said Donohue, who attended farrier school in Santa Cruz, California. "It's not a lost art if you realize how many horses there are in the state of Nevada. Just in these north valleys there are 400 or 500 horses. You look at Silver Knolls and look how many people have horses. In Lemmon Valley, there's a horse in every yard."

Donohue got his horse after a trailer carrying ten mares and one stallion overturned on U.S. 395 just north of Reno in 1977. It took a while. All the mares were captured shortly after the accident, but not the stallion who would become such an important part of Donohue's life. The

stallion was a wild mustang. He roamed the north valleys for a year and couldn't be caught.

"There was a guy out here working on a ranch, a cowboy," Donohue said. "He spent a year trying to catch him. He never caught him. They chased him down to Silver Knolls. He was on a couple of acres." Finally, Donohue built a twenty-by-twenty-foot corral and put food inside. "He'd go in there every day. He wouldn't let me close the gate."

But one day, the stallion let Donohue close the gate. "That's how we got together," said Donohue, who rode horses in rural areas outside New York as a youngster. "Truthfully, it's probably the most important thing that ever happened to me in my life. It changed so many things in my life, my way of thinking. It taught me to be close with nature. It taught me that animals can communicate with people."

Horses, even wild ones, trust Donohue, who rode Myriah among the mustang herds that roam open country in Washoe County.

"The two of them will go with the herd until they get tired of it, pull back and drop out," Zackery said. "It's amazing to see the two of them. Donohue's able to walk up to a horse in the wild. They come to him. I can't do that."

Donohue credits Myriah. "He was accepted with the herd and he had a human on his back," he said. "I'd ride him. The herd would wait. We'd take runs across the valley. He'd stop and the herd would go about its business. He was allowed into the herd with me on his back. He put me in the middle of wild horses."

Reno residents want a new image for the city

Rosa Molina, director of Latinos for Political Education in Reno, first worked as a hotel maid when she fled from El Salvador's civil war seventeen years ago.

Reno residents, old and new, are image conscious. They'd like the city to get one. Reno's image used to be easy. Gambling. Harolds Club and Harrah's. The Biggest Little City in the World. Virginia Street. The Arch.

"I'm concerned about Reno's identity," said Mercedes de la Garza, a designer and community activist who's lived in town since the mid-1990s. "That's what will make or break Reno. Everybody talks about it, but nobody does anything. That's something we need to do here."

Councilman Dave Aiazzi recalls the old image. "Everybody always knew what Reno was," he said. "Well, they knew what Reno was because of the casinos. That's how Reno got put on the map."

But that's the wrong image, according to a teenager who has lived in the area since he was three. "It's not really a place to grow up in. It's an adult town," said Nate Hogan, a seventeen-year-old student who takes a combination of high school and college courses in a special program at Truckee Meadows Community College. "The casinos set a bad image. Behind all the glamour, I don't think the casinos are that great. My

friends and everybody I've talked to haven't enjoyed growing up in Reno."

Emily Brown, a junior at Hug High, disagrees. "I don't think it's a bad image," said Brown, whose dad worked at Harrah's before teaching. "We've had it so long, it's hard to change."

But in the 1960s Las Vegas replaced Reno as Nevada's capital of glitz and glitter and Reno has been trying to find itself ever since. Government leaders and tourism officials have struggled to give the city an image. Outside consultants have been brought in. Plenty of suggestions have been made: feature special events, advertise the scenery, don't forget Lake Tahoe and clean up downtown.

"We've got to keep casinos and downtown growing," Brown said. "If we don't preserve that, our economy is going to go down. "

For better or worse, Reno is known to the outside world for casinos. "We were in California a couple of weeks ago," said Jodi Meyer, a junior at Bishop Manogue High. "We told some people we were from Reno and they asked, 'Do you gamble?' "

Despite all the ideas, the identity search

Lance Crump of Klondike, Texas, holds his sleeping three-year-old son, Lathan, at the Reno Rodeo

In Idlewild Park, Reno native David McCamant works on an acrylic painting while being ignored by Jack, his wire-haired terrier.

continues. "There is no vision," said Jeanille Hyde, a Reno native and retired teacher. "Our community leaders, they have no vision. I'm frustrated."

She's not the only one. "We don't have people in Reno believing it's a good place to live," Aiazzi said. "If we want to get Reno known, they are probably our best ambassadors. You have to have a downtown that everyone is proud of."

Instead, locals avoid the place. "We never go downtown," said Gail Dickson, a thirty-six year Reno resident. "It's dirty. It's dark." But others who live here like a lot of their surroundings — such as Tahoe — and believe they should be used to attract visitors.

"We have a region of many things here," Dickson said. "You go to Las Vegas and you can do one thing — gamble. We have this wonderful package of things." She is willing to give downtown redevelopment a chance, but she and others said some of the best of Reno is outside the city limits.

"Here we have all these casinos jammed into the downtown," Larry Lyons said. "You get people in here and you don't let them out. Everything they see is in this little section of downtown. There's an awful lot to do around here."

Index